EMDR Therapy Treatment for Grief and Mourning

EMDR Therapy Treatment for Grief and Mourning

Transforming the Connection to the Deceased Loved One

Roger M. Solomon

OXFORD
UNIVERSITY PRESS

OXFORD
UNIVERSITY PRESS

Great Clarendon Street, Oxford, OX2 6DP,
United Kingdom

Oxford University Press is a department of the University of Oxford.
It furthers the University's objective of excellence in research, scholarship,
and education by publishing worldwide. Oxford is a registered trade mark of
Oxford University Press in the UK and in certain other countries

Published in the United States of America by Oxford University Press
198 Madison Avenue, New York, NY 10016, United States of America

British Library Cataloguing in Publication Data

Data available

Library of Congress Control Number: 2023945989

ISBN 978–0–19–888136–0

DOI: 10.1093/oso/9780198881360.001.0001

Printed in the UK by
Ashford Colour Press Ltd, Gosport, Hampshire

Foreword

Those of you who have had the chance to listen to Roger Solomon teaching and presenting around the world will agree with me that he is an extraordinary, gifted therapist and teacher. I have known him for well over 10 years now and, after having had the privilege of working with him on many occasions and in a variety of settings, I can firmly say that Roger artfully models how to be present with our clients in the most challenging moments and what to do to help them face their deepest fears and pains.

EMDR Therapy Treatment for Grief and Mourning offers the reader the opportunity to take a close look at the work on grief and mourning that Roger has been developing in the last decades. It opens a window to his thorough and coherent thinking process regarding how to approach these extremely difficult moments and memories. Throughout the book, he teaches us how to accompany clients in moments of tremendous distress, how to encourage our clients to connect with these complicated emotions, and how to adapt EMDR therapy in the different phases so our clients can heal their pain.

Solomon focuses specifically on the application of EMDR therapy to the universal issue of grief and mourning, addressing beforehand the different models of grief, the impact of loss, and the development of traumatic bereavement and complicated grief, along with an in-depth discussion of EMDR therapy. A strong focus is placed on Attachment Theory and understanding the different attachment styles. Research has shown that attachment style is a determining factor of how a person deals with loss of connection to a loved one, which is a major clinical dynamic in grief and mourning. Of particular interest is how EMDR therapy often results in the emergence of heartfelt, meaningful memories. These memories form an 'adaptive inner representation' that provides the mourner with a positive sense of connection to the deceased loved one. This sense of connection can be further enhanced through additional bilateral stimulation.

Personally, I most definitely enjoyed how his engaging theoretical explanations are interwoven with practical case examples and partial transcripts of EMDR therapy sessions, covering history-taking, case conceptualization, target selection, Preparation & Stabilization, and trauma processing in an easy-to-understand manner. He emphasizes the importance of understanding how current triggers can be painful reminders of the absence of the loved one, and identifying what needs to be addressed, thus integrating a three-prong protocol throughout the application of the different phases of EMDR therapy to grief and mourning.

EMDR Treatment for Grief and Mourning is a wonderful gift for EMDR psychotherapists and a comprehensive guide for anyone interested in helping those who have lost their loved ones to walk the path of healing the pain of grief and complicated bereavement.

Dolores Mosquera
Institute for the Study of Trauma and Personality Disorders
A Coruña, Spain

Acknowledgments

This book is the result of the inspiration, encouragement, motivation, and, occasionally, a needed kick in the rear to get going, given to me from many people. First of all, I am grateful to have had Francine Shapiro in my life. I will always cherish and honor Francine, a person who has positively impacted my life and whose lifeforce is inherent in this book. I thank Isabel Fernandez, who first brought me to Italy to each EMDR therapy in 1999, coordinated the publishing of this book in Italian, and provided important feedback and inspiration. Her tireless work in providing leadership in the growth of EMDR therapy in not only Italy, but the world, is greatly appreciated.

Marilyn Luber dedicated many hours to reviewing and editing the manuscript at various points during my writing giving me the needed "kick" to articulate my own model, which is an integrative model with the Adaptive Information model as the base. Her editorial prowess is interwoven throughout this book. Barbara Hensley not only motivated me to write this book but provided many hours of editorial suggestions. Katy Murray, a walking encyclopedia of EMDR therapy, provided her editorial prowess. Naomi Zikmund-Fisher (who made me promise to spell her name right) and Hilary Searles provided editorial help and suggestions in the early stages of my writing. I thank my fellow EMDR Institute trainers who provided feedback and direction, including Wendy Freitag, Mark Nickerson, as well as Katy Murray. Atle Dyregrov, my friend of over 40 years, provided much help in the initial chapters of this book. I thank Onno van der Hart and Kathy Martin for their aid in writing the chapter on complex trauma. I thank Dennis Klass and Margaret Stroebe for reviewing the sections on their grief framework and allowing me to quote them. I thank Kris White for providing a case example. I thank my EMDR brothers Elan Shapiro and Ignacio (Nacho) Jarero for their contribution to recent event protocols.

Maria Fatima Caddia provided support and motivation not only in writing this book but in all my endeavors—I can never thank her enough.

Other people who have read sections of this book and gave me feedback include (alphabetically):

Sigmund Burzynski
Carol Carr
Helene Delucci
Atle Dyregrov
Gunilla Klensmeden Popper
Jack Harris
Marcus Heinimaa
Sari Honkanen
Antonino Longobardi
Ellen Ma
Candice Solomon
Anne Suokas
Tuija Turunen
France von Brussel

Contents

List of Figures   xi
List of Tables   xiii
List of Contributors   xv
My Journey with EMDR Therapy   xvii
The Development of My Interest in Trauma, Grief, and Mourning   xix
My Philosophy of EMDR Therapy   xxiii
The Scope and Focus of This Book   xxv
Structure of This Book   xxvii

Introduction   1

SECTION 1 EMDR THERAPY AND GRIEF AND MOURNING

1. **EMDR Therapy**   7

2. **Grief and Mourning**   20

3. **Impact of Loss: Internal and Interpersonal Changes**   31

4. **Traumatic Bereavement**   47

5. **Complicated Grief and Mourning**   54

SECTION 2 GRIEF AND MOURNING FRAMEWORKS

6. **Attachment Theory**   65

7. **Models of Grief: Continuing Bonds Model**   79

8. **The Dual Process Model of Grief**   83

9. **The "R" Processes of Mourning**   90

SECTION 3 EMDR THERAPY INTEGRATIVE TREATMENT MODEL

10. **EMDR Therapy Integrative Treatment Model for Grief and Mourning**   107

11. **Three-Pronged Protocol: First Prong—Past Memories**   113

12. Three-Pronged Protocol: Second and Third Prongs—Present
    Triggers and Future Templates   131

SECTION 4   EIGHT PHASES OF EMDR THERAPY

13. Phase 1: History-Taking and Treatment Planning   151

14. Phase 2: Preparation & Stabilization   169

15. Introduction to Reprocessing Phases   176

16. Phase 3: Target Assessment   184

17. Phase 4: Desensitization   195

18. Phases 5–8: Installation, Body Scan, Closure, and Re-evaluation   214

19. Grief and Mourning with Complex Trauma and Trauma-Generated
    Dissociation of the Personality   226

20. Closing Thoughts   245

Appendix 1: Eye Movement Desensitization and Reprocessing (EMDR)
    Therapy Treatment of Grief and Mourning with Death Caused by Covid-19   251
Appendix 2: Transcripts of Sessions   259
Appendix 3: Psychological First Aid   275
Appendix 4: Eye Movement Desensitization and Reprocessing (EMDR)
    Protocol for Recent Critical Incidents and Ongoing Traumatic Stress
    (EMDR-PRECI) and EMDR Recent Event Protocol (R-TEP)   279
Appendix 5: Additional Resources   281
References   283
Index   293

A scripted protocol summary to assist the clinician in applying the therapeutic framework presented in this text is available at www.oup.co.uk/companion/ Solomon.

List of Figures

Figure 10.1 Integrative Model for EMDR Therapy for Grief and Mourning   109

List of Tables

Table 2.1 Summary of Grief Reactions   29

Table 9.1 Six 'R' Processes of Mourning   91

Table 14.1 Criteria for Client Readiness   170

Table 14.2 Coping Strategies   173

Table 14.3 Highlights of EMDR Therapy with Grief and Mourning   174

Table 16.1 Elements of the Target Assessment Phase   185

Table 16.2 Examples of Positive and Negative Cognitions for
Theme of Responsibility   188

Table 16.3 Examples of Positive and Negative Cognitions for Theme of Safety   190

Table 16.4 Examples of Positive and Negative Cognitions for Theme of Control 191

Table 16.5 Examples of Positive and Negative Cognitions for Theme of
Connection and Belonging   192

List of Contributors

Onno van der Hart, PhD, is a psychologist and psychotraumatologist, and until 2017, a psychotherapist. He is an emeritus professor of Psychopathology of Chronic Traumatization. (He was president of the International Society for Traumatic Stress Studies (ISTSS).) With Ellert Nijenhuis and Kathy Steele, he wrote the book *The Haunted Self: Structural Dissociation and the Treatment of Chronic Traumatization* (2006).

Kathleen Martin, LCSW, EMDRIA Consultant and Trainer, ISSTD Fellow, is an international trainer on EMDR therapy and complex trauma. In her private practice in Rochester, New York, USA, she uses EMDR therapy extensively in her specialty of PTSD, trauma, and dissociation, and teaches workshops in the area. She has published numerous articles and book chapters focused on treating complex trauma and dissociation.

List of Contributors

My Journey with EMDR Therapy

My first full-time position as a professional psychologist was Police Psychologist with the Colorado Springs, Colorado, Police Department, 1979–1988. This was an important phase of my development where I first learned to work with trauma and grief. Then, I moved to Olympia, Washington, for the position of Department Psychologist with the Washington State Patrol, from, 1988–1994. I learned about EMDR therapy (then termed EMD) while reading Francine Shapiro's article in the *Journal of Traumatic Stress* (1989). I was highly skeptical about the idea of a client thinking about a negative memory and a therapist moving fingers in front of the client's face to reprocess a memory. But I was intrigued. The data were interesting, and the theory of stimulating the brain's inherent information processing system made sense.

In October of that year, I went to San Francisco for the International Society of Traumatic Stress Studies conference, and heard Francine speak about EMDR therapy. She showed a video of an EMDR therapy session with a Viet Nam veteran. Again, I was skeptical but intrigued.

After the congress, I went to Santa Cruz, California. Santa Cruz was the epicenter of an earthquake that had rocked the San Francisco Bay Area. I had been invited to provide Psychological First Aid and support for the mental health center staff and volunteers who had been providing direct clinical services. One of the volunteers was the same Viet Nam veteran that Francine had shown on video at the congress. He was also a mental health professional. I asked him if EMDR therapy had really helped him and he replied, "It did!" I asked him to show me. He asked me to think of something negative. I brought up a recent annoying experience, and he did two sets of eye movements (about 20 seconds each). At the end of the second set, I thought about the event and wondered why it had even annoyed me—and then I realized something had shifted. I was convinced and I signed up for the workshop in June of 1990. I immediately started utilizing EMDR therapy (called EMD at the time) and witnessed the amazing therapeutic results EMDR therapy brings.

My life changed. In 1993, as EMDR therapy was growing rapidly, Francine needed more trainers and selected 13 people to become trainers. In 1994, I started training internationally. As one of the early EMDR therapy trainers, I was fortunate to have the opportunity to travel to many countries. I had the privilege to meet, work with, and become friends with many of the current EMDR trainers, facilitators, and supervisor/consultants from around the world who have made EMDR therapy what it is today.

Sadly, Francine died on 16 June 2019. It has been my honor to proudly continue my affiliation with the EMDR Institute as Senior Faculty and Program Director. It is an important part of my identity. I think of Francine with love and gratitude for creating EMDR therapy, envisioning how it can help people all over the world, and impacting my life and identity in a way I could never have imagined.

The Development of My Interest in Trauma, Grief, and Mourning

Shortly after becoming the Police Psychologist with the Colorado Springs Police Department in 1979, I met a Federal Bureau of Investigation (FBI) agent (Jim Horn), the stress specialist from the Denver FBI Field Office. He asked me what I knew about "post-shooting trauma," the psychological trauma an officer experienced after a line-of-duty shooting. The FBI was hearing that up to 80% of police officers involved in a line-of-duty shooting were leaving law enforcement as a result of the trauma. Very little was known at the time. Posttraumatic Stress Disorder (PTSD) was officially recognized in the *Diagnostic Statistical Manual of Mental Disorders* (DSM) only in 1980. Jim and I started doing research that largely consisted of working with officers all over Colorado involved in traumatic incidents, including line-of-duty deaths and working with families of officers killed.

I continued to consult with the FBI and many other law enforcement and government agencies, including the Secret Service, Bureau of Alcohol, Tobacco, and Firearms, United States Department of Justice (United States Attorney's Office), Diplomatic Security, National Aeronautics and Space Administration, United States Army, several United States intelligence services, and the Polizia di Stato in Italy, as well as other first responder agencies. I provided direct psychological services after traumatic events and training to peer support teams (first responders with critical incident experience who provide Psychological First Aid to their peers involved in traumatic incidents). Incidents I responded to included: the Oklahoma City bombing, 11 September terrorist attack, the Shuttle Columbia tragedy (disintegration upon re-entry to Earth), mass casualty events, and numerous line-of-duty deaths and injuries.

In 1986 I was invited to participate in the 3-day program, *Concerns of Police*, and I worked with this group for the next 30 years. This was a national support group for families of police officers killed in the line of duty. Every 14–16 May, the families gather in Washington, D. C., for workshops and the availability of individual support sessions, with 15 May being a national memorial ceremony. In 1990, I started applying EMDR with spouses, adolescents, adult children, parents, siblings, and fellow officers of policemen killed in the line of duty. This brought together my ongoing experience with grief and mourning, with my growing interest on the impact of EMDR therapy on this human condition.

In 1995, I met Therese Rando, a psychologist with expertise (and many publications) on grief and mourning. We started collaborating and wrote several articles on EMDR therapy and grief and mourning. These articles focused on how EMDR therapy can facilitate movement through the psychological processes (termed "R" processes) important for assimilation and accommodation of the loss. In 2012, Marilyn Luber, noted editor of eight volumes of Scripted Protocols and a dear friend, pointed out how our articles needed to further discuss grief and mourning in terms of the eight phases of EMDR, including earlier memories triggered by the loss. I agreed with her. Childhood memories and attachment style (formed as a result of child-caregiver interactions) greatly influence how one grieves and goes through the mourning process (Kosminsky & Jordan, 2016). Reprocessing present triggers and installing future templates are necessary for comprehensive treatment. Further, I studied other frameworks enabling me to understand grief and mourning from a variety of perspectives. The result of much study and clinical work is this book which aims to illustrate how these theoretical frameworks can guide EMDR case conceptualization and treatment.

Another significant influence in my work was teaching EMDR therapy in Finland under the sponsorship of the Trauma Center in Helsinki, Finland. The Trauma Center had started to bring leading experts in trauma and dissociation to train there. Anne Suokos, the Director of the Trauma Center, insisted that Onno van der Hart and I meet and collaborate on how EMDR therapy could be guided by *The Theory of Structural Dissociation of the Personality* (Van der Hart, Nijenhuis, & Steele, 2006) for treatment of complex trauma and trauma-generated dissociation of the personality. I have been greatly enriched by Onno, as well as collaboration with Ellert Nijenhuis, Kathy Steele, Suzette Boon, Dolores Mosquera, Anabel Gonzalez, and Kathy Martin. I have included a chapter on complex trauma and grief and mourning since so many of our clients suffer from complex trauma and trauma-related dissociation.

A Convincing Experience

After taking the basic training in California, I went back to Olympia, Washington, and immediately started using EMDR therapy. I called up clients

I had previously treated for PTSD and asked them to come back in. I told them, "I have something I think could further help you." One of the troopers who accepted my offer was Sam (not his real name), whom I had treated successfully treated the year before (with basically a cognitive-behavioral approach). Sam had made a routine traffic stop at night when the driver came out with a gun. Sam had his flashlight in his hand, and shined the light in the gunman's eyes to distract him. Then, he drew his weapon and shot the suspect. What had been the worst part for Sam was that it was found the suspect had attempted to fire his weapon, but the firing pin had been defective. Sam realized he could have been killed, and this resulted in his PTSD. I did EMDR therapy on this incident with Sam, and achieved full processing results.

I asked Sam what he liked better, EMDR therapy or what we had done before and what he thought of EMDR in comparison with our previous work (which involved an exposure approach with emphasis on highlighting and reinforcing moments of resilience and capability to respond). Sam replied that the EMDR had taken the trauma out of his body, and he could think about the incident and really feel calm. However, he said he liked what we did before better because, "If I am involved in another critical incident, I know how to think about it and do not have to wait for you to come with your fingers." This experience drove home the importance of having experience and knowledge specific to the problems of the client. EMDR therapy is helpful, but must be integrated within a theoretical and treatment framework appropriate to the clinical population we treat. Hence, the purpose of this book is to educate the reader with a theoretical and treatment context appropriate for grief and mourning that guides EMDR therapy case conceptualization and treatment.

My Philosophy of EMDR Therapy

This book assumes the reader has been trained in basic EMDR therapy (both weekend 1 and 2). Though basic concepts are reviewed, they are not presented in depth. Reading the textbooks on EMDR therapy is very important, and having done so, the reader will be familiar with the EMDR procedures and strategies presented in this book.

I consider myself an EMDR purist and minimalist. By this, I mean I teach and practice EMDR therapy as taught by Francine Shapiro. I am flexible with the implementation of EMDR according to the needs of the client, a principle Francine emphasized. As she put it, "EMDR is not a cookie cutter." EMDR therapy and the eight-phase, three-pronged model is very flexible and is applied within the context of a therapeutic relationship that takes into account the unique needs of the client. It is important to track clients moment by moment, with clients' responses determining what happens next. There is a relationship between clients and therapists, and the pace, rhythm, and flow of the bilateral stimulation. I call this "the Art of EMDR therapy," the dance between clients and therapists nuanced with therapists holding clients in a compassionate presence, while accompanying them through the process. The therapeutic relationship is crucial in EMDR therapy as in all therapy, and perhaps even more so following a significant loss, a time when a person can be quite vulnerable. Therapists accompany clients through the difficult process of mourning. Indeed, the reprocessing of a loss can be very emotional and intense. If clients go through Hell, therapists accompany them, and together they go through to the other side.

An important therapeutic principle is that EMDR therapy facilitates an intrinsic healing process. Therefore, if there is a change reported by clients after a set of bilateral stimulation, therapists stay out of the way. Therapists simply say, "Go with that." However, if the processing gets stuck, then therapists need to talk and implement strategies to get the processing started. Many therapists over talk and get in the way. Clients are the agent of change, not therapists. This makes EMDR therapy very organic (as Francine liked to say) with our role to provide the atmosphere and encouragement for clients to have one foot in the past and one foot in the present, as they process their distressing experiences.

The Scope and Focus of This Book

The main focus of this book is on the death of loved one. However, it is applicable to any type of loss. Grief is the reaction to loss, and there are many types of losses, for example:

- *Break Up of a Relationship*: Though a relationship break up can certainly be a major loss similar to a death, the other person is alive. A death is a permanent loss, with the loved one gone, and never seen (physically) again. Where a break up is someone's choice, death is beyond the deceased's control or realm of choice (suicide is an exception).
- *Health and Medical Issues*: for example, loss of eyesight, hearing, and injuries resulting in diminished lifestyle.
- *Transitions*: for example, children grow up and leave the house, retirement, and change in lifestyle.
- *Material or Tangible Loss*: losses one can see such as, the house burns down.
- *Intangible Loss*: for example, loss of self-esteem if one doesn't get promoted at work.
- *Negative Event or Traumatic Circumstance*: Any negative event or traumatic circumstance involves a loss. With any loss there are painful reactions, and adaptations to life, and the resulting changing circumstances that need to occur.

Though the emphasis of this book is on death of a loved one, the EMDR therapy framework and treatment strategies presented are applicable to any loss. This book provides an integrative treatment approach for utilization of EMDR therapy with grief and mourning.

Structure of This Book

Four sections on EMDR therapy for grief and mourning are presented in the book.

Section 1: EMDR Therapy and Grief and Mourning

- Chapter 1 provides a brief overview of EMDR therapy including its utilization with grief and mourning.
- Chapter 2 describes grief and mourning, and includes *bereavement* definitions, progression through the grief and mourning process, and grief reactions.
- Chapter 3 further elaborates on the impact of loss, focusing on internal and interpersonal factors. A discussion of how the assumptive world of mourners gets violated, and the consequences; areas of life that are impacted, and mediators of mourning will be presented.
- Chapter 4 focuses on traumatic bereavement when grief is overpowered by the traumatic circumstances of death. Risk factors for traumatic bereavement will be presented and the treatment implications for EMDR therapy.
- Chapter 5 addresses complicated grief and mourning when grief reactions continue at clinically significant levels. The forms of complicated grief and clues when clients are suffering from complicated grief are presented.

Section 2: Theoretical Models to Guide EMDR Therapy Treatment

Several theoretical models help us understand grief and mourning, how it may become complicated, and how to guide clinical intervention and treatment planning with EMDR therapy.

- Chapter 6 highlights Attachment Theory, increases our understanding of complicated grief and mourning, and explains individual differences in response to loss (Kosminsky & Jordan, 2016). Research has shown that attachment style is an important determinant of how one grieves. The loss of a significant person in adulthood can evoke many of the same feelings and responses that accompanied separation from an attachment figure during childhood. Consequently, understanding Attachment Theory and how attachment style results from early child-caregiver interactions can guide EMDR clinicians in the identification and treatment of the maladaptively-stored information complicating the grief.
- Chapter 7 presents the Continuing Bonds model (Klass, Silverman, & Nickman, 1996), which suggests that we don't detach from the deceased loved one; instead, we create a new relationship and develop a continuing bond that maintains a connection with the deceased. This helps us understand the important role played by the emergence of positive memories of the deceased, which is commonly observed during EMDR therapy.
- Chapter 8 describes the Dual Process model (Stroebe & Schut, 1999, 2010) and ways people come to terms with the loss of a loved one. This model describes two categories of stressors. Loss Orientation (LO) refers to the mourner's focus on dealing with the loss experience itself (the grief work). Restoration Orientation (RO) refers to the mourner having to deal with the consequences of the loss, secondary stressors, and reorient to the world without the loved one. Healthy grief involves an oscillation between these two orientations. Mourner has to be able to confront the emotional aspects of the loss (i.e., LO) and at times to put the pain on hold to deal with the changes and challenges that are the consequence of the loss (i.e., RO). The clinician needs to help the client maintain a balance between these dynamics.
- Chapter 9 focuses on Rando's 'R' processes (1993), that discuss the psychological processes necessary for the assimilation and accommodation of loss. Solomon and Rando (2007, 2012, 2015) discuss how EMDR therapy can facilitate movement through these processes. This model provides a way to understand where a person is in the mourning process and where to intervene if the grief becomes complicated because of some compromise, distortion, or failure of one or more of the "R" processes.

These models complement each other and can be used to identify appropriate targets for EMDR therapy when working with loss. They are by no means an exhaustive list of frameworks for understanding grief and mourning. There are many rich resources covering all aspects of grief and mourning, including personal accounts, other theories/frameworks, and a plethora of treatment strategies and coping techniques. For the sake of brevity, I have chosen frameworks that have *personally* guided my work and are widely utilized in the field. In the body of the text, however, I will describe other conceptual frameworks that overlap with ones I present, not only because they are helpful, but to pay homage to their valuable contribution.

Section 3: EMDR Therapy Integrative Treatment Model

This section describes an overview of an EMDR therapy treatment model for grief and mourning according to the Adaptive Information Processing model, and how other models can integrate into this model. This integrative model presents a way to conceptualize treatment, and select targets for EMDR reprocessing.

- Chapter 10 presents a comprehensive model for EMDR treatment based on the Adaptive Information Processing model as an integrative framework.
- Chapter 11 deals with the three-prong protocol of EMDR therapy and discusses treatment of past memories.
- Chapter 12 also deals with the three-prong protocol of EMDR therapy and examines the treatment of present triggers and provides future templates.

Section 4: Eight Phases of EMDR Therapy

This final section focuses on the eight phases of EMDR therapy in the context of grief and mourning.

- Chapter 13 discusses Phase 1: History-Taking and Treatment Planning.
- Chapter 14 covers Phase 2: Preparation & Stabilization.
- Chapter 15 provides an introduction to the reprocessing phases.
- Chapter 16 focuses on Phase 3: Target Assessment.
- Chapter 17 discusses Phase 4: Desensitization.
- Chapter 18 covers Phases 5 through 8 (Installation, Body Scan, Closure, and Re-evaluation. This chapter also presents an additional step to

enhance the "adaptive inner representation" of the deceased to integrate the loss and enhance coping.

- Chapter 19 presents a framework for working with complex grief with because many of our clients have complex trauma and dissociative symptoms. Onno van der Hart and Kathy Martin are coauthors of this chapter.
- Chapter 20 presents my closing thoughts.

Appendices

In the Appendices, I cover added information that will be useful to the reader.

- Appendix 1 is on EMDR therapy in relation to loss from Covid-19. The stressful conditions of Covid-19 can compound the trauma of a loss. This was especially true under lockdown conditions when mourners may not have been physically present to say goodbye, and social distancing interfered with funeral and religious ceremonies. This appendix discusses EMDR therapy treatment in the context of loss because of Covid.
- Appendix 2 includes transcripts of EMDR therapy sessions. This appendix presents three cases illustrating EMDR therapy with mothers who have lost children: a baby to sudden infant death, a teenager to an auto accident, and a teenager to suicide. Dealing with stuck points, fear of losing connection to the loved one if one heals, and the formation of an adaptive inner representation are illustrated in these transcripts.
- Appendix 3 offers a description of Psychological First Aid and a brief summary of recent event protocols. Mourners may be in shock in the immediate aftermath of a loss. Psychological First Aid is a framework for reducing the initial distress of a traumatic event and fostering adaptive coping where appropriate. The principles of Psychological First Aid and stress reduction methods are described in this appendix.
- Appendix 4 is a supplemental discussion of EMDR protocols for recent events. EMDR therapy can be helpful shortly after a trauma to deal with the worst aspects and can be applied within the context of Psychological First Aid (see Chapter 15, which describes EMDR and focused reprocessing). Two other important protocols for dealing with recent events are the EMDR Protocol for Recent Critical Incidents and Ongoing Traumatic Stress ((EMDR-PRECI) Jarero, Artigas, & Luber, 2011) and the EMDR

Recent Traumatic Episode Protocol ((RTEP) Shapiro & Laub, 2013). A brief description and case example are provided.

- Appendix 5 describes other resources helpful in dealing with grief and mourning. There are many resources that are helpful to mourners and therapists that are beyond the scope of this book. Some of these resources are presented in this appendix.

Introduction

For most people love is the most profound source of pleasure in our lives while the loss of those whom we love is their most profound source of pain. Hence, love and loss are two sides of the same coin. We cannot have one without risking the other.

—Colin Parkes, 2015, p. 1

The death of a loved one can be a time of tremendous distress. Losing someone we love and cherish can also mean losing someone we looked to for security and balance in life, and who provided predictability and meaning. A loved one is not only part of our lives and external world, but part of our identity and our internal world. Whether the relationship was positive or negative, secure or insecure, peaceful or conflictual, the deceased shaped our assumptive world and contributed a role in defining who we are and what we are. In the immediate aftermath of a loss, especially when it is sudden and unexpectedly traumatic, it is difficult to fathom who we are without the loved one or how life can go on without that person. With the loss of someone we love, we lose our world—things will never be the same.

It is not only the primary loss of the loved one that affects us, but secondary losses—losses that are a consequence of the primary loss, thus compounding our hardship. For example, a spouse dies suddenly, and because of the drop in income, the surviving spouse and children must move to a new house. Secondary losses here include leaving the house and neighbourhood that have been 'home', the children going to a new school and leaving their friends behind, and, indeed, undergoing a major change in lifestyle.

Neimeyer (2013) views grieving as a process of reconstructing a world that has been challenged by the loss. The death of a loved one creates a crisis of meaning in the life of the bereaved. Mourners need to process the narrative of the death to 'make sense' of what has happened, including the implications for ongoing life. Adapting to the loss, shifting our identity, and rebuilding life can indeed be very challenging. Even when uncomplicated, bereavement may have significant psychological, behavioural, social, physical, and economic

EMDR Therapy Treatment for Grief and Mourning. Roger M. Solomon, Oxford University Press. © Roger M. Solomon 2024.
DOI: 10.1093/oso/9780198881360.003.0001

consequences (Osterweis, Solomon, & Green, 1984; Solomon & Rando, 2007, 2012, 2015). As therapists, our role is to accompany our grieving clients through the difficult transition of rebuilding a splintered world. This involves adapting to the external changes that confront the mourner (e.g., taking on new responsibilities previously fulfilled by the loved one), to a new sense of identity ('Who am I without the loved one?') and the far more difficult and subtle task of transforming the relationship from loving in presence, when the loved one was alive, to loving in absence, now that the loved one is gone.

This process is beautifully described in the movie Wind River (2017). Cory, whose daughter had died is talking to Martin, whose daughter has just been murdered.

> I'd like to tell you it gets easier, but it doesn't. If there's a comfort—you get used to the pain if you let yourself.... I got good news and bad news. Bad news is you'll never be the same. You'll never be whole. Ever. What was taken from you can't be replaced. Your daughter is gone.
>
> Now the good news—as soon as you accept that, as soon as you let yourself suffer, allow yourself to grieve ... You'll be able to visit her in your mind, and remember all the joy she gave you. All the love she knew.... that's what not accepting this will rob from you... .
>
> If you shy away from the pain of it, then you rob yourself of every memory of her, my friend. Every one. From her first step to her last smile. You'll kill 'em all... .
>
> Take the pain ... Take the pain, Martin. It's the only way to keep her with you.

The above interchange is a wonderful description of the grief process. The deceased loved one is gone and is not coming back, and the pain of this loss must be acknowledged and experienced. But rather than taking the pain as the 'only way to keep her with you', EMDR reprocessing of the loss often results in positive memories emerging that are heartfelt and comforting, giving the mourner a sense of connection. The positive memories, forming an adaptive inner representation of the loved one, can transform the connection to the loved one from one of pain to one of love. As described in Wind River, 'You'll be able to visit her in your mind, and remember all the joy she gave you, all the love she knew.'

But the pain can be too much. The late Giovanni Liotti whose adult son suicided (after battling major depression for many years) also described that the pain must be experienced so that love and its meaning can be felt:

Pain is the other, unavoidable side of love in a world haunted by illnesses and death such as ours. This is why, I think, no parent would really wish not to feel any pain, even when many years or a whole life has elapsed, after the loss of a beloved child. Indeed, it seems to me that such a pain after such a loss increases the experience of love and of its meaning—our only human Goodness—in our lives. Provided, of course, the pain is not utterly unbearable. (Giovanni Liotti, personal communication).

To avoid the pain, or if the pain is too much, complicates the grief, and robs mourners of their positive memories ('You'll kill 'em all', as described above in the Wind River excerpt). Indeed, the pain can be too much, which can complicate the grief, keeping mourners stuck in the pain of loss, unable to adapt to the loss and the new world where the loved one is absent.

The last statement of the Wind River dialogue can be misinterpreted: 'Take the pain . . . Take the pain, Martin. It's the only way to keep her with you.' Some people believe they have to hold on to the pain, it is their connection to the deceased and to lose the pain is to lose the connection to their loved one. This is not true. As we shall see with EMDR therapy, the pain of the loss can be processed, resulting in a transformation of the relationship with the loved one and results in remembering the loved one through meaningful, heartfelt memories.

Eye movement desensitization and reprocessing (EMDR) therapy is a therapeutic approach that research has shown to be effective with psychological trauma (Shapiro, 1999, 2001, 2018) and many other psychological disorders (Solomon & Shapiro, 2017). EMDR therapy can be utilized to treat the trauma of grief and facilitate the assimilation and accommodation of the loss (Solomon & Shapiro, 1997; Solomon & Rando, 2007, 2012, 2015). A major loss can indeed be distressing, and there can be many moments, situations, and memories that become dysfunctionally stored, especially when there is a sudden, unexpected, or violent death. The memories of getting the news (the knock on the door, the phone call, the doctor saying, 'we did all we could') can become maladaptively stored and are triggered when mourners try to think of their loved one. The loss can be so distressing that other memory networks with positive memories of the loved one cannot be accessed, experienced, and felt. This often results in a profound sense of disconnection ('I can't connect') because every time mourners try to think of their loved one, they are again reminded their loved one is dead.

EMDR therapy, by targeting distressing moments (e.g., getting the news), allows the processing of such pain and 'raw felt' emotions, and enables the linking in of adaptive information, which is evidenced by the emergence of positive memories with 'heartfelt' emotion. The positive memories and meaningful moments that emerge create an adaptive internalized representation of the lost person that allows a feeling of connection and psychological proximity. In other words, the clinical dynamic with EMDR therapy seems to involve moving from 'I can't connect', to 'I can connect', offering a pathway for clients to connect through love instead of pain.

Going through the mourning process depends on the bereaved person's ability to endure the emotional pain of recognizing that the loss is irrevocable—that the loved one is gone, never coming back. This can be too much for some people. Working through the raw, felt emotion of this realization can be complicated by past losses, unresolved trauma, and insecure or disorganized attachment styles. EMDR therapy can be effective in treating the factors that complicate grief and mourning, through reprocessing past memories, present triggers, and providing a future template for adaptive behaviour (Solomon & Rando, 2007, 2012, 2015; Solomon & Shapiro, 1997).

The main goal of this book is to guide EMDR clinicians in utilizing EMDR therapy with grief and mourning. EMDR therapists treating bereaved clients' need to be knowledgeable about different theoretical frameworks in order to understand grief and mourning, to comprehend what may be complicating the grief, and to devise treatment plan to alleviate pain, reduce dysfunction, work through conflicts, and promote adaptation. This book details how to utilize EMDR therapy with grief and mourning, and it provides theoretical frameworks to guide case conceptualization and intervention.

SECTION 1
EMDR THERAPY AND GRIEF AND MOURNING

1

EMDR Therapy

Eye movement desensitization and reprocessing (EMDR) therapy is an integrative, psychotherapeutic approach that emphasizes the brain's intrinsic information processing system and focuses on how experiences are stored. Current problems are viewed as resulting from disturbing experiences that have not been appropriately processed and have been stored in a state specific, maladaptive form (Shapiro, 2001, 2005, 2018). The heart of EMDR involves the transmutation of these dysfunctionally stored experiences into an adaptive resolution that promotes psychological health.

EMDR is guided by the Adaptive Information Processing (AIP) model, which explains the basis of pathology, predicts successful clinical outcomes, and guides case conceptualization and treatment procedures. The AIP model posits the existence of an information processing system that assimilates new experiences into already existing memory networks. These memory networks are the basis of one's perception, attitudes, and behavior. Perceptions of current situations are automatically linked with associated memory networks (Buchanan, 2007). When working appropriately, the innate information processing system "metabolizes" or "digests" new experiences. Incoming sensory perceptions are integrated and connected to related information that is already stored in memory networks, which allows us to make sense of our experience. What is useful is learned, stored in memory networks with appropriate emotions, and made available to guide the person in the future (Shapiro, 2001).

Reprocessing, which involves accessing the maladaptively stored memory while simultaneously applying bilateral stimulation (e.g., eye movements, tapping, or auditory tones), results in the linking in of adaptive information into the memory networks that hold the maladaptive information, forging new associations. Hence, processing is learning. EMDR can be utilized to target any distressing memory, including memories that do not meet standard criteria to be classified as traumatic (Afifi et al., 2012; Heim et al., 2004; Mol et al., 2005). Indeed, adverse child experiences (Felitti et al., 1998) and "seemingly small" memories (e.g., mother's angry look at a moment a child feels vulnerable) have a significant impact on present day functioning, and can be processed with EMDR therapy (Shapiro, 2018).

EMDR Therapy Treatment for Grief and Mourning. Roger M. Solomon, Oxford University Press. © Roger M. Solomon 2024.
DOI: 10.1093/oso/9780198881360.003.0002

There are over 44 controlled studies validating the efficacy of EMDR therapy for trauma treatment (Maxfield, 2019). EMDR therapy has been designated effective according to international practice guidelines of organizations and agencies such as the World Health Organization (WHO, 2013) and US Departments of Veterans Affairs and Defense (DVA/DoD, 2017).

The Eight Phases of EMDR Therapy

EMDR therapy involves eight phases (discussed further below) and is guided by a three-pronged protocol:

1. *Past Memories*—The first prong consists of processing the past memories underlying the current painful circumstances. For loss, this may involve moments of shock, denial, other dissociative symptoms, or the moment of realization. Such realization typically occurs when hearing the news about the death of the loved one, if not present at the moment of the death, or during the worst moment if they were present (e.g., hospital scenes, accident scenes). The moment of realization may be before the death ("When I saw her at the hospital, 3 weeks before she died, I knew we were going to lose her") or after ("One month after he died in a car accident, I went to see the car and realized there is no way anyone could have survived"). Past unresolved losses, trauma, or attachment issues can be triggered by the current loss and complicate the grief and mourning, and they need to be processed.

2. *Present Triggers*—The second prong includes processing the present triggers that continue to stimulate pain and maladaptive coping. It is important to address the current situations where symptoms, "stuck points," and/or particularly painful moments are experienced.

3. *Future Templates*—The third prong involves laying down a positive future template. This involves facilitating adaptive coping patterns and strategies in present and anticipated future stressful situations. After processing a present trigger, a future template for adaptive functioning in that situation can be incorporated. Clients may need to learn new coping skills first, which can then be actualized by the future template.

The standard EMDR protocol involves the eight phases briefly described below, and these will be discussed in depth in later chapters.

Phase 1: History-Taking and Treatment Planning

This phase involves obtaining a full history and conducting appropriate assessment with a focus on current issues and the past experiential contributors underlying present problems. The therapist and client work together to identify targets for treatment that include past memories, present triggers, and future challenges related to the presenting problem(s).

Phase 2: Preparation and Stabilization

Clients deemed appropriate for EMDR therapy treatment are prepared for memory processing. The goals in this phase include: (a) establishing a therapeutic alliance; (b) educating the client about symptoms according to the AIP model (e.g., current problems are the result of past maladaptively stored memories); (c) explaining the EMDR process and procedures, its effects, and what to expect; and (d) teaching clients, according to their needs, affect regulation and management methods that increase stability and enable a sense of self-mastery and control. Typical preparation procedures used during this phase are the Calm/Safe Place exercise, with clients imagining a scene that evokes a feeling of safety and/or calmness, enhanced with bilateral stimulation (Shapiro, 2001, 2018), and Resource Development and Installation (Korn & Leeds, 2002), where positive memories/images involving adaptive qualities and characteristics are identified and enhanced with bilateral stimulation. With some clients, the history-taking and preparation phases can be provided in a few sessions. However, for individuals with an history of complex trauma, more time may be necessary for history-taking and preparation phases to ensure comprehensive assessment, sufficient stabilization and adequate readiness to begin memory processing.

Phase 3: Target Assessment

The Assessment introduces the reprocessing phases of EMDR. The memory to be treated (termed the "target" memory) is accessed through eliciting clients' current experience of the past event by identifying the components of clients' experience. Clients identify the following:

   a. *Image*—the image (most often is a visual element, but can be of any sensory modality) that represents the worst part.

   b. *Negative Cognition (NC)*—A negative, irrational, and self-referencing belief (in relation to the memory). The negative self-referencing belief that arises when the disturbing experience is brought to mind might be something like: "I am not good enough," "I am vulnerable," "I am powerless," and "I don't belong."

   c. *Positive Cognition (PC)*—identify a preferred, constructive cognition (or positive, adaptive belief) to discover and verbalize clients' desired outcome, like, "I am good enough," "I am safe now," "I have some control/choices," "I do belong."

   d. *Validity of Cognition (VoC)*—elicit this measurement by asking, how true the PC feels in relation to the memory, on a scale from 1 to 7, where 1 feels completely false and 7 feels completely true.

   e. *Emotion*—ask for the emotion associated when the image and negative image are held together.

   f. Subjective Units of Disturbance (SUDs)—ask, how distressing the memory is, on a scale of 0 to 10 scale, where 0 is no disturbance or neutral and 10 is the highest disturbance you can imagine.

   g. *Location of Body Sensation*—find out the location of the associated bodily sensations.

Phase 4: Desensitization

This phase initiates the reprocessing of the targeted memory, and the associated negative memories that are maladaptively stored. The client focuses on the image, negative belief, and physical sensations associated with the disturbing memory, while simultaneously engaging in sets of bilateral stimulation. The bilateral stimulation initiates an associative process, with each new set evoking new associations such as new images, thoughts, feelings, and/or sensations about the targeted memory, and eliciting other events that are in the memory network. Clients are asked to "let whatever happens, happen." Unless clients get stuck in the process and require an intervention, clinicians simply check in with clients between sets of bilateral stimulation, instructing clients to "just notice" what comes up and "go with that," with sets of bilateral stimulation continuing until clients are no longer reporting a change in experience. Clinical effects are measured utilizing the SUD scale, with the goal being 0 (no experience of actual distress or neutral in the present given what actually occurred). An adaptive resolution in EMDR therapy is always ecological: that is, emotions are appropriate to the situation. Consequently, not all memories will process to "0." This is particularly relevant for grief, since there can be normal and appropriate feelings (e.g., sadness) and a SUDs of 2 or more. For example, a veteran whose close friend was killed went from a SUD of 8 to a SUD of 2, and could not go lower because "a good friend and person died."

Phase 5: Installation

Dr Shapiro's original studies (Shapiro, 1989, 2001, 2002) found that EMDR therapy resulted in spontaneous shifts from the negative beliefs that people hold about themselves in relation to the targeted memory, to an adaptive self-belief. Given the emergent, adaptive, positive perspectives that arise during processing, EMDR can be conceptualized as a paradigm for enabling resilience and coherence (Solomon & Shapiro, 2013). The Installation Phase harnesses this naturally occurring shift toward resilience and an adaptive resolution by pairing the PC with the distressing memory and fostering the processing through additional bilateral stimulation. Processing continues by enhancing the connection of the adaptive information with the dysfunctionally stored information, facilitating the generalization effects within associated memories networks. The VoC scale is used to measure treatment effects with the goal of a VoC of 7, or whatever is ecologically appropriate for the client.

Phase 6: Body Scan

EMDR therapy has a strong emphasis on nonverbal information, including imagery, smells, tastes and sounds, and the bodily sensations associated with the disturbing memory. When the processing of the target memory appears to be complete, clients are asked to close their eyes, hold in mind the PC, and bring their attention to the different parts of their body, starting with their head and working downward, while noticing any tension, tightness, or unusual sensation. If such a sensation is experienced, it is processed with bilateral stimulation. Processing is considered complete when no more disturbing physical sensations are associated with the memory. However, it is common for positive affective responses (e.g., strength and confidence) to emerge; they can then be enhanced with further bilateral stimulation.

Phase 7: Closure

At the end of the session, it may be important to provide grounding or relaxation strategies to return clients to equilibrium (e.g., using the calm/safe place exercise or other stabilization strategies learned during Phase 2 Preparation). In addition, clients are advised that processing may continue between sessions, and that it is helpful to take notes regarding memories, dreams and present triggers that occur during the week, so that they can be addressed at a subsequent session. Clients are also reminded to use the self-care techniques that were taught in the preparation phase of EMDR as needed. No specific "home-work" is assigned.

Phase 8: Re-evaluation

At the following session, clients are assessed as to their current psychological state, whether the therapeutic effects of the previous session have been maintained, and what other material (e.g., dreams, flashbacks, other memories) has emerged since the last session. The result of this assessment guides the direction of further treatment.

EMDR Therapy and Grief and Mourning

Research on EMDR and Grief and Mourning

The first article on EMDR therapy and grief and mourning was written by Solomon and Shapiro (1997). Since then, research has shown that EMDR therapy can be effective in the treatment of grief. Meysner, Cotter, and Lee (2016), in a randomly controlled study, compared EMDR therapy with integrated cognitive behavioral therapy (CBT), and found both interventions to be equally effective. Cotter, Meysner, and Lee (2017), presenting interview data from the same study, reported both groups showed increased insight, positive shift in emotions, more of a "mental" relationship with the deceased, increase in self-confidence, and increase in activity levels. However, there were some unique effects of each treatment, with those receiving CBT describing that acquiring emotional regulation skills (part of the treatment protocol) was helpful. This was not reported by the EMDR group, who were not taught the same emotional regulation skills (described as a "tool kit" for managing distress) as the CBT group. Unique to the EMDR subjects was that distressing memories were less clear and more distant. The authors noted that the EMDR group reported positive shifts in emotion, self-confidence, and an increase in activity, even though these changes were not targeted in therapy. The authors also reported that the CBT group reported a shift from grief to an anticipated future of hope and enjoyment. The authors attribute the difference to the fact that EMDR, though addressing future obstacles, did not address future goals whereas the CBT group promoted active work toward building good times. This points to the importance of addressing how the client is coping in daily life, as well as the emotional aspects of the loss. This is addressed in the Dual Process Model (Stroebe et al., 1999) discussed in Chapter 7.

Hornsveld et al. (2010), replicating previous studies showing eye movements reduced the emotionality of negative memories, investigated the effect of eye movement in the treatment of negative memories of loss. Recall of the negative memory plus eye movements was found to be superior to no stimulation or listening to music in reducing emotionality and ability to concentrate on the memory (which the authors point out may be related to the vividness of the negative memory). Sprang (2001) demonstrated the effectiveness of EMDR with mourning, by comparing EMDR and Guided Mourning (GM) for treatment of complicated mourning. Of the five psychosocial measures of distress, four (State Anxiety, Impact of Event Scale, Index of Self-Esteem, and posttraumatic stress disorder (PTSD)) were found to be significantly altered by the type of treatment provided, with EMDR clients reporting the greatest reduction of PTSD symptoms. Data from the behavioral measures showed similar findings. Further, positive memories of the loved one emerged during EMDR treatment, which did not occur with GM.

EMDR therapy has also been found to be effective in treating grief in combination with CBT. Denderen, Keijser, Stewer, and Boelen (2017) provided a treatment combination consisting of eight sessions involving both CBT and EMDR therapy in a sample of 85 people whose loved one was a victim of homicide. It was thought that the treatment combination would be beneficial to this grieving population who had a high percentage of complicated grief and PTSD (88% of the study's sample), The treatment protocol involved two introductory sessions, followed by three sessions of either EMDR therapy followed by CBT or CBT followed by EMDR therapy. In comparison with a waitlist control group, participants who received this treatment reported significantly fewer symptoms of both PTSD and complicated grief. Participants in both groups also showed a significant decrease in symptomology midway through treatment, when they had received three sessions of one of the two therapies.

Treatment order of EMDR or CBT did not make a difference in effectiveness in reducing symptoms. The results of this study, similar to Meysner, Cotter, and Lee (2016), suggests that EMDR therapy is as effective as CBT in the treatment of grief, and lends support to the notion that EMDR can be integrated into overall bereavement therapy.

Discussion of the utilization of EMDR with grief and mourning, including case examples, have been presented by Kimiko (2010), Murray (2012), Solomon (2018), Solomon and Shapiro (1997), and Yasar et al. (2017). Solomon and Rando (2007, 2012, 2015) discussed how EMDR therapy can be guided by Rando's (1993) "R" processes in the treatment of grief and mourning.

EMDR Therapy Is Natural

With processing viewed as learning and facilitating integration, EMDR therapy proceeds in a way that is natural for the person and will not take away anything that the client needs or that is appropriate to the situation (Shapiro, 2018; Solomon & Shapiro, 1997). As Francine Shapiro stated (2018), "EMDR does not eliminate or even dilute healthy, appropriate emotions, including grief. Rather it can allow clients to mourn with a greater sense of inner peace" (p. 232). Further, Shapiro (2018) said, "I cannot stress enough, however, that EMDR processing does not eliminate or neutralize appropriate emotions, and it does not forestall personal growth. Thus, when EMDR is used, a grief-stricken client will naturally—and in his own way—move toward acceptance of his loss, while simultaneously resolving impediments to recovery" (p. 234). Therefore, EMDR can be used to process disturbance, including what is considered to be "normal" reactions or uncomplicated grief. For example, it is normal to be upset by intrusive imagery of the funeral or hospital scenes. However, such recollections can be very painful. EMDR therapy can process these distressing moments and facilitate the decrease of the pain (i.e., integrate the memory) in a way that is natural and helpful for the person. Hence, EMDR therapy seems to process the obstacles (upsetting or traumatic moments) that can complicate the grief.

EMDR Therapy Is Not a Shortcut

EMDR therapy is not a short cut for movement through the processes of mourning or resolution of a trauma. Clinical observations indicate that

EMDR clients go through the same mourning processes as other clients, but may do so more efficiently because obstacles to successful integration and movement are removed. Hence, rather than skipping aspects of mourning or forcing clients through mourning processes by neutralizing appropriate emotions or truncating individual growth, EMDR promotes a natural progression by processing the factors that could complicate the mourning.

The Goal of EMDR Therapy with Grief and Mourning

Given that EMDR therapy promotes a natural process, the goal of EMDR therapy with loss is to enable adaptive progression through the mourning process. This involves reprocessing distressing and traumatic aspects of the loss utilizing the three-pronged protocol of the following: (a) past memories related to the death (e.g., "getting the news" of the loss, distressing images, and moments) and earlier trauma, loss, and attachment related memories that underly present response to the loss; (b) present triggers; and (c) future templates for each trigger.

The Emergence of Meaningful Memories and Formation of an Adaptive Inner Representation

The pain of realization that the loved one is truly dead and the connection is forever gone can be overpowering for clients. Mourners can be "stuck" in the pain of loss, finding the loss of connection unbearable, unable to go through the processes necessary for assimilation and accommodation. Access to memory networks containing positive memories of the loved one are blocked. This can result in mourners feeling a loss of connection ("I can't connect"), which can be quite distressing. EMDR processing seems to allow clients to experience, express and discharge the pain which is necessary for the eventual linking in of other networks with positive, adaptive information (e.g., healthy accommodation). When using EMDR with mourners, it is common to observe the emergence of memories of the deceased, along with associated affect (Solomon & Rando, 2007, 2012, 2015). This was also observed in the Sprang study (2001) cited above. These positive, heartfelt memories provide a sense of connection to the loved one. As Continuing Bonds theory (Klass, Silverman, & Nickman, 1996) points out, healthy adaptation occurs when mourners can internalize a representation of the deceased into their inner working model so that psychological proximity can substitute for the previous physical proximity. That is, the mourner moves from loving in presence to loving in absence (Attig, 2000). In this context, the memories that arise during EMDR are the building blocks of an adaptive inner representation.

Fairbairn (1952), highlighting the importance of memories, defines an inner representation (in relation to the deceased loved one) as: (a) those aspects of the self that are identified with the deceased, (b) characteristics or thematic memories of the deceased, and (c) emotional states connected with those memories. This inner representation, experienced through memories and their meaning to us, is what seems to emerge and form with EMDR. It is these heartfelt memories of the loved one that allow us to know and acknowledge the meaning of the relationship with the deceased and their role in our life and identity. This inner representation enables us to carry the connection with the loved one into the future. Clients seem to go from "I can't connect," with its consequent deep pain to a sense of connection ("I can connect") with the emergence of heart felt memories. The adaptive inner representation allows the deceased to continue to serve as an attachment figure and to be an important source of felt security in times of distress.

Case Example 1: A 44-year-old woman came into treatment 3 years after the death of her father. She still experienced distressing negative images of him at the hospital. Her therapeutic goal was not only to relieve her distress but to be able to have positive memories of him. He had suffered, was in pain, and she felt helpless. A major goal for her was to be able to think of her father and have positive images of him. During the processing, she got in touch with past memories of her father when he was healthy. She also remembered her father did not like their dog when she was growing up, and the father had joked about his upcoming death, "Spot (the dog) is up in heaven right now going, 'Oh no.'" Memories came up of all the things she did to help her father (e.g., work with hospital staff to make him more comfortable, hold his hand, read to him). At the end of the session, she realized she had helped her father as much as she could, and their last interactions were meaningful, and "I helped him." She was asked to think of her father, since the goal of the session was to have positive images of him. Images of her father smiling and of happy moments with him emerged. These images and positive feelings associated with them were reinforced with eye movements.

This case illustrates how processing painful moments can result in the emergence of positive, heartfelt memories. It is suggested that at the end of a processing session, clients can be asked to think of the deceased and describe what memories come up. If positive, these memories with heartfelt emotion can be reinforced with bilateral stimulation. This serves as an additional installation to enhance the adaptive inner representation. If negative, painful, or neutral images arise, it can, in the author's experience, be an indication that clients would benefit from further processing. It must be emphasized that the emergence of positive heartfelt emotions does not mean clients are through grieving. Rather, it appears to balance out the pain, enabling clients to continue to go through a normal mourning process, providing relief, a sense of connection, and positive meaning (Neimeyer, 2006, 2015).

Adaptive Perspectives

Reprocessing the trauma of the loss, results in new perspectives emerging that provide meaningful and new ways of thinking about the death. Although complicated grief can result from a significant loss, mourners may also experience adaptive outcomes and personal growth.

A significant loss shatter's one's world assumptions and can create a crisis in meaning. Neimeyer et al. (2009, 2013), in his model of Meaning Reconstruction, discusses the importance of finding meaning after a loss, and regaining a "self-narrative to embrace the reality of the loss" (2009, p. 2) that enables mourners to make sense of what happened, and assimilate and accommodate the loss into their assumptive world. Mourners can also experience posttraumatic growth (Tedeschi & Calhoun, 2008) and experience positive changes and adaptive perspectives that enhance their life and ability to adapt to traumatic circumstances. The examples below illustrate how EMDR therapy can help clients achieve such positive outcomes, finding new meaning and growing from the loss.

Case Example 2: A soldier was killed as a result of a suicide bomber in Iraq. The father, Gilbert, was tremendously distressed. EMDR was provided 8 months later, starting with getting the news. The session was very emotional, with Gilbert feeling deep sorrow and anger at his daughter's violent death. After a 90-minute session, the SUD for the original memory was 0, and he was able to complete the Installation Phase. (The Body Scan was skipped because it was thought other associations would emerge). The positive meaning that emerged was that "The terrorist did not take my daughter's life, my daughter gave her life in the line of duty." This shift in perspective was a turning point in the father's trauma recovery and adaptation to the loss.

This example shows how reprocessing the trauma of the loss resulted in an assimilation and accommodation of the loss, giving Gilbert a new and adaptive perspective on the death of his daughter.

Case Example 3: Trudy's 17-year-old son died in a car crash. He was not wearing a seat belt. Trudy received EMDR therapy treatment 10 months after the death. Though Trudy had always emphasized the importance of wearing seatbelts, she felt guilty for not doing enough to ensure her son wore his seatbelt. Three sessions were devoted to processing the trauma of the loss, and working through the intense sadness of her loss. An important part of her adaptation to the loss was a commitment to educate others, in memorial to her son, on the importance of wearing seatbelts. In the next months, she gave talks to community groups, high school students, and made videos that were posted on social media websites on the importance of wearing seatbelts. These activities were meaningful to Trudy, giving her life a new sense of purpose.

As Trudy put it, "My son did not die in vain if his loss helps just one person remember to put on a seatbelt."

This example illustrates how part of the adaptation to the loss was Trudy engaging in meaningful activities that also memorialized her son. Many mourners participate in activities that memorialize their loved one and/or provide meaning in their lives such as advocating for programs to prevent death (as in the case of Trudy) to having fund raising activities (e.g., cancer research in memory of a loved one who died of cancer), provide support to others with similar losses, or memorial events (e.g., golf tournaments, marathons). This provided Trudy a new sense of direction in life. Despite her pain, she could still engage positively in life, demonstrating posttraumatic growth. EMDR therapy, in reprocessing the trauma of the loss, helps mourners go forward in life and find meaning and new purpose.

Summary

In summary, EMDR is an evidenced-based, eight-phase, three-pronged protocol. EMDR therapy is guided by the AIP model, that states that present problems are caused by maladaptively stored memories. Consequently, treatment proceeds with processing memories underlying present problems, present triggers, and installation of a future template for each trigger.

The trauma of a loss may cause negative memories to be maladaptively stored, unable to fully process. Thinking of the loved one evokes the traumatic moments and anguish over the loss, making it difficult to progress through the mourning process. The goal of EMDR therapy with loss is to enable adaptive progression through the mourning process. EMDR therapy promotes a natural healing process that will not take away anything a client needs, or that is true. Typically processing the trauma and distress of the loss enables a transformation of the attachment relationship to the loved one through the linking in of adaptive information such as meaningful, heartfelt memories. This gives rise to an adaptive inner representation enabling mourners to move from a sense of "I cannot connect" to the loved one to "I can connect." However, negative memories involving the loved one also need to be identified and reprocessed. Further, such reprocessing enables mourners to assimilate and accommodate the loss, with mourners gaining an adaptive perspective and posttraumatic growth.

2
Grief and Mourning

Bereavement Definitions

First, let's talk about some important definitions pertaining to bereavement.

Bereavement comes from an old English term that means *rob* or *deprive*. *Bereavement* is a term commonly used to describe having suffered a loss, and is the period after a loss during which grief is experienced and mourning occurs.

Grief refers to a person's reactions to the perception of loss. Grief reactions include the following:

- *Feelings* about the loss and the deprivation it causes; for example: sorrow, sadness, and guilt.
- *Protest*: the mourner's protest at the loss; the *wish to undo the loss* and have it not be true; anger, searching, yearning, and preoccupation with the deceased.
- *Personal actions*: mourner's personal actions, such as crying, withdrawal, and increased use of substances.

Mourning differs from grief and refers to the process that one goes through in adapting to the death (Worden, 2009); that is, the assimilation of and accommodation to the loss. Mourning encompasses not only grief reactions, but also an active coping with the loss through adapting to the world without the deceased.

In adapting to the loss, mourners must reorient in relation to the lost loved one, their inner world, and their external world (Rando, 1993). Consequently, mourners need:

1. *To evolve from the former psychological ties that connected mourners to the loved one to new ties appropriate to the now altered relationship*. There must be a shift in the relationship with the deceased loved one. The adaptation involves transforming the relationship from loving the person in the "here and now" present, when their presence could be felt and

EMDR Therapy Treatment for Grief and Mourning. Roger M. Solomon, Oxford University Press. © Roger M. Solomon 2024.
DOI: 10.1093/oso/9780198881360.003.0003

experienced, to loving in absence now that the loved one is dead (Attig, 2000). Although we need to relinquish the aspects of life that are no longer valid because the person is dead and not coming back, mourning is not "letting go" and "moving on." Rather, the relationship continues as it transmutes into a new, inner representation of the deceased, composed of heartfelt memories and meaningful moments.

2. *To personally adapt to the loss.* The loss of a loved one can affect identity ("Who am I now?") and challenge basic assumptions about how the world works, or one's assumptive world. Mourners must revise their identity and assumptive world to the extent of the impact made by the death and its consequences.

3. *To learn to live adaptively in the new world without the deceased.* The focus here is on the external world and how mourners will now exist within it. For example, a widow may now have to raise her children alone, assume roles previously fulfilled by the spouse, and adapt to a new social environment.

Progression Through the Grief and Mourning Process

Stages of Grief and Mourning

Several people have conceptualized stages or phases of grief:

- Sigmund Freud (2017): (1) denial, (2) acceptance, and (3) detachment.
- John Bowlby (1969): (1) shock and numbness, (2) yearning and searching, (3) despair and disorganization, and (4) reorganization and recovery.
- Elizabeth Kubler-Ross (Kubler-Ross & Kessler, 2014): (1) denial, (2) anger, (3) bargaining, (4) depression, and (5) acceptance.

However, people do not appear to go through a strict sequence of stages of grief (Bonanno et al., 2004), but there is general agreement that people seem to experience *a cluster of reactions* accompanying bereavement (Osterweiss et al., 1984; Pearlman et al., 2014; Rando, 1995). These can be categorized in three broad phases that describe the unfolding reactions and adaptation to loss (Rando, 1993):

- *Shock/avoidance phase.* The most frequent immediate response following the death of a loved one is shock, numbness, and a sense of disbelief, which is sometimes referred to as an avoidance or shock phase (Pearlman et al., 2014; Rando, 1993). This is a natural reaction to a significant loss, particularly if it is sudden and unexpected. After some time, with many factors determining the timing and intensity of reactions, the numbness wears off and gives way to emotional pain.

- *Confrontation/emotional impact phase.* Referred to as the "confrontation" or emotional impact phase, this is the time when waves of distress may be experienced along with yearning, pining, and longing for the loved one. Sadness and despair, guilt, anger, and anxiety are common reactions as the mourner comes to realize that the loved is gone for good.
- *Accommodation phase.* Generally, with time, there is an "accommodation" phase with grief reactions gradually declining as mourners accept the reality of the loss and adapt to life without the deceased. As already noted, these are broad phases meant to describe the unfolding nature of grief and mourning.

Grief Reactions

Losing someone we love, whom we were attached to, and who was a part of our lives, is uniquely painful. It is helpful to describe grief reactions as *normal reactions* to an upsetting and sad situation, *not* signs of pathology. The acute reactions in the immediate aftermath of trauma or loss can indeed be intense and difficult to understand, and may be interpreted by some as signs of going crazy. It is important mourners know that whatever they are experiencing are normal reactions to an intense event, and they are not losing their mind or going "nuts." For example, talking to the deceased loved one, sensing them talking back, and continuing the dialogue can be understood as another way of working through the loss instead of a sign of denial. One father had a conversation with his deceased son most nights for the first three months following his death. He would ask, "Are you okay?" and get a sensed answer of, "I am at peace ... I'm doing fine." His friends told him he was in denial and that he had to accept the death. Such comments were distressing to him. He felt better when I explained that it is okay and quite usual to have such conversations and they could indeed be comforting. As will be elaborated later, having a conversation is not necessarily denying the loved one is dead and not coming back; believing that the loved one is coming back indicates a more complicated form of grief.

Reactions to a significant loss can be quite varied and encompass a broad range of feelings and behaviors. Worden (2018) states, "Each person's grief is like all other people's grief; each person's grief is like some other person's grief; and each person's grief is like no other person's grief" (p. 8). Some of the more common reactions, put into general categories of feelings, physical sensations, cognitions, and behaviors (Worden, 2018), will be discussed below. These lists of reactions are by no means exhaustive. Generally, the reactions are normal, as described above, but if they persist for long periods of time (usually defined as six months; Prigerson et al., 1995, 2009) with an intensity that interferes with functioning, it is an indication that person may be experiencing Prolonged Grief Disorder.

Grief Reactions: Feelings

There are many ways that grief can be expressed. The following are some of the most frequent.

- *Shock* is common in the immediate aftermath of a tragedy. The event may be too much to take in, and a person can feel numb, with a feeling of unreality and disbelief.
- *Numbness* is experienced early in the grieving process, usually when the person learns their loved one has died. Numbness occurs when there is overwhelm. To feel the full brunt of the emotional impact would be overwhelming, and numbness is a protection from this flood of emotions.
- *Sadness* is the most common and natural feeling after a loss. Feeling despair, down, blue, empty, a void, are common descriptors of the impact of a loss. Something precious has been lost, something is missing, a void is felt (e.g., "a hollowness in my chest"), and life can lose its color and meaning. Mourners may lose the desire to interact with others or engage in usual activities. Sadness draws us inward, and we want to put the world on hold, withdraw and slow down.
- *Anger* is a frequent reaction, and may have several sources (Worden, 2009). Anger may be experienced *in reaction to circumstances* or people that trigger a sense of vulnerability and helplessness. It can reflect mourners' feelings about being abandoned ("How dare you die and leave me!"). It can reflect the frustration that comes with the *powerlessness to prevent the death*. One wife was angry with her husband who died after a long illness. On one level, of course, she realized he did not want to die and that he had fought the good fight to stay alive. But she was angry at him for dying, leaving her to raise the children alone and at being left without her chosen companion. People may *regress* in response to loss, feeling helpless, vulnerable, and unable to exist without the loved one, and then experiencing anger in response to these feelings of anxiety (Worden, 2018). Anger can be *displaced*, or directed at some other person or circumstance in an effort to understand what happened and to feel in

Grief Reactions: Thought Patterns

A diversity of thought patterns may accompany grief. Certain cognitions are quite common in the immediate aftermath of grieving and usually fade after a short time.

- *Disbelief*: "It didn't happen." Or "It doesn't feel real."
- *Confused thoughts*: difficulty concentrating, jumbled thoughts, or forgetfulness.
- *Preoccupation*: Mourners can be preoccupied with thoughts of the deceased, how they died, how they suffered (particularly if the death was traumatic), wishing the death could be undone, or reuniting with the lost person.
- *Sense of presence*: Worden describes sense of presence as the cognitive counterpart to the experience of yearning. It is normal and quite common in the early phases of grief that mourners can experience the presence of the loved one. Worden (2018) states that in the immediate aftermath of a death, mourners may think the deceased loved one is still in the current area of time and space. Hence, yearning for the loved one can lead to illusionary experiences, such as smelling their cologne or perfume or perceiving their face in a crowd, hearing their voice, and having a dialogue with the loved one. In missing the person, one may be on alert for cues of their presence, wanting to experience them as present, and not ready to realize they are never coming back.
- *Illusions/hallucinations*: Visual and auditory hallucinations are commonly experienced by the bereaved. Transient illusionary experiences ("I saw him in a crowd … I heard her voice.…"), usually occur during the first weeks following a loss. Grimby (1993) reported that over 80% of elderly people experience hallucinations associated with their deceased spouse within a month of the death. It is as if the mourner's perception has not quite caught up with the knowledge of death. Kamp et al. (2018) reported that over half the bereaved report some kind of bereavement-related hallucination. However, bereavement-related hallucinations (particularly if persisting) may be an indicator of psychological distress and may be associated with complicated grief.
- *Negative beliefs and self-appraisals*: Negative beliefs across the themes of responsibility, safety, control, and belonging may be experienced. For example, *self-blaming* may occur for not being able to prevent the death, or for not doing more for the loved one. "It's my fault.…" "I am a bad/not good enough son/daughter, husband/wife, father/mother."

Memories of negative interactions and perceived wrongdoing may also occur. Themes of *vulnerability* such as "I am not safe … my loved ones are not safe" can also be triggered by the loss. Indeed, such realization of vulnerability can be difficult to cope with. Themes of *powerlessness and helplessness* may not only revolve around the inability to prevent the death or to do more, but about life without the loved one, such as, "I can't live without her." "I can never be happy." "I will never find love again," And "I don't know how to cope with the pain." Themes having to do with *belonging* can involve a lack of connection, a sense of being alone, or not belonging.

- *Difficulties in positive reminiscing*: The distress of losing a loved one can block access to positive memories. Mourners may think of the loved one, or try to bring up a positive memory, and the pain of the loss is triggered. As one mother put it, "I try to think of my son's beautiful face with his curly hair and then I realize he is dead, and I feel I have lost him again."

Grief Reactions: Behaviors

A number of grief reactions are reflected in our behavior:

- *Sleep Disturbances.* This is perhaps the most common reaction to the distress of bereavement. Sleep disturbances sometimes require medical consultation and medication, but in uncomplicated grief, they usually dissipate within a few weeks. If a sleep disorder persists, it may be a sign of a more serious depression or anxiety reaction, and further assessment is indicated.
- *Dreams of the deceased.* Dreams are very common, such as dreaming of the loved one being alive, or of the circumstances of the death. The themes can reflect issues mourners are dealing with, such as fear of being alone, guilt, and anger at abandonment. Exploring these in therapy may be helpful.
- *Sighing and crying.* These naturally accompany the sadness and distress of the loss.
- *Restless hyperactivity.* Another common sign of distress, with agitation and difficulty staying still, can accompany loss.
- *Appetite disturbances.* Another common reaction to distress, overeating or undereating, may be experienced in grief.
- *Absentminded behavior.* After a significant loss it may be difficult to focus, concentrate, or stay present, and the person may be forgetful and preoccupied.

- *Social withdrawal.* After a distressing event, a person may choose to withdraw from others. Being depressed and not wanting to socialize or deal with other people's reactions is common after a loss.
- *Searching.* From an attachment perspective, the loss of a loved one can trigger the same kind of separation distress a child experiences in the absence of the caretaker (e.g., parent). The attachment system can be activated following the death of a loved one, with the goal of restoring proximity and motivate search behavior and experiences. Mourners frequently engage in "searching" behaviors, which may include going to places where they went with the deceased loved one, visiting at the cemetery, eating the favorite foods of the loved one, or watching their favorite television shows in an effort to feel present with them.
  a. *Carrying objects reminding the survivor of the deceased.* Carrying objects, such as pictures or wearing jewelry or clothes to feel in touch and keep the memory fresh is also a common reaction, which can provide a sense of connection.
  b. *Treasuring objects belonging to the deceased.* Keepsakes and reminders of the loved one are normal and can enable the mourner to maintain a sense of connection. When I lecture on grief and am asked if it is pathological to hold onto possessions of the loved one, I ask what they think about keeping the tongue and jawbone of a loved one? After seeing people cringe, I explain that St. Anthony's tongue and his jawbone are both displayed in the Basilica of Saint Anthony of Padua, Italy, in elaborate gold reliquaries. (The rest of his remains are entombed in a separate chapel.) Although not usually as elaborate as Saint Anthony's memorial, people often keep memorials to their loved ones, to remember and connect with the positive feelings and to honor the heartfelt memories.
  c. *Avoidance.* Some people will avoid reminders of the deceased that may be too much to handle in the aftermath of a death, such as not going to places or doing activities that will trigger painful feelings of grief. Usually, with time, avoidance, as with all the reactions described, decrease. However, continued or excessive avoidance is a major symptom of complicated grief.

See Table 2.1 for examples of emotional, physical, cognitive, and behavioral reactions to grief.

Table 2.1 Summary of Grief Reactions

Emotional	Physical	Cognitive	Behavioral
Shock	Hollowness in the stomach	Disbelief	Sleep disturbances
Numbness		Confused thoughts	Dreams of the deceased
Sadness	Tightness in the chest/throat	Preoccupation	
Anger		Sense of presence	Sighing and crying
Guilt and self-reproach	Oversensitivity to noise	Hallucinations	Restless activity
	Shortness of breath	Negative beliefs/ self-appraisals	Appetite disturbances
Anxiety	Weakness in the muscles		Absentminded
Loneliness		Difficulties in positive reminiscing	Social withdrawal
Yearning	Lack of energy		Searching
Fatigue	Dry mouth		Carrying reminders of the deceased
Helplessness	Body aches (e.g., headaches,		Treasuring objects that belonged to the deceased
Relief	stomachache, and chest pain)		Avoidance
	Higher than usual pulse and/or blood pressure		
	Digestive problems		

The Difference Between Grief and Depression

People who are grieving can exhibit some of the classic symptoms of depression, such as sleep disturbance, appetite disturbance, withdrawal, and intense sadness. However, with grief there is not the loss of self-esteem that is common in depression. Freud (1917) said, *in grief, the world looks poor and empty, while in depression the person feels poor and empty.*

While a distinction needs to be made between grief and depression, some bereaved individuals develop a major depression following a loss (Zisook & Shuchter, 1993). Here the major symptoms are:

- Guilt (other than guilt regarding actions that were taken/not taken at the time of the death).
- Thoughts of death (other than the feeling that he/she/they would be better off dead or should have died with the loved one).
- Feelings of worthlessness, psychomotor retardation, and marked functional impairment.

Accordingly, treatment for depression, along with the complicated grief, needs to be provided.

Summary

This chapter defines those concepts that are part of the bereavement process. It tracks progress from grief though mourning and suggests that people do not go through a rigid progression of stages to deal with grief; individuals each find their own way. This chapter described grief as a person's reaction to the loss and mourning as the process of adaptation to the loss. But there seems to be agreement on a broad framework of a shock phase, an emotional confrontation phase, and an accommodation phase. Emotional, physical, cognitive and behavioral reactions to grief have been described. The difference between grief and depression has been illustrated.

3

Impact of Loss

Internal and Interpersonal Changes

Violations of the Assumptive World

The death of a loved one can be *traumatic*. Mourners are confronted with the permanent absence of someone who was a present and significant attachment figure in their life, or in the case of the death of parents, the recipient of their caregiving (Shear & Shair, 2005). This permanent change in an ongoing real relationship may be too much to assimilate in a person's world view (Janoff-Bulman, 1992; Shear & Shair, 2005; Solomon & Rando, 2007, 2012, 2015). Indeed, a major secondary loss (with the loss of the person being primary) is the *loss of one's assumptive world* (Rando, 1993; Solomon & Rando, 2007, 2012, 2015).

The assumptive world is a conceptual system that is based on a set of assumptions about the world, the self, and others. These assumptions compose a world view that helps us make sense of the world and our role within it. They enable us to feel safe, capable, and in control of what happens not only to us ('I can keep myself safe') but also to those around us ('I can keep my loved ones safe'). The assumptions can be so basic and fundamental that they are virtually automatic habits of cognition and behaviour (Janoff-Bulman, 1989), and we may not even know we have these assumptions until they are violated. When our assumptive world is challenged by traumatizing events, significant distress, and disruption may occur. Janoff-Bulman points out that a trauma can violate global basic assumption such as:

1. It is a benign universe (bad things are not supposed to happen, 'not to me').
2. It's a meaningful world that is fair, just, predictable, and where one has control.
3. The self is worthy (bad things don't happen to good people).
   Assumptions are not only global, but can be specific to the loved one. For example: 'We were supposed to grow old together.' And 'My brother

EMDR Therapy Treatment for Grief and Mourning. Roger M. Solomon, Oxford University Press. © Roger M. Solomon 2024.
DOI: 10.1093/oso/9780198881360.003.0004

was supposed to always be around to protect me.' Or 'I was supposed to always make sure no harm would come to my children.'

Colin Murray Parkes (2011) puts it this way:

> I know where I'm going, and I know who's going with me, except when we lose someone we love, we no longer know where we are going or who is going with us (p. 4).

This quote illustrates how we not only lose someone we love, but potentially a significant part of our assumptive world, necessitating the need for the assimilation and accommodation of the loss and rebuilding of one's world. In 1988, Parkes refers to mourning as a psychosocial transition that requires the mourner to adjust his or her assumptive world in order to come to terms with the death. He goes on to say, in regard to the death of a spouse:

> The death of a spouse invalidates assumptions that penetrate many aspects of life, from the moment of rising to going to sleep in an empty bed. Habits of action (setting the table for two) and the thought ('I must ask my husband about that') must be revised if the survivor is to live as a widow (p. 56).

Major issues are created when one's assumptive world is violated, especially when there is traumatic loss (Parkes, 1988; Pearlman et al., 2014; Janoff-Bulman, 1989):

- *Meaning of Loss*: Mourners may grapple with meaning, finding it difficult to make sense of what happened. Some may find meaning in various beliefs, such as believing the loved one is no longer suffering, or is now in a better place (e.g., in heaven), or died doing what he loved to do (e.g., a police officer killed in the line of duty). Some people develop a new purpose in life (e.g., helping others who died in similar ways), or emerge with enhanced resilience as a result of reprocessing and integrating the loss. However, for many survivors of traumatic loss, life loses its meaning. Mourners cannot make sense of what happened, how a tragedy like this could occur, or understand how the loved one could die in this way. The loss of meaning leaves mourners with intense and prolonged distress and feelings of powerlessness and vulnerability. As one wife of a soldier killed in battle said a year after his death, 'I can never be happy again.' Another spouse of a soldier put it this way, 'Every day is dark and there will always be places within me that light will never touch.'

- *Finality*: Mourners may have difficulty accepting the loss and fully understanding the finality of the loss and all of its ramifications. For example, one woman whose son was killed in a mountain climbing accident said, 'I know he is dead, but inside I feel like he is still alive.'
- *Causality, Responsibility, & Blame*: Mourners can be preoccupied with causality, responsibility, and blame. How it happened, why it happened, who should be held accountable, could anything have been done to prevent the tragedy, are issues that can preoccupy mourners. Some people attempt to learn everything they can about what happened, reading every document, or looking at all the pictures. As one mourner who frantically read everything available over and over again put it, 'I still can't accept it and am still trying to understand it.' If there is an identifiable perpetrator, naturally mourners may focus on justice and retribution. I have known many mourners (e.g., families of police officers killed in the line of duty) whose main focus in life becomes the trial and prosecution of the perpetrator, which in many cases can take several years. After it is over, the mourners may feel empty, ask 'Now what?', and again have to face the pain and grief that comes with realization of loss.
- *Intense Guilt*: Mourners can suffer intense feelings of guilt. Guilt is a common reaction, especially for parents who may have deep feelings of responsibility for their children, that are readily transformed into guilt after a child's traumatic death (Worden, 2018). In wanting to feel in control, people can blame themselves for factors that were beyond their control. For example, 'Because of what I did (or did not do), this is what happened ... If only I had done something different, it would not have happened.' It may be psychologically easier, despite the emotional pain, for survivors to blame themselves for an act of omission or commission, than to realize how powerless they really are. My first lesson in this came early in my career. A man and his wife were riding a motorcycle when it went over a small rock, bounced slightly, but the wife fell off and was killed. I met with the husband within three hours. He told me that he killed his wife. After he told me what had happened, we went through the sequence of events, moment by moment, and I pointed out how each significant moment was beyond his control (e.g., no one saw the small rock; he was focused on keeping the motorcycle upright). He looked at me with a look of anguish and said in a sad but determined tone, 'What you are saying is logical, but I am very emotional right now ... I killed my wife.' It then dawned on me that right then and there, he needed to blame himself in order to understand what happened and perhaps to feel in control. All I could do is nod my head and say, 'I understand.' In the next few

weeks, he was able to see the how unforeseen circumstances had caused the death rather than any fault of his.

- *Questioning One's Faith*: A traumatic loss can lead to mourners questioning their faith. Religious or spiritual beliefs may help people cope with loss, and may mitigate threats to meaning (Park & Halifax, 2011). However, an event that shatters one's assumptive world can trigger a crisis in faith (e.g., 'How could God let this happen?'). One mother of an infant who died was very religious and had always believed in a benign, loving God. After the death of her baby, she was in a dilemma—either God was punishing her or God was not loving as she had been brought up to believe.

- *Preoccupation with the Loved One's Suffering*: Mourners can be preoccupied with the deceased's suffering. Particularly when a death is sudden, unexpected, and traumatic, mourners may be preoccupied with the question of how much their loved one suffered. Was it painful? Was the loved one frightened? What were they thinking when they died? We all want to believe our loved ones died peacefully. Often, in the hope to mitigate the pain, a loved one is told, 'Death was instantaneous' or 'He didn't know what hit him', or 'She didn't feel a thing, it happened so fast.' However, there are times when the deceased did suffer, and the realization of this can be traumatizing for relatives. Many mourners may suffer deeply when thinking about how their loved one died. For example, relatives are often present at the trials of the murders who killed the loved one. These trials can be very graphic and descriptive of how the loved one was killed. In trying to understand what happened, many mourners can deeply identify with the deceased, and become traumatized as a result.

I have found eye movement desensitization and reprocessing (EMDR) therapy to be quite helpful in these situations, resulting in the mourner moving from 'He suffered' to 'He is not suffering now' or 'She is at peace now.' On 1 February 2003, the Space Shuttle Columbia disintegrated upon re-entry to earth. Originally, it was thought that the astronauts died instantaneously. However, during the investigation it became evident that the astronauts knew what was happening about 30 seconds before the disintegration occurred. This was very upsetting to those close to the astronauts. I worked with one mourner with EMDR therapy, targeting the moment the client found out the astronauts became aware of what was happening, keeping the focus on the person the client knew. The resolution was, 'He was probably angry as hell, and doing everything he could.' Thinking of the loved one as having an active response, rather than a passive resignation, was comforting to the client.

Areas of Life Impacted

A significant loss can affect all aspects of mourners' lives. Therapists not only need to focus on the emotional impact of the loss, but how it impacts daily life. Pearlman et al. (2014) describe five main areas.

Interpersonal Relationships

Impact on Family Life

A loss has a tremendous impact on how a family functions, particularly when there is a sudden death. If the loved one dies after a long illness, the family has had time to prepare, in comparison with an unexpected and sudden loss. If the person who passed was the main wage earner, the family must cope with new financial stressors. A loss in income creates hardship, and the family faces many difficult decisions pertaining to where they live, daily expenses, and the like. Dealing with insurance, legal issues, and taxes, for example, makes the loss more stressful and can be overwhelming while suffering acute grief. The surviving spouse will now have to take on new responsibilities regarding raising the children, handling finances, and take on the roles left vacant when the loved one died.

Loss of a Child

The loss of a child can put a tremendous strain on the marriage, and research has shown that divorce is more likely following the death of a child (Murphy, Johnson, & Lohan, 2003). However, it is a myth that divorce is inevitable. Most couples who do remain together following the loss of a child become closer and are more satisfied with their relationship, with men more so than women (Dyregrov, Gjestad, & Dyregrov, 2020).

Parental Grief

The grief of a parent can also interfere with attending to the needs of the surviving children. Partners may have different mourning styles. For example, one partner may need to talk about what happened and their feelings about the loss while the other may have a style where feelings are held inside and dealt with privately. A significant loss commonly affects a couple's sexual relationship. There can be lack of interest or loss of desire. On the other hand, sexual desire can increase. As one man expressed after the loss of his child, 'My need for intimacy increased after Joseph died ... my wife represented life, and I reached for life.'

The loss of a child or partner also creates problems in parenting. Some problems are unique to the parent who has lost a partner and now has to assume the responsibilities of the other. As one man put it, 'I had to learn how to brush my little girl's hair.' Other difficulties are unique to parents who have lost a child, and are in deep mourning as a result. It is difficult to be emotionally and physically available to other children after a significant loss. In fact, a child born after the death of a child can be significantly impacted by the parents' grief (Liotti, 1992). A parent can be calm one moment, experiencing despair and grief the next, and overreact to a child's behaviour the next. Interfamily conflicts may worsen.

Family members may also grieve differently, given the unique aspects of their relationship to the deceased. Children of different ages grieve differently. A young child may not understand the permanence of the loss, versus an older sibling who recognizes the permanence and feels lost without their role model and attachment figure. Surviving children, of course, have intense reactions both to the loss of a sibling as well as to the change in family dynamics. It is beyond the scope of this book to describe child grief, and ways it is expressed. Many resources exist for the therapist to provide appropriate support (see Dyregrov, 2008).

Extended Family Impact

Extended family relationships are also affected. One frequently encountered problem is that extended family members may find it difficult to acknowledge their loss and to talk about the deceased. Another common problem is that of conflicts between the survivor and in-laws. Issues involving advice (often unwanted), doing too much, not doing enough, for example, can arise as new boundaries and ways of relating are negotiated.

Structures of Daily Life

Life can be complicated after the death of a loved one. There are financial and household obligations to attend to. Work can be impacted with mourners experiencing intense emotions, difficulty with concentration and memory, and perhaps a lessening in motivation and/or in job satisfaction. Leisure and recreation activities may also be impacted. For example, activities that were enjoyed with the deceased may be difficult to engage in. Vacations, holidays, and a variety of family activities can be painful. In the case of death, following a long, protracted illness, the family may have difficulty remembering their daily life routines prior to the intense caregiving.

Spiritual or Religious Community

A traumatic death can evoke a crisis of faith, feelings of disillusionment, and participation in religious or spiritual activities. However, sometimes feelings of spirituality and participation increase. As one widowed man put it, 'In being closer to God I could feel closer to my wife.'

The Criminal Justice and Legal System

If the death of a loved one involved a crime, mourners will have to deal with the legal system. Whether it entails a criminal trial or civil lawsuit, dealing with the legal system is stressful. Legal proceedings can take years, with postponements and endless delays causing frustration and disillusionment. Families of people killed in a crime want justice and can become engrossed in trial preparation and proceedings. If a case gets settled or the perpetrator gets a lighter sentence than survivors think is deserved, it can create a secondary trauma and disillusionment. For example, a suspect who was drunk and involved in a fatality pleaded guilty in exchange for 1-year probation, which upset the survivors, who felt there was no justice. Going to trial, being scrutinized by attorneys, and being examined and cross-examined on the witness stand can be distressing. Having to hear the details about the death can also be harrowing. For example, one mother of a police officer who was killed was subjected to hearing about the gory details of the death, which created vicarious trauma.

Social Support

Social support is an extremely important resource for dealing with distressing life experiences. Supportive interactions are calming, enabling people to feel cared for, valued, and that they belong and have safety, and, indeed, lack of support is a risk factor for complicated grief.

Studies suggest three reasons for lack of support:

1. Potential providers of support can be impacted by the death and may be less effective because they are mourning as well.
2. Mourners tend to withdraw. Many mourners choose to avoid or to minimize contact with others. Some mourners feel too helpless to ask for support, or feel ashamed for needing help or are too sad to respond to the

overtures of others. Sometimes it is difficult to be with other people because of a perceived lack of understanding or feeling like a 'third wheel' and out of place.

3. The social ineptitude of other people.

Dyregrov (2003, 2004) concluded there were three categories of social ineptitude.

1. Anticipated support may fail to appear or others may offer little actual support. Good friends or relatives who have said, 'Call me if I can do anything to help' do not actually check on the person or respond if called.

2. Some potential *supports are uncomfortable with the death* and avoid contact. For example, police widows are often cut off from social contact with other police wives because they are a reminder of a tragedy that can happen to them.

3. Social ineptitude often comes in the form of *comments, advice, or actions viewed as unhelpful.* People say superficial platitudes that are a sure-fire turn-off, such as, 'I know how you feel', 'You can always find another partner', or 'God needed him more than you did.' Shortly after the miscarriage of a child, one person said to the father in an attempt to help, 'You knew this could happen, right?' All he could do was nod and walk away. Others may also have unwanted advice on how to live, raise the kids, or get back into the 'swing of things'.

Mediators of Mourning

A number of important mediators affect mourning (Pearlman et al., 2014; Worden, 2018).

Deceased's Relationship to the Survivor

Kinship identifies the deceased's relationship to the survivor (e.g., spouse, parent, child, sibling, or friend). A grandparent who dies peacefully of natural causes will be grieved differently than a child killed in a car accident. The loss of an old friend whom one has not seen in years will be grieved differently than a parent who lived in close proximity with day-to-day contact.

The death of a child results in more intense and prolonged grief and depression than the death of a spouse, sibling, or parent (Cleiren, 1991, Cleiren et al., 1994; Nolen-Hoeksema & Larson, 1999). Further, Cleiren (1992) found that the family relationship was the more important factor in determining the mourner's adaptation, with mothers of the deceased showing the worst outcome. Murphy et al. (2003) found that parents of murdered children had more posttraumatic stress disorder (PTSD) symptoms than parents of children who committed suicide or died in accidents. Otherwise, there were very few differences resulting from how the loved one died. Dyregrov et al., (2003) studying parents who lost children to suicide, accident, or sudden infant death syndrome (SIDS) noted that they all experienced severe distress. Further, they found that parents of children who died from suicide or accidents experienced significantly more problems than parents whose who lost infants to SIDS. Loss by suicide was not worse than other modes. These studies indicate that the sudden, traumatic death of a child results in long lasting distress for the parents, regardless of the mode of death.

Nature of the Relationship

The Strength of the Attachment
The intensity of grief is determined by the intensity of love. Who was lost and what was their place in the mourner's life?

The Security of the Attachment
The more the deceased was an important part of the security and well-being of the survivor, the more difficult coping with the loss can be. Studies show that widows with the highest levels of warmth and closeness had a more difficult adjustment in comparison to more conflictual relationships (Carr, 2008; Carr et al., 2000). Similarly, Pearlman et al. (2014) summarizing the research, concludes that individuals who had warm, loving relationships may be more at risk for traumatic bereavement.

The Ambivalence and Conflicts in the Relationship
Ambivalent relationships are those where negative feelings coexist in equal proportions to positive ones, or outweigh them. Commonly in relationships with a significant degree of ambivalence, the death results in a tremendous amount of guilt. However, some clients who have been in conflictual relationships report that they are glad the person is out of their life (Dyregrov, personal communication, 2022).

Conflicts with the Deceased

In a conflicted relationship where there has been an ongoing history of conflict, there is often unfinished business that never gets resolved or reaches closure before the death. The death can bring feelings of relief (from the conflict) on one hand, but also may burden mourners with the issues that were unresolved. Past arguments, residual anger and negativity, or unresolved problems can haunt mourners and may still need to be dealt with.

Dependent Relationships

Adaptation to life can be more difficult if mourners were dependent on the loved one for daily living functions and/or as well as for emotional support, problem-solving, and self-esteem.

Mode of Death

How the person died, as described above in the section on traumatic death, has an impact on grief and mourning. Traditionally, deaths are catalogued under the NASH categories: natural, accidental, suicidal, and homicidal (Worden, 2018). Pearlman et al. (2014) names these four, and also includes disaster. Below is a brief description of some of the issues. Death caused by Covid-19 perhaps fits under disaster, but being a pandemic, it is different and perhaps in a category by itself. It will be briefly discussed below, and more comprehensively in Appendix A.

Natural Death

A loved one can die suddenly of a physical cause such as a heart attack, illness, stroke, and the like. For some mourners, the pain the loved one felt, images of being hooked up to medical equipment and life support, and watching physical deterioration (especially if one is a caregiver), result in intrusive imagery and painful memories. There can be guilt associated with making the decision to take the loved one off of life support, that more could have been done to ease the pain, or that more time should have been spent with the loved one before they died.

Accidental Death

Automobile accidents, biking or hiking accidents, falls, drowning, fires, and choking are examples of accidental deaths. Sudden and unexpected death can be traumatizing. Children and adolescents have higher accident rates than adults, and hence are untimely. Often, accidents are viewed as preventable and something that should not have happened, which is very distressing.

Accidents can involve violent, painful death where there is mutilation and body disfigurement, and perhaps identification with the pain the deceased may have felt. Hospital experiences (e.g., waiting room, death notification, and gruesome images of the body) can also be harrowing. Making medical decisions (e.g., take the person off life support) and organ donation decisions can also be extremely painful. In cases where the accident was the fault of the deceased (e.g., through carelessness or substance abuse), survivors can experience guilt for not doing more to possibly prevent the death. An accident that resulted from the behaviour of the mourner (e.g., child playing with a gun, accidently running over a small child hiding behind the car) can be traumatizing, as well.

Disasters
Disasters can be natural, such as hurricanes or earthquakes, or deliberate, as with terrorism. Following a large-scale tragedy, there can be a prolonged time before relatives find out about the fate of their loved ones. It can also be difficult to get hold of the loved one's body, and sometimes no body is recovered. When the body is recovered it can be badly damaged. In addition to the loss of a loved one, there can also be a loss of property. Further, there can be the loss of the community. People who lose their houses can be in temporary quarters for weeks or months. One's community and a sense of safety may never be restored. Dealing with insurance companies, government agencies, assistance organizations, and other bureaucracies can also be frustrating, creating secondary injuries. With personal and community loss, there can be bereavement overload (Pearlman et al., 2014).

Suicide
It is a common belief that deaths from suicide lead to more problems, in comparison to deaths that come about in other ways. However, research (Dyregrov et al., 2003; Murphy et al., 2003; Sveen & Walby, 2008) shows that there are no significant differences in symptoms of mental health (e.g., depression, anxiety, or anger) for surviving loved ones, while Young et al. (2012) reported research indicating that those grieving loss by suicide are at significantly higher risk of suicidal ideation and behaviours. Sveen and Walby (2008) did find differences between survivors of suicide and other modes of death in terms of shame, stigma, rejection, concealing the cause of death, and blaming others. Suicide of a loved one can lead the survivor to feeling guilt and/or shame for not doing enough. Further, suicide can be viewed as the ultimate rejection and betrayal—the person has chosen death over life. There can be intense anger for using suicide as the way out and abandoning those close to them in this way. A suicide can invalidate the positive aspects of the relationship, intensify

the grief and prolong the mourning process. Feelings of humiliation, shame, guilt, rage, and inadequacy and a belief that, 'I was not important enough', add to the trauma of the loss and complicate the grief. There can be much unfinished business and unanswered questions for the mourners: 'Why? How could you do this to yourself? How could you do this to me?'

Suicide can be viewed as the ultimate taking of control of a difficult situation where the person saw no way out, with the person dying on their own terms, and, thus, represents a solution to a perceived unbearable situation. For others, suicide is perceived as a personal failure that makes no sense at all.

Homicide

Homicide is sudden, unexpected, and violent, all qualities that pose further risk factors. Further, a deliberate act of someone killing one's loved one can evoke feelings of rage and thirst for revenge. The mourner's feeling of powerlessness, not only in thinking of what their loved one experienced, but also in not being able to help, can indeed be traumatizing. Murder violates basic assumptions about safety and control in this world, and can result in PTSD among the mourners. Mourners may become hypervigilant and worry excessively about living loved ones. If a perpetrator is caught, dealing with the criminal justice system can be frustrating, with court delays, impersonal proceedings, and impersonal treatment. If no perpetrator is apprehended, the lack of closure and sense of injustice compound the trauma of the loss. Further, media coverage can be intrusive and insensitive, not only in the immediate aftermath of the murder but during legal proceedings.

Covid-19 Pandemic

Death caused by Covid-19 meets many of the criteria for a traumatic death (see Chapter 4), with grief and mourning further complicated by mourners' personal distress caused by the pandemic. The restrictions caused by Covid-19 include not having a live funeral, religious or spiritual gatherings, face-to-face comfort from family and friends, and significant distress caused by unwanted changes in one's daily life. Personal issues can be triggered by Covid-19 and need to be dealt with, along with issues related to the loss. This topic will be further discussed with in Appendix 1.

Proximity

Proximity is another variable that can mediate grief. How close was the loved one geographically? When the loved one lived far away, with visits few and far between, the death can seem unreal initially because not having contact is the norm. Not uncommonly, it can take a while for the reality to sink in because the deceased has not been part of everyday life.

Historical Antecedents

Mourners' histories of previous losses, traumas, and mental health issues have a direct bearing on grief and mourning. This will be illustrated in later chapters.

Gender of the Mourner

Overall, men appear to have greater difficulty than women in coping with the death of a spouse. Men who lose a spouse are more likely to become depressed than widowed women. In general, this may be because men rely primarily on their wives for social support, whereas women typically have more close friends. Studies have shown that widowers tend to decrease their social activity over time and may have more difficulty in maintaining and building social relationships following the death of their wives (Cleiren, 1992; Pearlman et al., 2014). Further, married women often have a large role in monitoring the husband's health practices such as medical appointments, taking medications, and diet. Consequently, it is important to talk with widowers about their support networks and how they handle health matters. In regard to loss of a child, studies show that fathers experience considerable distress, but that mothers report significantly more distress than do fathers.

Studies show mothers scored higher than fathers on many mental health indices following the death of a child, including depression, anxiety, somatic complaints, and cognitive functioning (Murphy et al., 2003). There are also differences in coping strategies that are most helpful in dealing with loss. Shut et al. (1997) found that widows benefited more than widowers following counselling that focused on day-to-day activities, whereas widowers benefited more from counselling that facilitated emotional expression. This may be because mothers typically cope by seeking support and communicating about their feelings and so benefit more from interventions that focus on dealing with everyday life. Fathers may be more likely to conceal and hold in their grief and, consequently, benefit more from interventions that help them express and deal with their emotions.

Personality Variables

A number of personality variables influence how a person deals with adversity. Self-esteem is a strong predictor for coping with traumatic grief (Murphy et al., 2002). Negative self-beliefs and low self-esteem also affect a person's ability to cope with tragedy (Boelen, van den Hout, & van den Bout 2006). Dispositional optimism (Nolen-Hoeksema, 2001) is the tendency to be optimistic. People scoring higher on this variable showed greater declines in grief symptoms following the loss of a loved one.

Coping Style

The thoughts and behaviours that a person uses to manage the external or internal demands of stressful situations have direct bearing on dealing with tragedy. Lazarus and Folkman (1984) report that coping styles of problem-solving coping and active emotional coping are most effective, while avoidant emotional coping is least effective.

Attachment Style

An individual's attachment style strongly influences how a person reacts to loss. Loss of a loved one can result in separation distress and activate the same responses to separation that the mourner may have experienced as a child. Understanding attachment style and the experiences involved in the formation of insecure attachment styles is paramount in treatment of complicated grief. This will be further discussed in Chapter 6.

Social Variables

The degree of perceived support from others, inside and outside the immediate family, is important in the mourning process. Studies have shown that perceived support is a buffer against stress, including the stress of bereavement (Strobe et al., 1999). Also, most studies find that those who have inadequate or conflictual social support do less well with bereavement. Stroebe, Schut, and Stoebe (2005), summarizing four longitudinal studies, found that those with more social support had lower rates of depression. However, these studies did not show social support accelerating adaptation to the loss or making adjustment easier. It seems that social support eases the trauma of loss, but does not accelerate the grieving process (Worden, 2018). There are a number of important social mediators.

Support Satisfaction
Satisfaction with support is more important than the availability of support. In fact, social support can be negative, and can sometimes make things worse. For example, friends or family may say, 'It's time to move on', or do not really want to hear about the mourner's difficulties, and such responses can make coping with loss more difficult.

Religion and Spiritual Beliefs
Most studies show that religious beliefs or practices are helpful to mourners and are associated with adjustment to the loss (Becker et al., 2007; Wortman & Park, 2008). Religious and spiritual traditions offer many resources for coping with death, including prayer (which can help maintain a rewarding connection to the deceased), social support, coping guidance, finding meaning in a loss, and rituals that can facilitate adaptive grieving. Many people, however, struggle with religion and may be angry at God or feel abandoned or betrayed or feel they are being punished for their sins. It is common for survivors to have a crisis of faith and feel life no longer has meaning. Religious struggle has been identified as a strong predictor of poor outcome following the loss of a loved. However, Tedeschi and Calhoun (2006, 2008) studying 'posttraumatic growth' found that in some cases people emerge from their religious struggle with more meaning and more satisfying spiritual lives.

Secondary Gain
Bill Worden (2018) points out that secondary gain is another mediator. 'A survivor might get a lot of mileage in his or her social network out of grieving, and this would have an effect on how long it goes on' (p. 75).

Concurrent Stress in Mourners' Lives
The loss of a loved one can lead to significant disruption of life. These secondary losses, such as changes in financial situation, having to move, and a host of other changes associated with the death of a loved one, compound the difficulty of adaptation.

Summary

This chapter described that a loss can violate a person's assumptive world, creating a crisis in meaning, causing difficulty in accepting the loss, preoccupation with causality, and guilt, questioning one's faith, and preoccupation with the loved one's suffering. All areas of life can be impacted. Grief and mourning result in a unique journey, and mediators that impact the mourning process have been addressed. This included a discussion of the mode of death (natural, accidental, disaster, Covid, suicide, and homicide).

4

Traumatic Bereavement

Traumatic Bereavement Definitions

According to Pearlman et al. (2014) *traumatic bereavement* is when the grief over a loved one is overpowered by the traumatic stress resulting from the circumstances of the death. A trauma is an overwhelming event that occurs when a person is confronted with actual or threatened death or serious harm that is perceived to be inescapable. In other words, a trauma is an event that overwhelms one's sense of vulnerability and control. A sudden, traumatic death, resulting from an event that is abrupt and occurs without warning, may result in traumatic bereavement.

Traumatic bereavement is characterized by enduring symptoms of both traumatic distress and separation distress. Trauma-related issues include numbness, shock, and violation of the assumptive world. Intrusive, avoidant, and arousal symptoms (typical of posttraumatic stress disorder (PTSD)) related to the circumstances of the death can occur as well. Separation distress is when acute emotional distress experiences occur resulting in the loss of a meaningful relationship. Typically, it involves normal, grief reactions such as yearning, pining, and loneliness. Also, it can result in intrusive, avoidant, and arousal symptoms related to the loss of the relationship.

Impact of a Traumatic Death

There are five major reasons that a sudden, traumatic death is *more devastating* than a death stemming from natural causes (Wortman & Pearlman, 2016):

1. *Destabilization*—the initial impact of the loss is likely to be more destabilizing and have the potential to be overwhelming.
2. *PTSD Symptoms*—Survivors of traumatic loss experience a different set of symptoms. Along with the symptoms that typically occur with death by natural causes (e.g., deep sadness and yearning), there may be

EMDR Therapy Treatment for Grief and Mourning. Roger M. Solomon, Oxford University Press. © Roger M. Solomon 2024.
DOI: 10.1093/oso/9780198881360.003.0005

symptoms of posttraumatic stress disorder (PTSD). These indicators include intrusive symptoms (e.g., flashbacks and nightmares), avoidance of reminders and realization of the death, and increased physiological arousal (e.g., sleep problems, anxiety). Survivors of traumatic loss face dual tasks of mourning the loss (which can be traumatizing itself) and dealing with the trauma of the death.

3. *Avoidance*—Trauma can interfere with attempts to remember and recollect the loved one, an important step in adapting to the loss. An important part of integrating the loss is experiencing heartfelt memories of the loved one. Distressing memories or images can interfere with this process and can be so disturbing that many mourners attempt to avoid thinking about their loved one. This makes reprocessing the trauma, and mourning the loss, more difficult.

4. *Ramifications of the Death*—Survivors of sudden, traumatic loss struggle more with the ramifications of the death in comparison to those whose loved one died of natural causes. In the weeks and months following the loss of a spouse, grief typically begins to diminish (Jordan & Litz, 2014). However, for survivors of traumatic loss, there may be little improvement in painful reactions and symptoms over time as mourners continue to struggle with the distressing and heartbreaking consequences of traumatic loss for many years, often for the rest of their lives. (Pearlman et al., 2014).

5. *Shattered Basic Assumptions*—Trauma can shatter the survivor's basic assumptions about the world, such as the world is safe, meaningful, controllable, predictable, and fair. As described above, the loss of a loved one, in and of itself, can be traumatic, and can shatter assumptions.

Risk Factors Associated with Traumatic Deaths

There are a number of *risk factors* that mediate the response to the death and influence the level of grief and mourning (Pearlman et al., 2014; Worden, 2018). These factors are likely to add to the traumatic impact of a sudden, unexpected death. The more of these factors involved, the more difficult it can be to comprehend what happened and to start coping with it. However, there are individual differences on the impact of these factors depending on the person's perception of the event, prior history of trauma and loss, and coping ability.

1. *Suddenness and Lack of Anticipation*—A sudden, unexpected death can be traumatic. Whether sudden or anticipated, the loss of a loved

one hurts. Even when expected the loss of a loved one can be a challenge to cope with because nothing truly prepares us for the finality of death. But for mourners who have no time to prepare, the challenge is greater. A sudden death is more difficult to make sense of and cope with. If you know something awful is going to happen, there is time to plan and brace yourself. If something awful does happen that was not anticipated, a person may be reeling in shock, trying to comprehend something that may be too much to take in at the moment. One's world can change in an instant with the news. There is no time to say goodbye or make peace with the person. There may not be the opportunity to offer comfort in the final moments or be comforted.

2. *Unnaturalness of the Death*—Emotional impact differs depending on the cause of death: for example, when someone dies a natural death (e.g., sickness in old age) surrounded by loving relatives the impact can be different than when someone dies from a gunshot during a home invasion or a car crash caused by an unlicensed drunk driver. The more unnatural or grotesque the circumstances (e.g., the body is badly mutilated), the more it can be beyond the mourner's comprehension and hence be traumatizing.

3. *Violence and Its Consequences*—Violent circumstances typically evoke shock, and/or horror. They potentially overwhelm one's sense of control, and violate the assumptive world. Violence can result in mutilation and gory images. Rynearson and Salloum (2011) report that in a large majority of violent deaths, such as suicides or homicides, the person dies alone, in the absence of loved ones. This puts mourners at risk for what is termed the "re-enactment story," with mourners trying to understand what happened and what the loved one was experiencing (e.g., suffering) before death. This can result in vicarious traumatization, further complicating the mourning.

4. *Physical or Emotional Suffering*—We all want to believe that the death of a loved one was instantaneous, and "he did not feel a thing." However, the reality may be that the loved one experienced fear, pain, and suffered. This can be traumatizing as mourners try to understand what the loved one went through; there is an added consequence of mourners feeling helpless and guilty because they could not do anything.

5. *Preventable Deaths*—There is a difference between a natural disaster (e.g., earthquake, hurricane) caused by nature, and human-induced events which *should not have happened*. Death by natural causes is indeed tragic, with added risk factors because of being sudden, unexpected, and violent. However, natural events are more understandable

and evoke less anger and violation to the assumptive world than human-induced events. Human-induced events include deaths that are regarded as preventable (e.g., negligence or carelessness). Mourners may struggle with how senseless the death was, and may experience strong feelings of anger over the death—it was preventable and *should not have happened.*

6. *Intentional Death*—Death caused by a perpetrator with intent to harm can go beyond the emotional impact of preventable deaths. Murder, suicide, beatings that result in death, terrorist acts, and other intentional acts of violence are more potentially traumatizing because they were deliberate and malicious. There can be a significant breach in the assumptive world that undermines faith and trust in people, creates the realization of evil, and evokes rage, powerlessness, and vulnerability.

7. *Randomness*—A random death, for example, being in the wrong place at the wrong time, can be frightening because it is perceived to be uncontrollable, and it violates our assumptions of normality. One cannot see it coming or protect oneself from such events. A large steam roller cylinder fell off a truck, bounded to the other side of the highway, and hit a car, killing its occupant. What are the odds? This was truly tragic and there were so many "if only" thoughts (e.g., "If only he had waited two more seconds before getting in the car ... or left two seconds before ..."). Often survivors blame themselves for random events because of the psychological dynamic that it is easier to believe they have control over their lives than to deal with the fact there can be little or no control. As Pearlman et al. (2014) puts it: "In such situations, the assumption of blame and of the consequent guilt is the price one pays to maintain the needed perception that the world is controllable" (p. 73). Similarly, often the victim is blamed. Blaming the victim removes the event from something random by identifying what the victim should or should not have done to prevent the tragedy: "If he had only worn his seatbelt" or "If she had not gone out alone at night." However, there are many other factors involved in the tragedy that are overlooked. The psychological dynamic underlying second guessing or blaming the victim is that it reinforces a personal sense of control: such as, "It can't happen to me, I won't make that mistake (or do what the deceased did)." However, such second guessing can be another traumatization and create ambivalence and guilt in the survivors.

8. *Multiple Deaths*—Examples of multiple deaths, situations where two or more loved ones die in the same event, include disasters, auto accidents,

or mass violence situations. This can create a "bereavement overload" (Rando, 1993, 2013) and is more difficult to deal with than the death of a single loved one or sequential deaths. The mourning for one person can complicate the mourning for another person, which can result in incomplete mourning for each loss and compound grief reactions. Further, there is the potential for survivors to feel survivors' guilt.

9. *Threat to One's Own Life/Confrontation with the Death of Others*—If the mourner's own life was threatened during the incident where the loved one died, several difficult issues in addition to the loss of the loved one must be faced. Involvement in the situation and the horror of the scene in and of itself can cause PTSD, particularly if it involves witnessing the death of the loved one. Mourners may have to confront their own vulnerability and realize they could have died. There may be gory images to deal with. Also, the situation may not have permitted mourners to say goodbye before the death. Further, there may be guilt that one could not prevent or minimize what happened or survivor's guilt.

10. *Untimeliness*—The death of a young person is untimely because it is happening at an inappropriate stage in the life cycle and does not follow the natural order of nature. For example, parents are supposed to die before children. Intense feelings of anger, injustice, and sadness are felt following the loss of a life that had unrealized potential. Untimeliness adds to the trauma of a loss (e.g., the untimeliness of a person dying just when she was close to achieving a life goal, a father dying just before his daughter's wedding or before the birth of a grandchild, or a daughter dying just after receiving a college scholarship).

11. *Ambiguous Deaths*—Having no physical body (e.g., not uncommon in disasters, airplane crashes, or mass casualty incidents such as 11 September) puts an additional burden on the mourners. Mourners may wonder, "Did my loved one really die?" Mourners know their loved one probably did die, but not having positive confirmation can impede the mourning process.

12. *Stigmatized Deaths*—death by suicide or by AIDS are often seen as stigmatizing, which may interfere with seeking and receiving social support.

13. *Death of a Child*—all losses are terrible, but research (Pearlman et al., 2014) has shown that the death of a child can have more impact than other losses.

Other factors that compound emotional impact:

1. *Death Notification*—The way survivors are treated by police, ambulance, and medical personnel also makes a difference. An insensitive death notification, impersonal treatment at the hospital, rudeness at the funeral home, and the like, add to the distress of the loss.

2. *Viewing the Body*—Viewing the body can indeed be distressing, even traumatizing, especially when there is disfigurement. Having to identify the body can be harrowing and compound the trauma of a significant loss. However, it may be more distressing when a person wants to view the body and is not allowed. Perhaps a criminal investigation prohibits viewing the body or well-meaning but badly informed relatives or friends strongly advice against it. This can interfere with closure and a chance to say goodbye. It is important that mourners have a choice. Overall, research shows that the determining factor in viewing the body has to do with whether the person was given a choice and encouraged to do what they chose (Wortman et al., 2016). If a person chooses to view the body, care should be taken by medical personnel to clean up the body: for example, wiping away blood or removing tubes). If there is tremendous damage perhaps just a hand or foot could be shown to prepare the mourner for the viewing. A sensitive medical professional can explain what might be seen in order to minimize shock and be available afterwards to answer questions. Many people want to spend time with the body of their loved one (e.g., holding them, hugging them, and talking to them). These loving acts should be respected.

3. *Prolonged Waiting for Confirmation of the Death or Failure to Find a Body*—Having to wait a long time for confirmation of the death and wondering if the loved one is alive compound the stress of a loss. This is magnified if the body is not found. In the case of a terrorist attack or airplane crash, bodies may never be found, making closure difficult. As one widow of 11 September wondered, "Did he really die?" "Is he wandering around somewhere because he lost his memory?" "Is he alive and suffering?" The lack of his body complicated her grief—while logically she knew he was probably dead, in her heart of hearts, she always wondered.

Treatment Implications for EMDR Therapy

A sudden, unexpected, and violent death can be traumatic to the mourner. When there are traumatic circumstances, there can be both traumatic distress and separation distress, and both must be addressed. The trauma of the loss, which is usually most acute and strongly felt, can complicate the mourning process and usually needs to be addressed first. As will be elaborated in Chapter 10, first targets for EMDR processing usually consists of the moment(s) of shock or realization (e.g., getting the news, distressing scenes). It is also important to deal with the separation distress that include painful moments of missing the person, adapting to life without the person, or feeling stuck in pain.

Summary

Traumatic bereavement occurs when one's grief is overpowered by the trauma of the circumstances. Trauma interferes with going through the mourning process, and the loss can interfere with dealing with the trauma. A sudden, unexpected, and traumatic death is more devasting than a death by natural causes. Risk factors for traumatic bereavement were discussed along with other factors, such as the death notification, viewing of the body, prolonged waiting or failure to find a body. A major treatment implication is that the trauma of the loss has to be dealt with, and is often the first target of treatment.

5

Complicated Grief and Mourning

Bereavement is a universal experience that can have adverse effects on mental and physical health. The loss of a loved one is very painful, but in the weeks and months following the loss, grief reactions begin to lessen. With uncomplicated grief, also called "normal grief," research has shown that by 6 months, most bereaved individuals get through the initial sense of disbelief that comes with being overwhelmed and are able to accept the loss as a reality, move on with their lives, and proceed with daily life (Prigerson et al., 2009, 2021). Most people eventually re-establish a new equilibrium after loss, without developing any prolonged impairment (Jordan & Litz, 2014; Wortman & Silver, 1989).

Some studies show between 10% and 20% of bereaved people suffer from severe and disabling grief for a prolonged period of time (Prigerson et al., 2009). However, a meta-analysis showed that nearly half of bereaved adults suffered from Prolonged Grief Disorder (PGD) following an unnatural loss (Djelantik et al., 2020). Studies suggest that complicated grief reactions can last for several years and predict morbidity (e.g., suicidal thoughts and behaviors, incidence of cardiac events, and high blood pressure), adverse health behaviors (e.g., increased use of tobacco and alcohol), and impairments in the quality of life (e.g., loss of energy) (Boelen & Prigerson, 2013). Complicated grief also impacts physical health, with medical consequences such as high blood pressure, heart disease, and sleeping difficulties (Gallagher-Thompson et al., 1993; Germain, Buysse, & Shear, 2005).

Consequently, it is important that mourners suffering from PGD be assessed and treated.

Defining Terms for Complicated Grief and Mourning

Defining *complicated grief and mourning* is, well … complicated. There are several terms for the *complicated grief/mourning* conceptualized in the literature, such as *complicated grief, traumatic grief, complicated mourning, pathological grief,* and *Persistent Complex Bereavement Disorder.* ICD-11 recognizes the

EMDR Therapy Treatment for Grief and Mourning. Roger M. Solomon, Oxford University Press. © Roger M. Solomon 2024.
DOI: 10.1093/oso/9780198881360.003.0006

diagnosis of PGD. In 2020, the American Psychiatric Association approved the inclusion of PGD in the DSM-5-TR.

A major difference is that PGD can be diagnosed at 6 months for ICD-11 and 12 months for the DCM-5-TR. The reason for the 1-month criteria was to be sensitive to concerns about pathologizing normal grieving and diagnosing too soon after the death.

With so many terms and concepts, for brevity and to avoid confusion, I will mostly use the term *complicated grief* because it is widely used in the academic literature. However, I will occasionally use the term *complicated mourning* or *complicated grief and mourning* to describe how variables and events can interfere with adaptation or when citing an author who uses a particular term.

The Loss Itself Can Be Traumatic and Complicate Grief and Mourning

Complicated grief and mourning come in many forms. But, in all its forms, complicated grief and mourning occurs when mourners attempt the following: (a) to deny, repress, or avoid aspects of the loss, its pain, and full realization of the implications of the death, and/or (b) to hold on to, and avoid relinquishing the lost loved one (Rando, 1993). The loss can be too much to realize, and mourners may know the loved one is dead, but cannot accept that it is true. Hence, the loss of a loved one, in and of itself, can be of traumatic proportions, resulting in complicated grief and mourning.

Bowlby (1980) used the term "*segregated systems*" to describe how mourners can oscillate back and forth between knowing the loved one is permanently gone and another frame of mind where this reality of the death cannot be accepted. Trying to hold on to the deceased is also a form of denial, not wanting to accept the loved one is truly gone and never coming back. Mourners may continue to visit the grave, keep the deceased's belongings, not change anything associated with the deceased, or continually have memorials and rituals. Though a normal and positive way to connect to the loved one when mourners accept the loved one is dead and not coming back, such behaviors are signs of complicated grief when they are a way to hold onto the loved one and avoid full realization of the death in all its ramifications. Further, mourners may show a general reluctance to make adaptations to life in the absence of the loved one (Prigerson et al., 2021).

Separation Distress

Complicated grief is characterized by an intense yearning and longing for the loved one who has died; that is, separation distress. Mourners may wish life could revert back to the time the loved one was alive. Without the loved one, mourners feel empty, have little hope for the future, and may be preoccupied by sorrow and regret concerning the loss. With ruminating on the death, and difficulty concentrating on things other than the loss, mourners may feel disconnected from others, creating a sense of alienation and isolation. Recurrent, intrusive, and distressing thoughts regarding the loved one's absence make it difficult for them to move beyond an acute state of mourning, and leave mourners feeling life lacks purpose and meaning. It becomes difficult for people suffering from complicated grief to move on with their lives, and engage in other interpersonal relationship and potentially rewarding, meaningful activities. As one mourner described, 2 years after the death of his wife, "When Sally died, part of me died, and life is empty. I have no more joy or enthusiasm for living." Such sentiments are normal after the death, but if the intensity is not decreased and is interfering with functioning after 6 months, it is a sign of complicated grief.

Complicated Grief Is Different Than Depression or PTSD

Complicated grief reactions can be very similar to depression: however, there are important differences. Jordan and Litz (2014) point out that the major difference between complicated grief (specifically PGD) and depression is the extent to which symptoms are specifically about the loss of a loved one (i.e., PGD) versus a more generalized and free-floating sadness (i.e., depression). With depression, there is pervasive misery and pessimistic rumination, whereas the dysphoria of PGD centers more on the separation from the loved one, and the primary cognitive symptom is intense preoccupation with the lost loved one (Jordan & Litz, 2014). In depression, there is a broad loss of interest in life and inability to imagine that life could be pleasurable or rewarding, whereas with PGD there is continuing interest in the deceased loved one and the belief that the return of the loved one would bring satisfaction. Also, global guilt or sense of personal worthlessness, which is part of depression, is not part of PGD, although there can be the inappropriate self-blaming in regard to the death. Further, people with PGD avoid stimuli that are reminders of the reality of the loss, compared to a more general avoidance and withdrawal which is typical of depression.

Jordan and Litz (2014) also point out that *PGD is conceptually different from PTSD*. PTSD is characterized by fear, horror, powerlessness, guilt, and shame, along with hyperarousal and exaggerated reactivity. PGD, while sharing some of these same reactions, however, is characterized primarily by yearning, loss, or emptiness. With PTSD, intrusive thoughts and images are fixated on the death event and involve reactions of threat and fear, which results in mourners avoiding internal and external reminders of the death. In PGD, on the other hand, individuals may experience both voluntary and intrusive (nonvoluntary) thoughts about the relationship, including positive content longed for by the bereaved, and avoidance is mostly limited to those triggers that remind mourners of the reality or permanence of the loss. However, the similar symptoms of PGD and PTSD is noted. In fact, the results of a factor analysis (O'Connor et al., 2010) suggest that the intrusive component of PTSD can largely account for the construct of complicated grief. Hence, EMDR therapy, an evidence-based treatment for PTSD, is indicated for treatment of complicated grief.

Complicated Grief and Attachment Style

Complicated grief can have its roots in insecure attachment styles. Zhang et al. (2006) noted that complicated grief is fundamentally an attachment disturbance. Risk factors include person-related variables such as childhood abuse and neglect, separation anxiety in childhood, insecure attachment style, and marital closeness (Shear et al., 2011; Zhang et al., 2006). Consequently, EMDR treatment not only needs to deal with the trauma related to the death and its circumstances, but also the child-caregiver interactions that underlie the insecure attachment style. Chapter 6 will further discuss attachment styles and how they impact grief and mourning.

Complicated Grief Comes in Many Forms

Bill Worden (2018) presents a paradigm to describe complicated grief symptoms under four categories:

1. Chronic grief reactions
2. Delayed grief reactions

3. Exaggerated grief reactions
4. Masked grief reactions.

Chronic/Prolonged Grief Reaction

Chronic or prolonged grief reaction describes grief that is *excessive in duration* and does not come to a satisfactory conclusion. Mourners are aware that the grief is too much and not resolving. It is common for people to seek treatment several years after the death because they are still suffering or not able to adapt to the loss. For some, treatment requires facing the fact that the loved one is irrevocably gone. For others, exploring and clarifying confusing and ambivalent feelings toward the deceased is important. The relationship with the deceased may have been conflictual and unresolved, and arguments and issues may still haunt mourners. For others, past losses and traumas may have been triggered and need to be identified and reprocessed. People who were highly dependent on the loved one may need to deal both with past underlying memories that resulted in dependency as well as with the learning of new skills to deal with life circumstances. As will be elaborated below, the loss of an important attachment figure can trigger the same reactions that accompanied separation in childhood. Hence, attachment style provides a context for understanding present grief reactions.

Delayed Grief Reactions

Delayed grief reactions, sometimes called inhibited, suppressed, or postponed grief reactions, are characterized by a minimal emotional reaction at the time of the loss. People may experience grief reactions only later, perhaps triggered by another loss or stressful incident. For example, a person may have a minimal reaction over the loss of a parent, but experiences an excessive reaction later when a distant cousin dies. In such a case, the initial death may have been "too much," and pushed aside and avoided, but can be triggered when there is a later distressing event. What characterizes delayed grief is the intensity of the felt reactions when it is finally experienced. It is often due to previous unresolved loss or trauma.

Delayed reactions may be experienced because at the time of the death, the mourner may have been busy with funeral planning, taking care of others, or doing other tasks that kept them externally focused. When the tasks are completed (e.g., funeral is over, the estate is settled, finishing the trial, or if there was a court case), the grief that may have been suppressed or inhibited becomes felt. For example, when a man was murdered and the suspect brought to trial, the legal process lasted 14 months, with the wife attending all hearings and the trial. Finally, the suspect was convicted and sentenced to life in prison. After an initial feeling of joy that justice was finally achieved, depression and sadness set in. This was initially confusing, but then the wife realized she had not been feeling the loss of her husband during the trial. The legal process had given her something external to focus on and a way to avoid the emotional impact of the loss. With the trial over, she started to have grief reactions and go through the mourning process.

Grief can appear to be inhibited or absent because of an avoidant attachment style where thoughts and feelings related to the loss are avoided or minimized. People may have a coping style of avoiding distressing emotions and thoughts and in grief minimize the impact of the loss or the importance of the relationship. It is also possible that grief is absent because there may not have been a strong bond and, consequently, the loss has minimal impact. For example, one woman was not upset about her mother's death. There never was a deep attachment, and the woman had never relied on her mother. The woman felt sad for her mother's death, but with the lack of closeness, and impact of the loss was minimal. However, as Bonano et al. (2004) point out, grief may appear to be minimal because the person is resilient and coping. There can be sadness and distress at a loss, but a person may simply not express it, coping with it quietly and inwardly, but successfully.

Exaggerated Grief Reactions

Exaggerated grief reactions are when mourners experience an intense, overwhelming reaction or is engaged in maladaptive behavior. People are aware that their distress is related to the loss, and they seek therapy because their experience is disabling. Exaggerated grief responses, as Worden elaborates, include major psychiatric disorders that develop following a loss such as clinical depression, anxiety disorder, PTSD, phobias that are centered on death (e.g., a serious fear of death), or serious substance abuse.

Masked Grief Reactions

In masked reaction, people experience intense reactions that interfere with functioning, but they do not recognize that these symptoms are related to the loss. Parkes (1972, 2006) describes that symptoms can be viewed as affective equivalents of grief. Reactions are "masked" as a physical symptom or a maladaptive behavior. When the loss is too much and individuals cannot experience the grief directly, medical symptoms or psychosomatic complaints may develop. For example, pain or somatoform disorders can be symbolic of unexpressed grief. Both exaggerated grief and masked grief may result in a formal psychiatric or medical diagnosis, but with exaggerated grief, people know the symptoms began around the time of the death and are related to the loss. On the other hand, people experiencing masked grief do not associate their medical, emotional, or behavioral symptoms with a death. Worden points out that once therapists help clients make the connection and start dealing with underlying loss issues, there is improvement in the physical or emotional symptoms.

Complicated Grief and Mourning Clues

Worden (2018) outlines a number of clues that indicate clients may have unresolved grief.

- *Clue 1*: clients cannot speak of the deceased without experiencing intense and present grief.
- *Clue 2*: a relatively minor event triggers an intense grief reaction.
- *Clue 3*: themes of loss come up during the session.
- *Clue 4*: clients may be unwilling to move the material possessions of the deceased.
- *Clue 5*: clients have developed physical symptoms after a loss, particularly if they are similar to those of the deceased before death, or if physical symptoms occur annually (e.g., the anniversary of the death, holiday season, or the loved one's birthday).
- *Clue 6*: people who make radical changes to their lifestyle following a death, withdrawal from their family, friends, or activities associated with the deceased may be symptomatic of unresolved grief.
- *Clue 7*: Clients who present a long history of below threshold (subclinical) depression, including persistent guilt and low self-esteem may have unresolved grief. Worden also points out the opposite can be a clue to unresolved grief— clients experience a false sense of euphoria following the death.
- *Clue 8*: Clients have a compulsion to imitate the dead person, particularly if the person does not have a conscious desire or competence for

this behavior. This may come from the need to compensate for the loss by identifying with the deceased, and somehow internalize the lost loved object. This may extend to taking on mannerisms and characteristics of the deceased even though these may have been rejected in the deceased's lifetime.

- *Clue 9*: self-destructive impulses, which can be due to several factors, including unresolved grief.
- *Clue 10*: unaccountable sadness occurring at a certain time each year (e.g., anniversary of the death, birthday of the deceased) can also a be sign of unresolved grief.
- *Clue 11*: a phobia about death or illness may relate to a specific illness that resulted in the death of the loved one.
- *Clue 12*: Signs of significant grief can be assessed from how people behaved at the time of the death or after. If people have suffered a significant loss, ask them what it was like for them at the time of the loss. Extreme or unusual behavioral and emotional reactions (e.g., dissociative phenomena, avoiding the funeral and significant other), though understandable at one level, may be predictive of complicated grief.

Assessment Instruments

Several instruments can help assess complicated grief. The most widely used instrument is the Inventory of Complicated Grief (ICG) (Prigerson et al., 1995), which has 19 items. An extended 34-item version of this instrument is the ICG-R (Prigerson & Jacobs, 2001). Both the ICG and ICG-R are both well-validated but do not include some of the Persistent Complex Bereavement Disorder (PCBD) criteria (e.g., "difficulty in positively reminiscing about the deceased," "maladaptive appraisals about oneself in relation to the deceased or the death," "a desire not to live in order to be with the deceased"). Lee (2015) introduced the Persistent Complex Bereavement Inventory to assess PCBD. Prigerson et al. (2021) presented validity data for a 13-item inventory, PG-13 (revised).

Treatment Implications for EMDR Therapy

Complicated grief is characterized by separation distress, with the loss itself being traumatic. Further, complicated grief is more likely to occur when the death is experienced as sudden, unexpected, violent, untimely, or is perceived as preventable (Holland & Neimeyer, 2011; Shear, Boelen, & Neimeyer, 2011). Consequently, as with traumatic bereavement, complicated grief has two important components that must be addressed: traumatic distress and separation distress. As will be elaborated on in Chapter 10, the trauma of the loss can be treated by conceptualizing the loss as a traumatic event and initially focusing treatment on the moment of traumatic impact (e.g., getting the news of the death or distressing images or scenes). Consequently, EMDR therapy can be helpful in treatment of complicated grief. Further, separation distress can be treated by focusing on the present triggers that exacerbate the distress. Further, given that attachment style accounts for the variation in response to loss (Kosminsky & Jordan, 2016), underlying memories contributing to the separation distress, such as child-caregiver interactions, can be targeted and reprocessed with EMDR therapy.

Summary

Complicated grief has many forms, but at the root is the inability to fully realize the loss and its permanence. Mourners may deny or avoid aspects of the pain or attempt to hold on to, and avoid relinquishing, the tie to the deceased. Complicated grief is different than depression and PTSD, but has many overlapping symptoms. Different forms of complex grief were discussed, and clues about when clients are suffering from complicated grief were described. Complicated grief may contain both traumatic distress and separation distress, and both can be treated with EMDR therapy.

SECTION 2
GRIEF AND MOURNING FRAMEWORKS

6

Attachment Theory

A major clinical dynamic in grief and mourning revolves around the loss of connection to the loved one. Research has shown that attachment style is an important determinant of how a person deals with loss of connection to a loved one: therefore, it is important to understand attachment styles.

Part 1 of this chapter involves basic information that the reader familiar with attachment may want to skim or skip. Part 2 of this chapter presents a more in-depth view of Attachment Theory that is pertinent to understanding how attachment style influences a mourner's reaction to loss.

Attachment Theory: Part 1

Attachment styles form early in life with child-parent bonding. Infants come into the world hard-wired to attach to caregivers for physical protection and for a psychological sense of safety (Bowlby, 1960). When there is threat or insecurity, the young child's inborn, instinctually guided reactions are manifested in three kinds of behavior:

1. Seeking, monitoring, and attempting to *maintain proximity* to a protective attachment figure by crying, calling, clinging, and crawling (Wallin, 2007).
2. Using the caregiver as a *secure base* from which to explore unfamiliar places and engage in new experiences.
3. Fleeing to the attachment figure as a *safe haven* when there is perceived danger and moments of alarm. When soothed, the child can continue to explore and pursue non-attachment activities.

Consequently, an attachment figure is someone who allows proximity, serves as a secure base, and is a safe haven in times of need. During infancy, primary caretakers (usually the parents, as well as grandparents, older siblings, and day care workers) can serve as attachment figures. In later childhood,

EMDR Therapy Treatment for Grief and Mourning. Roger M. Solomon, Oxford University Press. © Roger M. Solomon 2024.
DOI: 10.1093/oso/9780198881360.003.0007

adolescence and adulthood, a wider range of relationship partners serve as attachment figures. This includes other relatives, romantic partners, friends, coaches, teachers, therapists, and close co-workers. In this light, as Holmes and Slade (2018) point out, attachment figures can include any intimate relationships where affect regulation or co-regulation—of both negative and positive affect—are at its core.

Attachment Classification

Mary Ainsworth made a significant contribution to our understanding of attachment with her "strange situation" research (Ainsworth, Blehar, Waters, & Wall, 1978). This was a structured laboratory assessment, lasting 20 minutes, where mothers and their infants (between 12 and 18 months old) were observed in a pleasant room filled with toys. In a series of 3-minute episodes, the infant would explore the room in the mother's presence. Then, there were two separations from the mother, two reunions, and the infant's exposure to a stranger (a trained baby watcher). The underlying assumption was that the combination of an unfamiliar setting, separation, and introducing a stranger would trigger the infant's attachment system. Three distinct attachment patterns were observed: secure, insecure avoidant, and insecure ambivalent/resistant. A fourth, disorganized, attachment pattern was identified and added later by Main and Solomon (1990).

These attachment styles are described below: (1) secure, (2) avoidant, (3) ambivalent/resistant, and (4) disorganized. Also, the adult equivalent attachment style will be briefly described. Bartholomew and Horowitz (1991) and Brennan, Clark, and Shaver (1998) conceptualized four attachment styles of adults similar to infant attachment styles: (1) secure, (2) dismissive/avoidant, (3) anxious/preoccupied, and (4) fearful/avoidant.

Secure Attachment Style

Secure infants were able to explore when they felt safe, and to seek solace in connection to the attachment figure when they did not. Distressed by the separation, they actively sought the mother when she returned, were almost immediately reassured upon reconnection with the mother, and readily resumed play. Mothers of secure infants tended to be responsive and sensitive to the infant's signals and communication. For example, the mothers were quick to pick the babies up when they cried and held them with tenderness and care, but only for as long as the infants wished to be held. These "good enough" (Winnicott, 1965) mothers were able to attune to their infants, were accepting rather than rejecting, were cooperative rather than controlling, and were emotionally available rather than remote (Ainsworth et al., 1978; Wallin, 2007). The majority of infants (60%) were securely attached (Ainsworth et al., 1978).

Securely attached adults have little or no difficulty becoming emotionally close to others and can behave flexibly in their relationships (Bartholomew & Horowitz, 1991). They tend to feel secure in their relationship and can trust the availability of others. They are not worried about acceptance from others, or about being left alone.

Avoidant Attachment Style
Avoidant-attached infants were incessantly exploring and were clearly unmoved by mother's departure or return. However, they were not calm—their heart rates were as elevated during the separation episodes as those of their visibly distressed but secure peers. Further, the rise in their level of cortisol pre- to postprocedure was significantly greater than that of secure infants. Though seemingly at ease, they experienced a higher level of distress. It was as if these avoidant infants had concluded that their attempts at comfort and care would not be effective in gaining the attention of the mother—in a sense, they had given up. These infants went limp when held by their mother, rather than seeking or attempting to cuddle.

Mothers of avoidant babies actively rebuffed the infant's attempts at connection. Inhibition of emotional expression, apparent dislike of physical contact, and brusqueness were all signatures of a parenting style that seemed to produce avoidant infants. In the Ainsworth et al. (1978) study, 20% of the babies had an avoidant attachment.

The adult equivalent is called *dismissing*. Dismissing adults may either fear intimacy or may lack interest or motivation to have an intimate relationship (Bartholomew & Horowitz, 1991). Consequently, Bartholomew and Horowitz distinguished between a dismissive-avoidant and a fearful-avoidant style. Dismissive-avoidant style emphasizes independence and self-reliance, downplaying the importance of close, intimate relationships. Fearful-avoidant adults with a fearful-avoidant attachment style may be tense and frightened about close contact with others. Although desiring close contact, they may have distrust and fear of other people, with difficulty in relying on others. Fear-avoidant style is consistent with disorganized attachment.

Ambivalent/Resistant Attachment Style
The ambivalent/resistant infants appeared to abandon exploration completely in favor of seeking connection with the mother. These infants remained continuously preoccupied with mother's whereabouts and were either angrily

or passively inconsolable or resistant to consolation upon reunion with the mother. Upon reunion, the angry infants would alternate between actively seeking connection to mother and expressions of rejection (e.g., leaning away from mother's embrace to throwing full-blown tantrums). Passive infants appeared capable of faint or implicit bids for comfort and connection, with their helplessness and misery limiting ability to approach mother directly. The reunion did not appear to ameliorate the ambivalent infants' distress nor terminate their preoccupation with mother's whereabouts. If was as if these infants were seeking a mother who was not there even though she was present. These infants had mothers whose presence was unpredictable and only occasionally available. These mothers were not verbally or physically rejecting, but their responsiveness to the baby's signals was insensitive. Also, the mothers seemed to discourage the infant's autonomy, which may contribute to the inhibition of exploration that characterized these babies.

The adult equivalent has been called preoccupied/anxious (Bartholomew & Horowitz, 1991). Adults in this category are preoccupied with seeking emotional closeness to others. They need contact with others and may feel unworthy and insecure unless they have close contact with other people.

Disorganized Attachment Style

The infants that did not fit the above classification were later assigned into a disorganized attachment category (Main & Solomon, 1990). These authors reviewed the tapes of infants in the "strange situation" and found that most of the unclassified infants displayed brief, 10–30-second responses in the parent's presence that were inexplicable, contradictory, or bizarre. For example, some infants backed toward the mother, froze in place, collapsed to the floor, or crawled to the mother but kept on going, or appeared to fall into a dazed, trance-like state. These babies were seen as lacking a coherent and consistent strategy for dealing with the stress of separation. They seemed to alternate between avoidant and ambivalent behaviors. Main and Solomon (1990) contended that disorganized attachment results when the attachment figure is both the source of safety and the source of danger. That is, the child is wired to turn to the caregiver in moments of alarm, but is caught between contradictory impulses both to approach and to avoid. The result of such a *biological paradox* (Wallin, 2007) is disorganization. The mothers of disorganized babies in *the strange situation* were observed to be frightening to their children (e.g., looming in the child's face, talking too loudly, approaching too suddenly, and threatening or abusing their infant). Further, these mothers seemed to be frightened of their own infants, observed in freezing behavior, backing away in fear, or appearing to be numb and expressionless in a trance-like state. Indeed, as Wallin (2007) points out, the mother being frightened by the infant's distress may be the result of her own abuse or neglect, or unresolved trauma or loss being triggered. The combination of maternal behavior where the object of proximity and safety is simultaneously the source of fear leaves the baby in the continuing conflict of needing to simultaneously approach and avoid at the attachment object. Main referred to this conflictual psychological state as *fright without solution*. In contrast to the more organized strategies of secure, avoidant, and ambivalent infants, disorganized attachment reflects a collapse of strategy (Wallin, 2007), which can be the precursor to complex trauma and dissociative disorder (Liotti, 1992).

As mentioned above, the adult equivalent is a fearful/avoidant style, with the adult wanting contact but frightened in regard to close contact. The desire for close contact is compromised by distrust and fear of other people.

For sake of brevity the terms used to describe attachment style will be *secure, anxious* (to also describe ambivalent and preoccupied attachment), *avoidant*, and *disorganized*.

Quality of Communication Between Infant and Caregiver

In differentiating between secure and insecure attachments, quality of communication was of utmost importance (Ainsworth et al., 1978). Understanding this, highlights the importance of nonverbal communication and how *seemingly small* moments can indeed be quite impactful. With secure attachments, the infant could express the need for comfort after separation, relief at being soothed during the reunion, and was ready to resume play. Communication was collaborative and contingent. As Wallin (2007) describes it, "One party signals while the other answers with behavior that says in effect, I can sense what you're feeling and respond to what you need" (p. 21).

Communication had a different quality in the insecure mother-infant interactions. Avoidant infants, upon separation, did not express the marked distress that was indirectly revealed through elevated heart rates and cortisol levels. Upon reunion, these infants did not express their need to be comforted. In essence, avoidant infants inhibited virtually all communication that invited connection. Avoidant infants seemed to have no desire for proximity and appeared to ignore the affectionate overtures of the mother. The opposite was true for ambivalent infants. These infants seem to amplify expressions of attachment, and virtually from the beginning of the separation conveyed preoccupation with the mother's availability. They were very distressed upon separation, with very little relief upon reunion. Communication of the need for attachment seemed to persist at a high level regardless of the mother's attempts to soothe (Ainsworth, 1969; Main, 1990, 1995).

The relevance for EMDR therapy is an appreciation for the subtle, seemingly small but quite impactful, interactions between caregiver and infant that determine attachment style. Attuned mirroring between caregiver and infant (e.g., loving gaze between parent and baby) is important in the development of secure attachment. Seemingly small negative interactions (e.g., Mother having an annoyed face or Father looking away during a moment of distress) have much relevance for development of insecure attachment styles, and can be targeted with EMDR. Although preverbal or early childhood experiences may not be stored as semantic memories, they resonate and are perhaps stimulated by later semantic memories (Lanius et al., 2004).

Attachment Theory: Part 2

Development of Attachment Styles

Attachment styles are reflections of the infant's need to adapt to the character of the parents. Infants will do what is needed to nurture the best possible attachment to the caregiver. When an infant or child is in distress, the attachment system is activated, and the child seeks proximity to the caretaker. If the caretaker is able to provide comfort, soothing, and to meet the child's needs, the attachment system is deactivated and reset and the child becomes ready for exploration, play, and interaction with others (Bowlby, 1960). This is the basis for a secure attachment. But if instead the child's initial distress signals (e.g., crying) are met in a rejecting, angry, or impatient manner, or are ignored and not dealt with, secondary strategies arise to reduce distress (Bowlby, 1982; Mikulincer & Shaver, 2016). The secondary strategies involve either (a) hyperactivation or (b) deactivation of the attachment system.

Hyperactivating Strategies
Hyperactivating strategies are characterized by an escalation of the intensity of protest. The child may cry louder and harder, become physically agitated, thrash about, and otherwise intensify the distress signals in an effort to get the caregiver's attention. They may attempt to maintain proximity through clinging, crying, protesting, and showing distress when imminent separation is perceived. This strategy is likely in relationships where the attachment figure is unpredictable—sometimes responsive and sometimes not. The goal is to get the attachment figure, viewed as unreliable, to pay more attention and

to provide protection and support. Hyperactivating strategies are a precursor to an anxious attachment style.

Deactivating Strategies

Deactivating strategies are a reaction to an attachment figure's unavailability, resulting from attachment figures who disapprove of and punish closeness, and expressions of need or vulnerability. These strategies involve suppression of behavior and affect (Mikulincer & Shaver, 2016), a shutting down of awareness of discomfort and signaling behavior aimed at bringing the caregiver into proximity. The child not only stops expressing discomfort, but may stop feeling it. The primary goal of deactivation strategies is to keep the attachment system down-regulated to avoid the distress and frustration caused by the unavailability of attachment figures. Deactivating strategies are the precursor of an avoidant attachment style.

These secondary strategies become the child's best strategy for restoring or maintaining proximity to the caregiver (Kosminsky & Jordan, 2016; Mikulincer & Shaver, 2016). As a way of coping with attachment distress, the child appraises and learns about the caregiver's availability, affect tolerance, and ability to meet their needs. If the caregiver is not available, dismissing, or punitive, then the best strategy for survival is to deactivate attachment needs. If the caregiver is sometimes available and sometimes able to meet needs, then a hyperactivating strategy to maintain proximity and safety is the best strategy for survival. The identification of the child-caregiver interactions that led to hyper- or hypoactivation strategies is important in treating the adult's present-day problems with affect regulation, self-esteem issues, and relationship problems. Many of these negative experiences are way below the posttraumatic stress disorder (PTSD) definition of trauma, but still pack a significant emotional punch. As one man with an avoidant style stated, "I always felt I was expected to handle problems on my own," and had memories from age 5 years of feeling helpless in dealing with negative social situations in kindergarten. Another man, with an anxious attachment style, stated, "I have always felt insecure in making decisions on my own," and had memories of being 4 years old, with his mother frowning at his choices and telling him what a better choice would be.

Loss Throughout Development

Loss in Childhood

The loss of an attachment figure can be a devastating event that triggers intense and all-encompassing distress, which Bowlby (1969, 1980) called *separation distress*. Bowlby conceptualized that when young children separated from their primary caregivers for extended periods of time would pass through three predictable states: protest, despair, and detachment. Protest is the child's initial response to separation and is characterized by children's resisting separation from the major source of safety, protection, and comfort. Behaviors such as crying, calling, and clinging in an attempt to regain contact, accompanied by anxiety and anger, are adaptive reactions geared toward preventing the loss. If protest does not restore proximity, the protest reactions decline, and children experience despair, depressed mood, decreased appetite, sleep disturbances, and pain expressions. Bowlby (1980) saw the despair phase resulting from the failure of the protest to restore a sense of security. Despair subsides over time and turns into a third phase of separation which Bowlby initially labeled *detachment*. Though marked by apparent recovery and gradual involvement and interest in other activities and relationships, detachment is not a neutral termination of the attachment bond, but reflects suppression of thoughts and emotions related to the lost attachment figure, Bowlby noted.

Loss in Adulthood

Bowlby (1980) thought that adults who lose or are separated from long-term attachment figures, such as romantic partners, experience reactions similar to those of infants reacting to separation (separation distress) from an attachment figure in childhood (Kosminsky & Jordan, 2016). Also, adults may react to the loss of a loved one with strong protest: anxiety, anger, yearning, preoccupation with the missing person, and lack of interest in other activities. However, in the case of adult bereavement (assuming adaptation), Bowlby (1980) called the final phase of separation distress as "reorganization" instead of detachment because adults do not necessarily defensively detach from a loved one and suppress feelings, thoughts, and memories of the deceased. Instead of detachment, Bowlby (1980) observed a transformation of the relationship and a rearrangement of the representation of self and the deceased loved one, so that the deceased can serve as a symbolic source of comfort and love, while life goes on. This reorganization involves two major psychological tasks. First, the death has to be accepted, and second, mourners need to maintain some form of a symbolic attachment to the deceased, integrating the loss of the relationship within a new reality of returning to everyday life activities. The hierarchy of attachment figures shifts, so that attachment (e.g., proximity seeking) can be geared toward real people and activities to provide safety, security, and comfort.

Attachment Theory and Caregiving

Along with describing *attachment* as the child's inborn motivational system to attach to a caregiver, Attachment Theory also emphasizes the importance of caregiving. We are wired to provide care to children, that is, to protect, to provide comfort and support in distress, and to ensure physical well-being. While parents are the main caregivers during infancy and early childhood, adults both provide and receive care in their attachment relationships, and being an effective caregiver can be as important as receiving care, producing a sense of well-being (Shear et al., 2007).

Mikulincer and Shaver (2016) point out the differences on the attachment and caregiving sides of a severed relationship: "The attached person longs for the lost attachment figure's supportive presence and provision of comfort and security; the caregiver who loses a child tends to long for opportunities to care for the child and make restitution for previous failures of adequate care" (p.3). Consequently, the death of an attachment figure may also be experienced as a failure of caregiving. This can result in feelings of failure, self-blame, and survivor guilt, especially for parents of a child who has died. It is not uncommon for bereaved people to rebuke themselves for failing to prevent the death and/ or to make it easier (Shear et al., 2007).

Attachment Theory and Complicated Grief Reactions

Complicated grief reactions (e.g., Prolonged Grief Disorder) occur when mourners cannot accept the death or return to everyday life activities (Bowlby, 1980). Instead, mourners attempt to deny, repress, or avoid aspects of the loss, its pain, and full realization of the implications of the death, and/or to hold onto and avoid relinquishing the lost loved one (Rando, 1993). Similarly, Kosminsky and Jordan (2016) assert that grief can be complicated by mourners' inability to accept that connection is no longer possible. The clinical dynamic of "I cannot connect," is too much for mourners and has its roots in the attachment history of the mourners.

Kosminsky and Jordan (2016) provide an attachment-based explanation for chronic mourners' inability to accept that connection is impossible. The painful state experienced by mourners in reaction to the loss can be likened to children who are preoccupied with reestablishing a tolerable level of proximity to a caregiver. Loss of a loved one activates the attachment system, with mourners wanting connection, to re-establish proximity, and potentially experiencing emotional dysregulation along with yearning and longing for the loved one (Shear et al., 2007). The loss evokes many of the same reactions that accompanied separation from an attachment figure in childhood (Kosminsky & Jordan, 2016). Consequently, attachment style is a major determinant of how people grieve and accounts for variations in the grief response

(Burke & Neimeyer, 2013; Kosminsky & Jordan, 2016; Parkes & Prigerson, 2010; Wayment & Vierthaler, 2002).

A major clinical dynamic in grief and mourning revolves around the loss of connection to the loved one. Loved ones may have been a mirror that reflected a sense of identity, meaning, and security, and the sudden void and loss of connection can be too much for survivors to bear. Further, especially with insecure attachments, the death can evoke the conflictual emotions and distress that accompanied attachment trauma (both large and small). Our response to death of an attachment figure is very deep-rooted, in a sense, hard-wired from infancy, possibly evoking the same feelings and responses that accompanied separation during childhood (e.g., the fear children may feel when the mother leaves the house). Given that attachment style results from caregiver-child interactions, Attachment Theory can guide EMDR clinicians in identifying and treating the negative memories related to attachment-related issues.

Attachment Style and Grief Response

Securely attached people are indeed impacted and saddened by the death of a loved one, but are likely to have an easier time adapting in comparison to those with insecure attachment styles (Mikulincer & Shaver, 2008). Secure attachment facilitates reorganization of inner models of self and others and makes adaptation to the loss more likely (Mikulincer & Shaver, 2011). Securely attached individuals can recall and think about a lost loved one without extreme difficulty, and can acknowledge their grief and talk about the loss in coherent manner. The old adage *time heals all wounds* applies. Individuals with insecure attachment, however, may have more intense and persistent grief.

Being careful not to overgeneralize, and acknowledging there is much individuality and variability, research has shown that people with *anxious attachment styles* are more likely to be hyperaroused and to show clinging behavior, loneliness, and rumination about their loved one, as well as overwhelming negative affect which can complicate the mourning process (Kosminsky & Jordan, 2016; Mikulincer & Shaver, 2016; Wayment & Vierthaler, 2002). Anxiously attached people, particularly with a history of dependency, tend to experience intense anxiety, anger, sorrow, yearning, failure to accept the loss, and difficulty establishing a new life structure (Mikulincer & Shaver, 2011).

Though the role of *avoidant attachment* in bereavement is less clear. Fraley and Bonanno (2004) found that bereaved adults with a dismissive-avoidant style showed a similar symptom picture to those with a secure attachment style. It may be that the dismissive-avoidant attachment style never permitted close attachment, which can lessen the impact of a loss. In such a case, absence of grieving may actually reflect a lack of deep involvement with the deceased. However, the apparent lack of anxiety about the loss may also be a result of downplaying the need for support from others, in line with the general agency of this style, and a belief there is little to be gained from reaching out to others (Parkes & Prigerson, 2010).

Avoidant defenses inhibit anxiety and sadness, and the avoidant person may minimize the importance of the loss, deny emotional impact, and attempt to stay away from thoughts and memories of the deceased (Mikulincer & Shaver, 2011). People with an avoidant attachment style, utilizing hypoarousing strategies, tend to be numb and shutdown, but when triggered, may feel that they are being flooded with unwelcome, distressing emotion. They may look as if they are doing well, but may actually be experiencing internal distress (Parkes & Priegerson, 2010). Daily activities previously enjoyed with the deceased can become painful and unwanted reminders of the loss. This can trigger distress and a need to avoid and suppress thoughts and feelings, which can complicate the grief.

Fraley and Bonanno (2004) found that *fearful-avoidant* adults (corresponding to the disorganized attachment style of childhood) had a difficult time adapting to their loss, in comparison with the secure and dismissive-avoidant style groups. It seems that people who have experienced abuse or neglect in childhood, develop a fearful-avoidant or disorganized attachment style in adulthood, and are more likely to experience traumatic bereavement following a sudden death, or loss of a significant loved one.

Implications for EMDR Therapy

Attachment styles develop in the context of child-caregiver interactions. *One can understand attachment styles as memory networks organized around child-caregiver interactions, stored as memories, that guide relationships and provide a foundation of emotional information about self and other.* Loss of a loved one evokes many of the same reactions that accompanied separation from an attachment figure in childhood. Treatment of complicated mourning, therefore, involves not only treating the trauma of the current loss, but identification and processing of these past maladaptively stored memories that were formative in the development of individual attachment styles and that underlie current difficulties. Anxious, avoidant, and disorganized attachment styles are not only determined by the major distressing experiences that become maladaptively stored (e.g., abuse or neglect) but also the ubiquitous and *seemingly small* but impactful moments, such as, "Mom did not look at me when I was upset," or "Dad would get irritated with me when I asked him for something."

Consistent with Bowlby, EMDR facilitates the psychological tasks important for adaptation to the loss: (a) acceptance of the loss and (b) development of a symbolic attachment to the deceased. First of all, EMDR therapy helps process the trauma of a loss, enabling integration and acceptance of the loss. Regarding Bowlby's second point, EMDR therapy seems to result in the emergence of heart-felt memories enabling an adaptive inner representation, providing a symbolic attachment to the deceased. As guided by Attachment Theory, difficulties in dealing with these two tasks can be overcome by identifying and processing past memories related to problematic child-caregiver interactions.

Case Examples
SECURE ATTACHMENT

Case Example 1: Zelda's husband was in an auto accident and died 2 months later of complications. Zelda had been married 8 years and had two children. One year after her husband's death she came in for EMDR therapy. She described it had been a sad year, but she believed she was adapting. She devoted much of her time to her children who were upset but managing in school and remained in close contact to the extended family and their friends. She had started back to work 4 months after her husband died, and in the last 3 months, resumed her usual routines that included playing tennis weekly with friends, and at least twice a week she met a friend or group of friends for lunch or dinner. The image of her husband at the morgue still haunted her, and she would think of it whenever she saw ambulance or passed the hospital. She described a normal upbringing, with parents she felt loved her and provided for her. She always had friends growing up. She met her husband in college, and the couple had been happily married.

Zelda appeared grounded in the first session and responded well to a safe/calm place exercise. After another session of history taking, and explaining EMDR therapy, the scene at the morgue was targeted. In the initial sets of bilateral stimulation Zelda cried, as she recounted seeing her husband in the morgue. She also described going home after that, being with family and friends, and the funeral. Then memories of her husband alive came to mind. For example, the couple had recently celebrated her birthday with dinner and dancing. She said she could almost feel his embrace when dancing with him. At the end of the session, she reported the image of her husband in the morgue had faded and she no longer felt distress at thinking of this scene. Thinking of her husband brought a smile to her, and she said she felt solid, and blessed their time together.

This client with a secure attachment met criteria after two sessions to start EMDR memory processing. Processing proceeded smoothly, ending with the emergence of positive, meaningful memories. Though the client did not meet criteria for PTSD and was functioning adaptively, EMDR was helpful in processing the distressing scene at the morgue. EMDR therapy does not interfere with the mourning process, but enables it by processing distressing memories and obstacles that could complicate the grief. As is typical of EMDR therapy with grief, positive memories arose, illustrating the adaptive inner representation.

ANXIOUS ATTACHMENT

> Case 2: (Contributed by Kris White). The father of this 34-year-old man died. The client was very upset, fearful, and indeed desperate. When targeting the memory of hearing the news about his father, the processing got stuck with the client's feeling of anxiety. The therapist did a "floatback," and memories of his mother, and the fear he felt in her presence came to mind. The mother was a frightening figure for the client: however, he felt secure with his father. When his father died, his childhood fears surfaced, complicating his grief and interfering with the mourning process. After processing memories regarding his mother, the client was able to adapt to the loss of his father.

AVOIDANT ATTACHMENT

> Case 3: A woman, aged 25 years, came into treatment 2 years after her father died. He had a degenerative disease, and had been bedridden since she was 8 years old. She found herself less emotional and more distant from others since her father died. After this was pointed out to her by friends, she came into treatment. She described her father as an intelligent man with broad interests. She enjoyed the conversations with him during his last years. On one hand, she missed him. However, she had always felt distant from him. Since his death, thinking or being reminded of her father would lead to feeling numb and shut down. She did not have many childhood memories (not uncommon with an avoidant attachment style), but did describe her father was gruff and critical of her. She would try to help her bedridden father when needed, but mostly tried to stay away from him. Given his illness was a major preoccupation for her mother, she often felt alone and on her own. After several sessions of history taking, EMDR initially

focused on an intrusive and sad memory of being at her father's bedside when he died. After several sets, processing became blocked, with the client feeling numb. The client was directed to go back to target, and the block was explored by asking what was the benefit of having blocked feelings. With exploration of this issue, the client started to realize how harsh, critical, and impatient he was when she was growing up and being emotionally distant from him and shutting down were primary ways of coping with her father's negative behavior toward her. Returning to target and continuing reprocessing resulted in the memory of being at the bedside of her father having a low SUD, but with more awareness of the negative childhood memories. The session was incomplete and ended with grounding exercises. Subsequent sessions of focused on the reprocessing of distressing memories related to her father, memories where she felt alone and on her own, and relevant present triggers and future templates.

Disorganized attachment style will be dealt with in the Chapter 19 on complex trauma.

Summary

Research has shown that attachment style is an important determinant of how one deals with loss of a loved one and explains individual differences (Kosminsky & Jordan, 2016). Attachment styles result from interactions with caregivers. In terms of the Adaptive Information Processing system (AIP), *attachment styles can be conceptualized as memory networks organized around child-caregiver interactions that guide relationships and provide a foundation of emotional information about self and other.* The loss of a significant loved one in adulthood may evoke many of the same feelings and responses that accompanied separation from an attachment figure during childhood. Treatment of complicated mourning not only involves treating the trauma and distress of the loss (e.g., focusing on the moment of shock or realization of the loss) but also the identification and processing of these maladaptively stored memories that were formative in the development of one's attachment style and underlie current difficulties. Present triggers also need to be identified and reprocessed, and a future template for each trigger provided.

7

Models of Grief

Continuing Bonds Model

Another important model of grief is *Continuing Bonds* (Klass, Silverman, & Nickman, 1996). These authors questioned models of grief where the end result is detachment from the deceased, "closure," or "moving on." For example, Freud, in his classic work *Mourning and Melancholia* (1917/1957), viewed the work of mourning (grief work) as the mechanism through which the bereaved person relinquishes the bond with the deceased loved one. Through repeated exposure to reminders of the finality of the death, bereaved persons come to accept its reality and de-invest (*decathect*) their libido (attachment energy), freeing it up for investment in other relationships.

From an attachment point of view, we will see that the goal of grief work does not involve detachment from the loved one. Rather, the goal is a *reorganization*, a *transformation* of the relationship that accommodates the reality of the death and results in the *development of a continuing bond* that endures throughout life. Mourners maintain a psychological connection with the deceased loved one (Marwit & Klass, 1996). This continuing bond is expressed behaviorally and socially with friends and family through talking about the loved one, remembering (informally, as well as in more formal rituals) and sharing the pain (Klass, personal communication, 2022). In the beginning, continuing bond behaviors seek to maintain a physical proximity. There may be dreaming about the loved one, talking to them, thinking about the loved one, and visiting places where there is a feeling of closeness to the person. However, these can be reminders that the loved one is gone, and over time, we come to accept and adapt to this new reality. However, the bond continues. Rituals, memorials, ceremonies, engaging in meaningful activities that honor the loved one, carrying on their legacy, and recounting fond memories bring comfort and ongoing connection. Continuing Bonds theory shows us that grief is ongoing, not something that ends, but continually evolves with our loved one still part of our life, carried through memories. The relationship with the deceased loved one is not static, but matures along with the person.

EMDR Therapy Treatment for Grief and Mourning. Roger M. Solomon, Oxford University Press. © Roger M. Solomon 2024.
DOI: 10.1093/oso/9780198881360.003.0008

How one relates to the loved one changes as one grows older with different perspectives at age 21, 30, 40, and so on.

Internal Working Models

The concept of internal working models, usually used in describing the experience of children with their caregivers, is also useful here. Through ongoing interactions with the caregiver and consolidation of information on both availability and responsiveness, the child develops an internal working model (IWM) that enables the child to feel the attachment without physical proximity. Hence, the IWM provides a connection with the attachment figures when there is separation. As Bowlby (2005, 2008) describes these inner working models have a lasting effect and influence expectations regarding relationships, including how people react when someone with whom they are deeply attached to dies. Much like children who learn to tolerate separation from the caregiver because of the internalization of the relationship (e.g., IWM), mourners come to develop a new inner model of the relationship with the deceased that enables mourners to adapt to the permanent separation created by the death. The internalized loved one can continue to be a source of felt security and comfort as well as a base for exploration into the new world and finding meaning in life. In this way, the relationship with the deceased transforms itself with the development of a new internal model, where a meaningful connection is experienced through the heartfelt memories. This occurs often during EMDR memory reprocessing.

Healthy adaptation, however, requires acknowledgement of the death and the accommodation of inner working models to include the permanence of the loss. For some, accepting the permanence of this loss may be unbearable, even traumatizing. Mourners may feel *stuck* in grief because they cannot *connect* with the loved one who is forever gone. Further, the deep pain itself can be the connection to the loved one, and mourners may fear (consciously or unconsciously) that losing the pain is akin to losing the connection (see Appendix 2). Some try to deliberately force a bond through keeping the loved one's possessions exactly the same, continuing to visit places frequented by the loved one, or having imaginal conversations in order to feel comforted (as if the deceased were alive, and not fully realizing the deceased is gone and not coming back). However, research (Fields, Gao, & Paderna, 2005) has shown that such deliberate behavioral or imaginal attempts of trying to connect to the loved one do not seem to contribute to long-term coping. There is a difference between such forced behavioral manifestations of a continuing bond and having an internal sense of felt-connectedness. The felt sense of connection can be symbolic; for example, the deceased can be remembered as a positive role model, a source of wisdom, a loving companion, or someone who accompanied them during important moments in life. This felt sense of connection that is experienced through meaningful, heartfelt memories can be integrated into the mourner's identity, and allows the loved one to continue to play a role in the mourner's personal life. In this light, the mental representation of the deceased can continue to evolve as part of a meaningful ongoing connection for mourners (Neimeyer et al., 2006).

The Continuing Bond Can Be Negative

The memories that emerge during EMDR and that form the internal representation can be negative. Dennis Klass (personal communication, April 15, 2020) states: "The continuing bond is <u>continuing</u>; that is, many of the same dynamics in the relationship can continue. So, difficulties or pathologies remain, though the death may give the living person more room to modify the bond, or in some cultures like ours, to separate rather fully from the toxic relationship.... I think we often make the mistake of talking about continuing bonds as if they are always good. If we know anything from a century of modern psychology it is that love is a complex thing."

Case examples illustrations of the continuing bond are numerous in this book, as seen in the emergence of positive memories that form an adaptive inner representation.

Case Example 1: Portia was pregnant with twins, and was walking downtown when a bombing attack occurred. She was close to the explosion, and tried to protect herself. She felt something tear inside and put her hands over her stomach. She then had a miscarriage. Twenty years later, Portia entered EMDR treatment. She had previously received some psychotherapy for posttraumatic stress disorder (PTSD), but her trauma was triggered by the death of the general of the invading army, motivating her for continued therapy. Treatment the first 2 years dealt with traumatic experiences occurring during the war. One session of EMDR therapy dealt with the loss of her twins. She felt guilty for not being able to protect them better. She blamed her arms, which she had wrapped around her stomach to protect her pregnancy during the explosion. With reprocessing, the putting her hands over her stomach became a moment of holding her

> *twins, a moment of connection. After this session she could think of her lost babies with the "holding moment" and have a sense of real connection.*

Implications for EMDR Therapy

Mourners may feel significant distress because there is a felt loss of connection to the loved one. The pain of irrevocable loss can be unbearable. Assuming clients meet readiness criteria for memory processing, EMDR therapy results in the reprocessing of the emotional pain that comes with the realization that the loved one is permanently gone. The reprocessing of the *raw felt emotion* enables the linking in of adaptive information, including the emergence of positive, heartfelt memories. These memories of the deceased enable an adaptive inner representation (as elaborated in Chapter 1) to emerge that includes a sense of felt connection. Hence, an important clinical dynamic is clients moving from, *I can't connect* to *I can connect*, with the bridge being the heartfelt memories.

The continuing bond, however, can be composed of negative memories that underlie negative self-beliefs and identity issues, and can complicate the mourning process. EMDR treatment consists of identifying and reprocessing these negative memories. For example, the father of one man died. The main impact for his man was, "Now I will never be able to show him I am good enough." Treatment through his mourning process started with reprocessing negative childhood memories underlying his belief, "I am not good enough." The goal of treatment was to emancipate the mourner from the identity emanating from this maladaptively stored information. EMDR therapy leads to individuation and differentiation from the attachment figure who was the source of negative identity. (As the above-mentioned client concluded: "My father had his own problems ... I am not responsible for his behavior or the way he treated me ... I can separate who I am from how he treated me ... I am good enough.")

Summary

Continuing Bonds theory emphasizes the attachment to the deceased continues. With EMDR therapy, the continuing bond is shown through the emergence of positive memories which form an adaptive inner representation. However, negative memories are also part of the continuing bond and need to be reprocessed to promote healthy mourning and adaptive functioning overall.

8
The Dual Process Model of Grief

The Dual Process Model: Loss Orientation and Restoration Orientation

Stroebe and Schut (1999, 2010) conceptualize a Dual Process model (DPM) where healthy adaptation to loss involves oscillation between *coping with the pain* related to the loss (*a Loss Orientation (LO)*) and *avoiding the pain* while dealing with psychological and practical daily life challenges issues pertaining to a future life without the deceased (a *Restoration Orientation (RO)*). These orientations are characterized by the following:

- *LO* involves dealing with the emotional reactions arising from the loss, with mourners engaged in yearning, searching, remembering, having imaginal conversations, experiencing the presence of the loved one, and dealing with situations or reminders where mourners have to face the loss of the relationship (Zech, 2016).
- *RO* involves turning away from the grief in order to deal with the secondary stressors: that is, the changes that are a consequence of the loss. This involves dealing with issues such as changes in financial circumstances, household duties, dealing with new responsibilities, and adjusting to shifts in identity (e.g., from husband to widower).

In the DPM the experience of coping occurs in an oscillatory pattern, with intervals of turning away from grief to deal with life changes (secondary stressors) as much of a part of the mourning process as moving toward and through the grief (Strobe & Schut,1999, 2010; Kosminsky & Jordan, 2016). That is, bereaved people oscillate between confronting the loss (LO) and dealing with the painful emotions, and avoiding the loss by resting and taking time off from grieving (RO). This enables mourners to move in and out of intense grief and deal with life changes necessitated by the loss. This oscillation is essential for optimal psychological adjustment. The ability to be flexible in dealing with both LO and RO stressors is crucial.

EMDR Therapy Treatment for Grief and Mourning. Roger M. Solomon, Oxford University Press. © Roger M. Solomon 2024.
DOI: 10.1093/oso/9780198881360.003.0009

One can understand the DPM model in terms of attachment theory. LO involves the activation of the attachment system and the bereaved confronting the emotional aspects of the loss. RO involves deactivation of the attachment system, with mourners able to put away the grief to deal with everyday life issues. When a loved one dies, the loss is irreversible, and the loved one can no longer provide safety and comfort, so that primary strategies for seeking comfort and attachment are no longer relevant. Secondary strategies, namely attachment system activation and deactivation, must come into play. As Mikulincer and Shaver (2017) describe, experiencing the deep pain of the loss (activating strategies) stimulates memories of the loved one along with the realization the person is gone and not coming back. This drives mourners to explore and appreciate the meaning and significance of the lost relationship, reorganize their bonds to the loved one from loving in presence to loving in absence, and integrate the loss. Deactivating strategies, where there is momentary detachment from the loved one, compartmentalizing, and turning away from grief, enables the reorganization process by allowing people to focus on their changing roles, responsibilities and life situation. Therefore, healthy grief involves oscillation between confrontation of the loss (LO) and periods of avoidance and respite (RO). Mourners will, at times, confront the loss and, at other times, avoid it. These dynamic processes of confronting and coping with the emotional impact of the loss and, other times, seeking respite from it makes for a healthy grieving process. There are times to confront the grief fully and times when it is important to take a break and focus on daily life tasks and practical needs. For example, a woman who was a teacher was mourning the loss of her mother. She described how emotionally difficult it was to cope with feelings of loss when she was home, but she found that going to work and focusing on her teaching was helpful. This is a good example of oscillation between LO and RO.

Oscillation between LO and RO breaks down when mourners are overly focused on either activating or deactivating strategies. Mourners using activating strategies (anxious attachment style) at some level have the belief (or at least the hope) that if they protest long and hard enough, the loved one will return. Complications with the over focus on LO include chronic grieving, where there is an unrelenting and intense grief, rumination, and preoccupation with thoughts of the deceased. There may be little progress towards accepting and coming to terms with the loss. Mourners using deactivating strategies (avoidant attachment style), on the other hand, strive to do what they can do to avoid being reminded of the loved one, will deny strong feelings about the loss, and suppress these thoughts if they arise. However, the painful feelings regarding the loved one, even if outside of conscious awareness, still impact mourners and can be triggered by reminders. In extreme cases, these individuals show inhibited, absent, or delayed grief (see Chapter 5), denying the need for grieving over the loss of an attachment figure and preferring to cope alone. This leaves the loss unintegrated and fragmented, and mourners suffering in silence.

Implications for EMDR Therapy

The DPM model illustrates the importance of taking a broad view of intervention, exploring not only how clients are dealing with the emotional impact of the loss (LO), but also how clients are able to put away the grief to deal with the changes in life, such as, taking on new roles and responsibilities resulting from the death (RO). In other words, it is important to evaluate the oscillation between LO and RO.

Over-Focusing on Loss Orientation

Some clients who are overly focused on LO—as with an *anxious attachment style*—may be helped by reprocessing the traumatic moments and images of the loss, such as hearing the news about the death, hospital scenes, or funeral scenes, that often intrude and disrupt functioning. This can help the client oscillate toward RO, shifting away from the emotional focus on the loss, and deal with the changes caused by the death.

For some clients, however, the yearning, sadness, and impact of the loss is too much and can leave them 'drowning' in emotion. Doing emotional work too soon can deepen distress and increase rumination and depression. Clients have to first have sufficient affect regulation and stabilization to put the anguish of grieving on hold and stay in active coping mode. Consequently, there may be more improvement, with movement toward RO, with an initial focus on affect management, Resource Development and Installation (RDI) (Korn & Leeds, 2002), problem-solving skills, finding ways to distract from the grief for some periods of time (e.g., hobbies, time with friends, movies, or meaningful activities), and learning new strategies and skills for coping with the changes (secondary stressors) resulting from the death.

Also, clients may need to learn to skills to adapt to new roles and deal with challenges posed by the death. Margaret Strobe stated (Personal communication, 11 September 2020): '....the secondary stressors, the changes that come about as a result of the loss, have to be dealt with as well as facing one's loss of the person. These RO tasks are arduous, and part of coping with the bereavement experience specifically—they need to be confronted. Clinicians can identify the obstacles that make dealing with RO tasks difficult, and target the present triggers that evoke the difficulty. As will be explained in more detail in Chapter 14 on Phase 2: Preparation and Stabilization, after sufficient preparation, stabilization and affect regulation, processing the trauma of the loss (e.g., initial emotional impact) can help clients function more adaptively. Then, reprocessing present triggers and providing future templates for each trigger can help clients cope with the changes and new challenges. Earlier memories (e.g., attachment-based memories) may underlie present difficulties. These memories should be explored and reprocessed when clients have the capacity for dual awareness during the reprocessing.

Case Example 1: Teresa's husband died of a heart attack at home. Six months after his death, she entered treatment. She was experiencing posttraumatic stress disorder (PTSD) symptoms from witnessing the death of her husband. Teresa, with two children (aged 8 and 11 years) had her hands full taking care of the children and working. She was also quite distraught, yearning for her husband, and felt overwhelmed by the loss and the difficulties of managing her household alone. Treatment initially focused on affect regulation, problem-solving skills (e.g., prioritizing and planning for the day), and time management. Teresa found it difficult to ask friends and family for help. Her reluctance stemmed from not feeling worthy of receiving help. Her parents divorced when she was 5 and she had lived with her mother. The mother was often bothered when Teresa would ask for help, and though the mother would help she appeared angry while doing so. These types of interactions led to her negative self-belief, 'I am not worthy.' After 2 months of affect regulation strategies, including the safe/calm place, RDI, and breathing exercises, EMDR memory reprocessing started with her witnessing her husband's death. The next priority was helping Teresa with RO. Childhood memories related to, 'I am worthless', that made it difficult for her to ask for help were identified, such as her mother's being angry when she needed help, were reprocessed. Present triggers, such as not asking friends or family member for help with the children (even though she knew they would help) were then targeted, following by future templates of being able to ask for help. After these sessions, Teresa was able to ask her friends and family for help. Her affect regulation increased with her ever-increasing self-esteem ('I am worthy') resulting from reprocessing attachment-based memories. Further, Teresa also became more adept at time management as she learned she could count on people to help her. With further treatment, she increasingly became more able to put aside her grief to deal with the challenges of adaptation.

Teresa was stuck in LO, with difficulty putting her grief on hold to oscillate to RO and deal with secondary stressors. A major obstacle was not being able to ask for help. Providing affect regulation strategies and RDI built up her adaptive capacity to maintain dual awareness, which is important for EMDR memory processing. After reprocessing the trauma of the loss, sessions focused on helping her deal with secondary stressors, with being able to ask for help a priority. After reprocessing attachment-based memories that contributed to 'I am not worthy', Teresa was able to oscillate to RO tasks and better engage in LO tasks.

Over-Focusing on Restoration Orientation

Clients stuck in RO (as with avoidant attachment) avoid the emotional impact of the loss and may need to gradually approach thoughts and feelings about the death. Affect management strategies should be taught to the client as needed. Exploring the history of the relationship, memories of the loved one, and what is missed can be approached at the clients' pace. It is important to explore and reprocess relevant past memories related to the development of an avoidant attachment style. For example, as a result of negative interactions with the caregiver or neglect, children may learn that shutting down, avoiding and not expressing emotions and needs is the best survival strategy. Further, reminders of the deceased which trigger emotion can be too much for clients. After sufficient affect regulation, the situations, people, or circumstances that trigger emotional pain need to be reprocessed, and followed with a future template for adaptive behaviour.

> Case Example 2: Jeff's mother died after an extended illness. Five months later Jeff, aged 27 years, entered treatment. Jeff had difficulty experiencing and expressing his feelings. He described he was keeping busy with attending to her estate, including readying her house for sale and dealing with legal matters. Whenever he would think of his mother, he would become sad, and quickly find something to do. However, he did notice he was experiencing body aches that seemed to become more frequent and were associated with thinking of his mother or being reminded of her. Jeff described his parents, emphasizing that he should be independent and find solutions himself. Consequently, he felt alone in growing up and when in distress, he learned to cope by himself. He also over-ate when stressed. He described he always had difficulty expressing emotions, and this also was a problem in his relationships. Often, women he dated would break up with

him because he seemed emotionally shallow. Sessions initially focused on listening to Jeff describe his mother's illness, her death, and his reactions. Probing for emotions was gentle and the therapist was accepting of his level of response. Initial sessions taught safe/calm place and breathing exercises to deal with tension. After 3 months, Jeff was able to describe the painful aspects of his childhood. As a child, he tried to handle his problems by himself, as was expected of him. However, he did not know what to do a lot of the time, and felt inadequate. He also felt alone, and learned how to keep busy to cope with his distress. A pivotal moment in therapy was when Jeff got in touch with a painful memory when he was 10 and his football coach told his mother he had a weight problem. His reaction was, 'Why couldn't my mother be the one to notice this and help me?' Jeff was tearful when he disclosed this memory. The next session EMDR processing began with this memory. Over the course of therapy, Jeff was more and more able to experience and express his emotions, including his grief for his mother. EMDR therapy was also utilized to reprocess distressing moments related to her death (e.g., moments she was suffering, the moment he knew she was going to die, and when she died). Therapy proceeded with EMDR reprocessing of childhood memories, more recent disturbing memories, present triggers, and installing future templates for each trigger. He continued to become more comfortable experiencing and expressing emotions. This was also evident in his social life, with Jeff's becoming better able to communicate with others and have more fulfilling relationships.

This example illustrates how an avoidant attachment style can interfere with the oscillation between LO and RO. Jeff was stuck in RO, overly focused on the tasks associated with his mother's death. It had always been difficult for him to express and experience emotions, and this was the case as well with the death of his mother. Treatment focused on gradually exploring his reactions to his mother's death and his childhood experiences. After getting emotionally in touch with a distressing childhood memory, EMDR treatment began, resulting in being increasingly able to experience and express emotions, including the grief for his mother.

Summary

The DPM emphasizes the importance of oscillation between dealing with loss-related stressors (LO) and the stressors resulting from adapting to the changes that result from the loss (RO). Mourners need to move back and forth between dealing with the emotional impact of the loss and putting the grief on hold, so they can deal with the practical matters. Clients stuck in LO may need affect regulation strategies to lower emotional arousal and, when ready, they need to reprocess the trauma of the loss, present triggers, and install future templates. It may also be helpful to reprocess early childhood memories relevant to an anxious attachment style to enhance capacity to move into RO and deal with life's new challenges. Clients stuck in RO may need to approach emotions and memories of the deceased slowly. Affect regulation strategies may be helpful. When clients can maintain dual awareness and stay present with emotions, reprocessing memories related to the death, along with present triggers, and installing future templates are possible. Further, reprocessing early childhood memories relevant to an avoidant attachment style may help clients oscillate into LO.

9

The "R" Processes of Mourning

Introduction to Rando's Six 'R' Processes of Mourning

Rando (1993) delineated six processes of mourning that are important for the healthy accommodation of a loss called 'R' processes (see Table 9.1). The 'R' processes are useful in helping clients and clinicians understand where clients are in the mourning processes and what has to be done to facilitate accommodation of the loss. Consequently, *complicated mourning*, within this framework, is defined as not being able to accomplish these processes. The 'R' processes provide clinical direction about what is important for the assimilation and accommodation of the loss and provides a framework to understand where people may be stuck and has implications for processing. The 'R' processes are divided into three phases—avoidance, confrontation, and accommodation, and consist of six separate processes (see Table 9.1).

The *Avoidance Phase* involves the initial reactions of shock, numbness, and disbelief that often accompanies a sudden, unexpected, or distressing loss. With time, the shock reactions wear off and the mourner starts to emotionally confront and deal with the emotional impact of the loss as in the *Confrontation Phase*. With more time, the mourner typically begins to adapt to the loss. This is termed the *Accommodation Phase*. Within each phase there are psychological processes, or operations, that are important in assimilating and accommodating the loss.

The 'R' processes are not a stage theory, rather they provide clinical direction and considerations for clinicians. During treatment, the 'R' processes tend to segue from one to another, with the earlier 'R' processes being a prerequisite for the later ones. However, people do not go through these processes in a linear fashion. As discussed in Chapter 3 there are many factors that influence the response to loss. Each person's bereavement experience and treatment needs are unique. Often, clients need to go back and again process issues and stuck points related to earlier 'R' processes. Consequently, clinicians must continually assess clients' movement through the 'R' processes, while

EMDR Therapy Treatment for Grief and Mourning. Roger M. Solomon, Oxford University Press. © Roger M. Solomon 2024.
DOI: 10.1093/oso/9780198881360.003.0010

Table 9.1 Six "R" Processes of Mourning

Rando (1993)	
Avoidance Phase	**RECOGNIZE** the loss • Acknowledge the death • Understand the death
Confrontation Phase	**REACT** to the separation • Experience the pain • Feel, identify, accept, and give some form of expression to all the psychological reactions to the loss • Identify and mourn secondary losses **RECOLLECT** and re-experience the deceased and the relationship • Review and remember realistically • Revive and re-experience the feelings **RELINGUISH** the old attachments to the deceased and the old assumptive world
Accommodation Phase	**READJUST** to move adaptively into the new world without forgetting the old • Revise the assumptive world • Develop a new relationship with the deceased • Adopt new ways of being in the world • Form a new identity • **REINVEST**

understanding in which process mourners may be blocked and reprocess relevant past memories, present triggers, and future templates relevant to such blocks.

This framework emphasizes what is important for assimilation and accommodation of the loss but does not elaborate on the developmental issues that can complicate mourning and compromise proceeding through the 'R' processes. Consequently, this framework can be supplemented by both attachment theory and the Adaptive Information Processing (AIP) model. With past caregiver-child interactions shaping attachment style, the AIP model emphasizes the importance of past maladaptively stored memories on present symptoms, including response to loss. Attachment theory provides a developmental perspective to understanding mourners' responses to loss and why mourners may be stuck in an 'R' process. Consequently, it is important for clinicians to understand that blocked processing of a memory that encapsulates a 'stuck point' may be due to previous losses, trauma, or memories relevant to attachment style. The underlying memories need to be identified and reprocessed along with present triggers and future templates.

The 'R' Processes

Phase 1: Avoidance Phase

The First 'R' Process: Recognize the Loss

In the first 'R' process, the task is to recognize the loss of the loved one, consists of two parts:

- Acknowledging the death.
- Understanding the death.

First, the mourner needs to *acknowledge that the death* has occurred. This is counter to the natural urge to deny death's reality and to avoid confronting it. Typically, there are repeated confrontations with the reality of what has happened before mourners can really recognize and assimilate it. For example, mourners may go to call their loved ones, and again realize that they are dead. It can take some time to fully comprehend on an emotional level that the loss is permanent. Second, it is important that clients *understand the death*: what happened, how it happened, and the reasons for the death. This understanding enables clients to take in its reality. Such understanding can be quite difficult in the event of traumatic death, such as suicide, situations where nobody is found (e.g., airplane crashes), or other horrific circumstances where there are gaps in the information. Many mourners experience significant anguish if they do not have this information.

Implications for EMDR Therapy

Acknowledging the death and understanding it in all its implications (e.g., the loss is permanent) can be very upsetting and traumatizing. Initially, mourners may find it difficult to fully comprehend the loss and experience numbness and a sense that the loss is 'not real'. However, at some point the emotional impact gradually begins to be felt. For many people, the realization of the loss is too much and very painful. At the beginning of the mourning process, when the loss is too much to realize, emotional support, psychological first aid, education about grief and mourning, and teaching clients coping skills and stress reduction methods as needed may be appropriate.

Eye movement desensitization and reprocessing (EMDR) therapy can focus on reprocessing the loss as a traumatic event, assuming clients meet readiness criteria, with the goal of integrating the trauma of the loss and enabling clients to progress through the next 'R' processes. The starting point can be the moment of shock or realization of the loss (e.g., getting the news). These can be quite painful sessions as mourners experience the raw felt emotions that come with the realization that the loss is real and permanent.

> Case Example 1 Matti: Matti's wife was killed in a car accident. Mattie, aged 34 years, had been married for 2 years. The couple had no children. Matti entered treatment 3 months after his wife died. After four sessions of history-taking and preparation & stabilization, EMDR therapy focused on reprocessing the trauma of the death notification, with the traumatic moment of the police coming to his workplace and telling him. Reprocessing this moment was very distressing as Matti emotionally confronted his wife's death. He tearfully recounted going to the hospital, seeing his wife's body, and saying goodbye to her. At the end of the session, he could think of his wife's laughter, some of the jokes she liked to tell, and other positive moments in their life together.

EMDR reprocessing started with the moment of the traumatic impact, getting the news. It was an emotional session, ending with positive memories of his wife reemerging. Afterwards, Matti was starting to react to the separation, which is the second 'R' process. The arising of memories of his wife is also important in adapting to the loss, as will be discussed below with the third 'R' process.

Phase 2: Confrontation Phase

This phase consists of the second, third, and fourth 'R' processes:

- *React* to the separation.
- *Recollect* and re-experience the deceased and the relationship.
- *Relinquish* old attachments to the deceased and the old assumptive world.

The Second 'R' Process: React to the Separation

The second 'R' process has to do with reacting to the separation from the loved one. With the reality of the death acknowledged, the mourner must react to this new reality and begin to cope with it. The mourner must do the following tasks:

- Experience the pain.
- Feel, identify, accept, and give some form of expression to all the psychological reactions to the loss.
- Identify and mourn secondary losses.

EXPERIENCE THE PAIN

Mourners must experience the pain resulting from the absence of the deceased. It is natural not to want to feel the pain, but it is there and must not only be acknowledged but embraced. Indeed, as the Dual Process Model teaches us, there are times to put the pain away so daily life can be dealt with. Then, mourners have to oscillate back and experience the pain. The reprocessing of memories of the loss can be very intense with clients experiencing the 'raw felt emotion' that accompanies the realization that the loved one is gone forever. However, doing so is important and enables clients to move into the next process that follows.

FEEL, IDENTIFY, ACCEPT, AND GIVE SOME FORM OF EXPRESSION TO ALL THE PSYCHOLOGICAL REACTIONS TO THE LOSS

This is crucial because unacknowledged and unexpressed emotions are major precipitants of complicated mourning (Rando, 1995). With EMDR reprocessing, the emotional pain is identified, experienced, and expressed. Doing so sets the stage for the emergence of meaningful, positive memories and accompanying heartfelt emotions, which in turn help transmute the relationship from external attachment to an adaptive inner representation. However, as will be noted in the third 'R' process, the memories that come up can be negative, bringing to mind the ambivalence and conflicts that were never resolved.

MOURNING SECONDARY LOSSES

Secondary losses must also be identified and processed. The loved one is the primary loss, but other losses result as a consequence. Daily routines taken for granted may now be changed, the sense of security and predictability provided by the deceased is gone. Seemingly small things, like riding to work every day with the loved one, can have a major impact now that it will no longer happen. These losses need to be identified and processed.

Implications for EMDR Therapy

The reprocessing of the trauma of the loss often brings intense 'raw felt' emotions, as mourners feel the pain of the loss. Present triggers that evoke painful reminders of the loss (e.g., separation distress) can also be processed. These are the people, places, and situations that remind mourners of the death and evoke painful separation distress. Also, situations and present triggers that encapsulate secondary losses also need to be processed.

> *Case Example 2 Matti: Matti experienced many painful moments in his daily life, with one of the most painful moments being cooking dinner alone. Matti often met with his family and friends for meals, but there were still many nights when he ate alone. The loss of cooking with his wife is also a secondary loss for Matti. A moment where he was cooking a meal his wife liked very much was targeted with EMDR therapy. This was an emotionally intense session with Matti again feeling the pain of his wife's sudden death, and the distress of being alone and missing her. The reprocessing resulted in moving from a negative cognition of, ' I cannot manage', to 'I can manage', with a future template of seeing that he had many options to cope with his loss and could live with eating dinner alone. Treatment also focused on adapting to life without his wife, including engaging in meaningful activities (playing tennis, playing chess online) and keeping up his social contacts.*

The above example illustrates how present triggers—situations that evoke distress—can be targeted. Further, as illustrated above, a future template should be installed for each trigger.

The Third 'R' Process: Recollect and Re-experience the Deceased and the Relationship

In order to adjust to a loss and adapt to new realities, mourners' attachment to the deceased and to the old assumptive world must alter and evolve. Mourners need to do the following tasks:

- *Review and remember the deceased and the relationship realistically, including all attachment ties, such as needs, emotions, thoughts, behaviours, dreams, and expectation.*
- *Revive and re-experience the feelings associated with these memories.*

REVIEW AND REMEMBER REALISTICALLY

In this first operation, all aspects of the loved one and the mutual relationship must be recalled (i.e., the positive, the negative and the neutral). To ensure clients are not left with emotional material that is problematic, it is important clients review and remember the deceased realistically. Otherwise, mourners may be left with connections to the deceased that may not have been appropriately resolved. Major issues that occurred in the relationship do not necessarily go away with the death, and painful, disturbing or conflictual memories involving the deceased must be addressed. There are the heartfelt positive memories, and the negative memories. The memories with a care-giver that underlie negative self-esteem and identity issues, giving rise to insecure attachments can interfere with the mourning process. The continuing bond/inner representation that evolves with the deceased is composed of memories and the meaning we give them (Fairbairn, 1952). The inner representation needs represent the deceased as a real person, the good and the bad, the positive and the negative. The inner representation is what mourners interact with when thinking of the deceased. An idealized and inaccurate representation where mourners have to avoid or deny some aspects of the relationship leaves mourners vulnerable to having maladaptively stored information triggered, resulting in present problems and difficulties in adapting to the loss.

REVIVE AND EXPERIENCE THE FEELINGS

The feelings associated with the memories must also be experienced. These feelings were the 'glue' underlying the mourners attachment bonds or ties to the deceased while they were still living (Rando, 1995; Solomon & Rando, 2007, 2012). Reprocessing the memories that encapsulate these feelings helps mourners experience, acknowledge, and integrate the emotions so that they lessen in intensity and ultimately allow adaptive information to link in. This paves the way for the next 'R' processes: relinquishing ties to the loved one, and old assumptive world, so that new ones can evolve.

Implications for EMDR Therapy

EMDR therapy often results in positive meaningful memories arising, forming an adaptive inner representation, as illustrated in previous sessions with Matti. However, conflictual memories that continue to haunt the mourner must also be reprocessed.

> *Case Example 3 Matti: Matti experienced many good memories of his wife that gave him a warm feeling when he thought of her. However, he felt guilty about losing his temper with her occasionally. They would eventually make up and resolve the issue, but he felt bad about yelling at her when her life would be suddenly taken away from him. Reprocessing this memory was emotional with the result being he could remember, with fondness, the two of them making up.*

Matti experienced many positive memories of his wife, which is important in the formation of an adaptive inner representation. It was also important to process conflictual memories which continue can be an obstacle to going through the mourning process. The resolution for Matti was being able to see the conflictual situation holistically, including the positive moments of making up.

Transition from the Confrontation Phase to the Accommodation Phase: 'R' Process 4 and 5

The fourth and fifth processes have to do with relinquishing old attachments that are no longer valid because of the death; ('R' Process 4) and moving adaptively into the new world without forgetting the old ('R' Process 5). These two processes come under different phases in Rando's scheme—Phase 2, Confrontation, and Phase 3, Accommodation, respectively (see Table 9.1). Dealing with the feelings that accompany relinquishing ties that no longer are valid is a painful process. For this reason, the fourth 'R' process is part of the Confrontation stage. This type of realization enables mourners to transition into the new world without forgetting the old. As mentioned at the start of this chapter, the processes segue from one to another, and this applies particularly to Processes 4 and 5. As will be discussed below, utilizing EMDR to process difficulties with relinquishing attachment (fourth 'R' process) naturally segues to an assimilation and accommodation of the loss, and moves adaptively into the new world (fifth 'R' process).

The Fourth 'R' Process: Relinquish the Old Attachments to the Deceased and the Old Assumptive World

Healthy adaptation to the loss of a loved one requires transforming former attachments to both the deceased and to the assumptive world which has been rendered obsolete by the death. Complicated mourning develops if old attachments to the loved one and the accompanying assumptions about the world, still based on the loved one being alive, do not evolve, leaving mourners stuck in a now unrealistic assumptive world. The mourners' attachments and ties to the deceased loved one may have been quite numerous and may involve feelings, thoughts, beliefs, needs, behaviour, socialization patterns, memories, hopes and dreams, assumptions, and expectations. These attachments are often central parts of mourners' identities and worldview, and the loved one, now deceased, can no longer fulfil these vital and mutually defining interactions.

Much pain is caused not only by the loss of the person, but also by the realization that one's world has changed significantly. The death of a loved one shatters elements of the assumptive world that were based upon the living existence of that individual. It can also shatter or violate more global assumptive world elements as well. For example, the death of an innocent child may make mourners question whether God is all-loving or that there is control over bad things happening. Since one's assumptive world strongly influences how a person lives and makes sense of life, having to let go or revise elements of the assumptive world can be disorienting and traumatizing for mourners. Individuals are thrown into a new, undesired, and often unrecognizable world.

Not surprisingly, there is often great resistance to relinquishing former attachments that are still based on the loved one being alive. Giving up what has provided a sense of control and predictability in life triggers vulnerability and powerlessness. It is not uncommon to fear there will be loss of all connection to the loved one. Sometimes, the pain of the loss is the connection to the loved one, so that they believe losing the pain effectively means losing the connection. Sometimes, mourners resist because the ties to the loved one have defined parts of their identity (e.g., 'My child has died; I can no longer be a mother.'). Or mourners do not think it is possible to relinquish the attachment and live in a world without the deceased and/or the former worldview (e.g., 'I can't live without him/her' or 'I can't live knowing things like this happen.'). The losses to self are too great.

It is helpful to explore the attachment by identifying the meaning or meanings of the relationship with the deceased. This includes specifying what was lost when that loved one died. Asking what is missed the most can be a useful question in understanding what was lost and helps identify the negative irrational self-belief that accompanies the loss at both personal and global levels. For example, with the death of a spouse, not only is a life companion taken away (e.g., 'I'm alone and not safe'), but also the stable world that it enabled (e.g., 'I'm not safe in the world'). These are the same issues that need to be explored when the loved one is stuck in any of the 'R' processes. After acknowledging the death, reacting to the death, and recollecting and re-experiencing the deceased and the relationship, mourners can better appreciate what is different in their world, what is missed and is forever gone, and can then continue to modify the assumptive world and to adapt to the loss.

It must be emphasized that relinquishing former ties does not mean that the deceased is forgotten or unloved. Rather it means that the ties are modified and transformed to assimilate and accommodate the new reality that the loved one is dead and cannot return mourners' emotional investment or meet their needs as before.

Implications for EMDR Therapy

EMDR therapy can focus on moments (present triggers and future templates) that encapsulate difficulties and obstacles to letting go of the old world and relationship.

> *Case Example 4 Matti: 1 year after his wife's death, Matti was coping adequately with the loss of her life. His work life was going well, and his contacts with his family and friends were meaningful. However, the first anniversary was triggering a lot of distress. He felt lonely and missed his wife. It was difficult to imagine how he could ever be with anyone else. EMDR processing focused on a specific moment when he acutely felt alone (drinking coffee in the morning 3 days before), with no end in sight. Reprocessing led to a further realization that his wife was gone and he would have to go on without her. He knew this before, but now felt this at a deeper level with more of an acceptance of the finality of her death. With further reprocessing Matti was able to say, 'I miss my wife, but I know life is not over . . . someday there will be a hand for me to hold.'*

The above example with Matti saying, 'Someday there will be a hand for me to hold', is an example of how reprocessing an obstacle to relinquishing an old tie that is no longer valid, given the death of the loved one, results into an adaptation into the new world, without forgetting the old. Matti did not forget his wife as the reprocessing led to a deeper acceptance of her loss and enabled him to look to the future and know 'life is not over'. The future template was imagining having his morning coffee with a feeling of optimism that indeed, life is not over.

Phase 3: Accommodation Phase

Phase 3 in Rando's framework consists of the fifth and sixth 'R' processes:

- 'R' 5—readjust to the new world without forgetting the old world.
- 'R' 6—reinvest emotional energy

Please continue to bear in mind however that 'R' Processes 4 and 5 are intricately linked.

The Fifth 'R' Process: Readjust to Move Adaptively into the New World Without Forgetting the Old

The fifth 'R' process concerning readjusting to move adaptively into the new world without forgetting the old consists of the following subprocesses:

- Revise the assumptive world.
- Develop a new relationship with the deceased.
- Adapt new ways of being in the world.

Form a New Identity

While mourners may want to keep the world as it was before the death of the loved one, gradually it is learned that this cannot happen. With every reminder of the loved one, there is increasing realization that the loss is permanent. Typically, a significant part of the world and identity feels gone and mourners experience a void in an unpredictable universe. These distressing moments (e.g., when the void was experienced) can be targeted. With reprocessing the painful moments and the linking in of positive, heartfelt memories, mourners come to appreciate and internalize the meaning of the attachment and adapt to the new world without forgetting the old.

As mourners release the old and now untenable attachments that occurred in the fourth 'R' process, a gradual accommodation to the loss can occur. Internal and external changes evolve that enable adaptation to the death. This segues closely into the fifth 'R' process of evolving a new world that does not forget the old.

REVISING THE ASSUMPTIVE WORLD

The death, especially a sudden, unexpected, and violent death can shake the foundations of people's assumptive world (Neimeyer, 2017). Adaptation to the loss, and reconstructing meaning in life, requires these violated assumptions be modified, replaced, or integrated with new information. Assumptions specific to the loved one being alive also have to be revised. After the death of a partner, mourners can no longer rely on them for safety, comfort, or companionship. Adapting to the new world, and letting go of the old, can be an arduous journey filled with fear and resistance. Moments where there is difficulty letting go of the old world and entering the new can be targeted.

DEVELOPING A NEW RELATIONSHIP WITH THE DECEASED
Mourners may experience yearning, pining, and sadness at the death of a loved one. There is often despair at the loss of connection and the thought that they must move on, breaking all ties with the loved one. Though death ends a live, it does not end the relationship, which is transformed. An inner representation, composed of heartfelt, meaningful memories, develops which becomes a basis for a sense of connection. However, the connection (and inner representation) can also be negative and create an inner struggle, that needs to be dealt with. EMDR therapy can be part of the treatment process; targeting the memories related to the conflicts, struggles, and 'unfinished business' associated with conflictual relationships. As stated earlier, EMDR therapy will not take away appropriate emotion or what is true. For example, it will not absolve people from appropriate guilt or responsibility in the conflictual relationship with the deceased.

ADOPTING NEW WAYS OF BEING IN THE WORLD
With the death of a loved, one mourners must learn to live in a world that is now fundamentally different. The closer mourners were to the deceased and the more their lives revolved around one another, the more challenging adapting to the new world will be. Mourners need to find new ways of meeting needs and fulfilling roles and duties that the deceased used to take care of. Mourners may need to learn new skills, adapt new roles, enhance their social support system, find other ways of getting needs met (e.g., ask for help from trusted friends and family), and otherwise learn to navigate in life without someone who was an intricate and stable part of their lives.

FORMING A NEW IDENTITY
With letting go of the old world and relationship and transitioning to the new, without forgetting the old, their identities shift. A mother whose baby died reflected, 'Who am I now that I can't be a mother?' A man whose wife died felt he no longer knew who he was, 'I was married with a woman who was like a mirror, and I saw myself through her.... That mirror is gone, and I don't know whom I am ... part of me died with her.' With time, the mourner develops a perspective on what is the same and what is different, on what has been lost, and what has been gained. Changes in life must be recognized and mourned. New aspects of the self develop with adapting to the new world and must be affirmed by oneself and the surrounding social network.

Implications for EMDR Therapy

Moments (present triggers and future templates) that encapsulate the difficulties in moving into the 'new world' can be targeted.

> *Case Example 5 Mattie: In a later session, Matti focused on a difficult moment of going to a dinner party alone, where he felt awkward as a single person, very much missing being a part of a couple. Reprocessing this present trigger resulted in Matti's expressing his sadness about his wife's death, and missing companionship. He knew he was ready for companionship and his wife would want him to be happy. Fond memories of his wife came up, and he felt thankful for the time they had together. Now he felt ready to date. A future template was installed where he imagined he could comfortably ask a woman out for coffee.*

In the above example, Matti was able to revise his assumptive world as evidenced by his readiness for companionship. Further, he could now feel his wife would want him to be happy. Hence, he is entering the new world, but not forgetting the old as experienced in fond memories arising along with feelings of thankfulness. He is adapting new ways of being in the world, as a single person, now ready to date. Hence, he is ready to REINVEST.

The Sixth 'R' Process: Reinvest

This sixth and last 'R' process involves mourners reinvesting in the new life without the loved one. The emotional energy that was previously invested in the loved one needs to be reinvested elsewhere, such as in other relationships, activities, new roles, and updated goals. Reinvestment does not have to duplicate what was lost (e.g., a widow or widower does not have to marry again). Rather, the emotional energy can be channelled into fulfilling directions. Moving on with life does not mean forgetting the loved one or that the loss is no longer important. It means that mourners are now able to love in absence or have made peace with the past (reprocessed previous trauma, losses, and conflicts with the deceased), and can adaptively go forth with a meaningful and productive life.

Implications for EMDR Therapy

The mourner's areas of difficulty can be identified, explored, and dealt with. Specific moments that represent obstacles to reinvesting can be targeted. It is also important that the therapist assess what new skills are needed, and whether past memories are interfering with present functioning and adaptive adjustment. If so, these past memories need to be reprocessed along with present triggers and future templates provided for each trigger.

> *Case Example 6 Matti: 5 months after the last session Matti scheduled an appointment. He had started dating a woman he felt comfortable with and enjoyed spending time with her. However, he felt uncomfortable with enjoying a new relationship. He reported he did not feel guilty, just that there was something wrong after having been married, as if he were letting his wife go. A moment where he felt this uncomfortable feeling, was when he was talking to her on the phone the week before, and this was targeted. The result was Matti could feel that his wife would always be part of his life, and had given him many positive life experiences to take forward into life, and that it was okay to go forward with his life. A future template of talking to his new girlfriend was comfortably installed.*

This example illustrates how a present trigger representing Matti's reluctance to reinvest can be targeted. Initially moving forward gave Matti a feeling he would forget his wife. The result of processing was an awareness of how valuable and helpful his relationship had been in his life, and he could carry this forward and reinvest in his own life.

Summary

The 'R' processes provide a clear and concise clinical direction for clinicians to understand and guide clients through the mourning process and can be facilitated with EMDR therapy. Starting at the beginning of the initial shock or realization of the death, clients come to be better able to recognize the loss (first 'R' process) and start to comprehend the loss is permanent. In doing so, clients can start to experience the emotional pain that accompanies the realization of the permanence of the loss (the second 'R' process). Memories arise pertaining to the loved one, including positive, heartfelt memories that enable an adaptive inner representation, further integrating the loss and facilitating the transformation of the relationship from loving in presence to loving in absence. Conflictual memories triggered by the loss have to be reprocessed to deal with and come to terms with loss and the relationship (the third 'R' process). Mourners start to adapt to life without the loved one, relinquishing ties to the loved one and the old assumptive world that are no longer valid because the loved one is dead (the fourth 'R' process). Stuck points can be reprocessed to enable the transition to the new world without forgetting the old (the fifth 'R' process). This sets the stage for the mourner to reinvest in life (the sixth 'R' process).

SECTION 3
EMDR THERAPY INTEGRATIVE TREATMENT MODEL

10

EMDR Therapy Integrative Treatment Model for Grief and Mourning

In Francine Shapiro's (2018), *Protocol for Complicated Grief*, she states that reprocessing should be initiated only once the initial shock and numbness of the loss has passed. She makes it clear that only once the client is able to experience the emotional impact of the loss and has the capacity, "for dual awareness and to stay present with the emotional pain" (p. 253), should eye movement desensitization and reprocessing (EMDR) targeting and reprocessing begin. She recommends that the following experiences may need to be targeted and reprocessed:

1. The moment of realization of the loss.
2. Other actual events (e.g., loved one's suffering, distressing events taking place after the death).
3. Intrusive images.
4. Nightmare images.
5. Present triggers.
6. Issues of personal responsibility, mortality, or previous unresolved losses.

Integrative Model for Treating Grief and Mourning

This chapter and the following chapters on EMDR processing are an elaboration of Shapiro's Protocol for Complicated Grief, Rando's Three Phases (Avoidance, Confrontation, and Accommodation), and six "R" processes, the Dual Process model (Loss Orientation and Restoration Orientation), and Continuing Bonds Theory. The focus in this chapter is an integrative look at case conceptualization and target identification based on the Adaptive Information Processing (AIP) perspective of past, present, and future and

EMDR Therapy Treatment for Grief and Mourning. Roger M. Solomon, Oxford University Press. © Roger M. Solomon 2024.
DOI: 10.1093/oso/9780198881360.003.0011

these other models. Section 4 will describe the eight phases of EMDR therapy in more depth.

Case Conceptualization and Treatment Planning for Grief and Mourning

Case Conceptualization and Treatment Planning for Grief and Mourning

Figure 10.1 is a summary of an integrative model highlighting EMDR therapy with grief and mourning, informed by other models, leading to case conceptualization and a treatment plan. Please note that this is not a linear process, but a flow that is centered on EMDR processing (past, present, and future) and informed by other frameworks. Use of these target suggestions and conceptual frameworks are used based on the needs of the client and their unique grief and mourning experience. The following expands on Figure 10.1.

Death of a Loved One (Traumatic and Separation Distress)
The death of a loved one can be a major loss that can lead to traumatic bereavement and complicated grief with mourners experiencing both *Traumatic Distress* and *Separation Distress*. Traumatic Distress results from overwhelming circumstances, such as a death that was sudden and unexpected, violent, or intentional. *Separation Distress* is the emotional distress experienced when a person dies with whom there was a meaningful bond.

EMDR therapy can address both aspects of distress.

Phase 1, Client History and Treatment Planning; Phase 2, Preparation and Stabilization
The first two phases of EMDR therapy are Client History and Treatment Planning, and Preparation and Stabilization, which are elaborated in Chapters 13 and 14. When the client meets readiness criteria (to a "good enough" level), memory processing (EMDR Phases 3–8) can proceed.

EMDR Therapy Targets (EMDR Therapy, Phases 3–8)
PAST MEMORIES
As Figure 10.1 depicts, EMDR therapy may initially focus on the traumatic impact of the loss. The trauma of the loss is usually targeted first because it often takes over the client's world, preventing adaptation. However, other distressing moments may be more impactful (e.g., hospital or

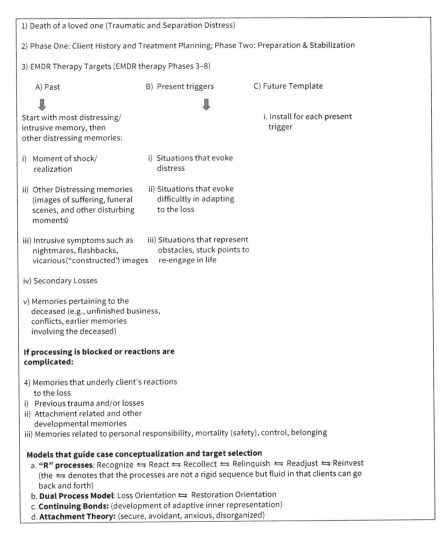

1) Death of a loved one (Traumatic and Separation Distress)

2) Phase One: Client History and Treatment Planning; Phase Two: Preparation & Stabilization

3) EMDR Therapy Targets (EMDR therapy Phases 3–8)

A) Past	B) Present triggers	C) Future Template

Start with most distressing/ intrusive memory, then other distressing memories:

i. Install for each present trigger

i) Moment of shock/ realization

i) Situations that evoke distress

ii) Other Distressing memories (images of suffering, funeral scenes, and other disturbing moments)

ii) Situations that evoke difficultly in adapting to the loss

iii) Intrusive symptoms such as nightmares, flashbacks, vicarious ("constructed") images

iii) Situations that represent obstacles, stuck points to re-engage in life

iv) Secondary Losses

v) Memories pertaining to the deceased (e.g., unfinished business, conflicts, earlier memories involving the deceased)

If processing is blocked or reactions are complicated:

4) Memories that underly client's reactions to the loss
i) Previous trauma and/or losses
ii) Attachment related and other developmental memories
iii) Memories related to personal responsibility, mortality (safety), control, belonging

Models that guide case conceptualization and target selection
a. **"R" processes**: Recognize ⇆ React ⇆ Recollect ⇆ Relinquish ⇆ Readjust ⇆ Reinvest (the ⇆ denotes that the processes are not a rigid sequence but fluid in that clients can go back and forth)
b. **Dual Process Model**: Loss Orientation ⇆ Restoration Orientation
c. **Continuing Bonds:** (development of adaptive inner representation)
d. **Attachment Theory:** (secure, avoidant, anxious, disorganized)

Figure 10.1 Integrative Model for EMDR Therapy for Grief and Mourning

funeral scenes). Further, as will be discussed in this chapter, if other memories pertaining to the deceased, such as previous traumas or losses, or attachment-related memories are more prominent or dominate the clinical picture, then, these memories should be processed first. Targets may include:

1. Moment of shock (e.g., initial impact of the loss or realization).
2. Other distressing memories associated with the death (e.g., images of suffering, funeral scenes, and other disturbing moments).

3. Intrusive symptoms (e.g., nightmares, flashbacks, and vicarious (constructed) images related to the death).
4. Secondary losses.
5. Memories pertaining to the deceased (e.g., unfinished business, conflicts, and earlier memories involving the deceased).

After addressing all the past targets that are appropriate, make sure to process:

PRESENT TRIGGERS

Current distressing moments, events, and stuck points that reflect difficulties in coping and pose obstacles to proceeding through the mourning process:

1. Situations that evoke distress.
2. Situations that evoke difficulty in adapting to the loss.
3. Situations that represent obstacles and stuck points to re-engagement in life.

Future Template

A future template for adaptive coping should be provided for each present trigger. However, the client may first need additional education and/or skills, before going to install a future template.

Note: Proceeding with past memories, present triggers, and/or future template is not a rigid, linear order. Often it is helpful to reprocess some significant past memories then proceed to present triggers and future template, then go back to reprocessing other past memories, then present triggers and future, and so on. Going sooner rather than later to reprocessing present triggers and installing future templates (depending on client response) can enhance adaptation. Though beyond the scope of this book to describe, there are circumstances where clients are not ready to approach past memories, and it is appropriate to start with affect management and resourcing strategies, and the reprocessing of present triggers, before reprocessing the worst memories (see Shapiro, 2018).

If Processing Is Blocked or Reactions Are Complicated

Memories That Underly Client's Reactions to the Loss

When processing is blocked or there is complicated grief, work with the following targets: Previous losses, traumas, and attachment-related and other developmental memories underlying maladaptive responses to the loss (e.g., memories formative in insecure or disorganized attachment style) can be reprocessed when relevant to the clinical picture. Also, it is helpful to take into account the memories related to the clinical themes that underlie Negative Cognitions, such as responsibility, safety (mortality), control, and belonging. When dominating the clinical picture, these memories should be addressed first.

Models That Guide Case Conceptualization and Target Selection

Complementary conceptual frameworks that can also guide EMDR case conceptualization and treatment planning are the following:

Rando's (1995) "R" Processes

The "R" processes delineate the processes important for adaptation to the loss and provide a framework for evaluating where a client may be stuck. It must be emphasized that the "R" processes are not a linear model where each process is discrete. In fact, during EMDR therapy the processes tend to blend together which will be discussed below.

Dual Process Model (Strobe & Schut, 1999)

The *Dual Process* model alerts clinicians to evaluate the extent to which clients are able to deal with their grief reactions (Loss Orientation) and put them aside (oscillate) to deal with stressors caused by the death (Restoration Orientation) and function adaptively in everyday life.

Continuing Bonds (Marwit & Klass, 1996)

Continuing Bonds Theory highlights how the bond with the deceased is *transformed* rather than lost, and continues. Consistent with this theory, in EMDR therapy there is often the emergence of heartfelt, meaningful memories during reprocessing, forming an adaptive inner representation that provides a sense of connection to the deceased. Negative memories also have to be acknowledged and reprocessed to provide an accurate and balanced inner representation and treat complications in the grief and mourning process.

Attachment Theory

Attachment Theory describes how attachment styles develop as a result of early child-caregiver interactions. This is consistent with the Adaptive

Information Processing model (e.g., present problems are the result of maladaptively stored memories). Attachment style plays a significant role in mourners' responses to loss. Consequently, early childhood attachment-based memories may underlie complications and challenges in grief and the mourning process.

This framework will be elaborated in the Chapters 11 and 12.

11

Three-Pronged Protocol

First Prong—Past Memories

This chapter focuses on *past memories*, the first prong of the three-prong protocol of eye movement desensitization and reprocessing (EMDR) therapy. Suggestions for specific targets and sequencing are offered. Present triggers and future templates are discussed in Chapter 12.

Note: The numbers in this chapter follow the structure of Figure 10.1 in Chapter 10.

Choice and Flexibility in Selecting Targets

There is choice and flexibility in selecting and ordering targets for EMDR reprocessing. The model elaborated on below is flexible and fluid, with targets for reprocessing determined by the clients' needs and responses to loss. For example, a starting point for processing is the trauma of the loss, the moment(s) of shock/realization. However, this can be modified depending on whether past trauma or losses may be influencing the current clinical picture. For example, a woman's husband was killed in a car crash, which also triggered childhood memories of her father's death. Several days before her father committed suicide, he told her that he was thinking about killing himself. This presents the choice of beginning with the present trauma of her husband's death (e.g., when she got the news) or the childhood trauma and loss of her father (e.g., when her father told her he was suicidal). The death of her husband was most present and therefore was the first EMDR therapy target. However, if memories pertaining to the father had been painful and intrusive, they could be the starting point (Solomon & Rando, 2007, 2012, 2015; Worden, 2018).

The four models of grief described in this book (Attachment Theory, Continuing Bonds, Dual Process model, and 'R' processes) are integrated into

EMDR Therapy Treatment for Grief and Mourning. Roger M. Solomon, Oxford University Press. © Roger M. Solomon 2024.
DOI: 10.1093/oso/9780198881360.003.0012

the Adaptive Information Processing (AIP) case conceptualization to illustrate how they can guide treatment planning.

Beginning EMDR Therapy Treatment

The death of a loved one can be traumatic because of the circumstances of the death (e.g., sudden and unexpected or other risk factors) or because the deceased was an integral part of the mourner's life. Clients may experience shock and numbness with the death feeling unreal. This has been described as the Avoidance Phase (Rando, 1993). In the immediate aftermath of a death, clients need psychological first aid, support, and information on grief, mourning, and coping (see Chapter 14 on Preparation & Stabilization and Appendix 3 on Psychological First Aid). Clients need to *recognize the loss* (first 'R' process), which involves the subprocesses of *acknowledging the death* (e.g., it is real) and *understanding the death* (i.e., what happened, reasons for the death).

In the weeks and months following the loss, the emotional impact begins to be experienced. The Avoidance Phase transitions to the Confrontation Phase, with mourners moving into the second 'R' process, *react to the separation*, and EMDR memory reprocessing can begin. During EMDR reprocessing, clients may experience intense raw felt emotion. EMDR therapy often goes to places 'words do not go', with the shifts during reprocessing experienced first at an emotional, physical, and sensation level before, or along with, cognitive information. Consequently, it is important that clients meet readiness criteria for memory processing (see Chapter 14 on Preparation & Stabilization).

EMDR therapy Phases 3–8 can first focus on processing the loss as a *traumatic event* with the goal of integrating the trauma of the loss and enabling clients to progress through the next four 'R' processes (see Chapter 9). Commonly during reprocessing positive, meaningful memories arise, giving the client a sense of connection to the deceased, a continuing bond (see Chapter 7). In terms of the Dual Process model (see Chapter 8), targeting the distress/trauma of the loss deals with Loss Orientation stressors, enhancing the client's ability to deal with the secondary stressors engendered by the loss (Restoration Orientation). Depending on clients' symptoms and reactions to the loss, it may be important to process past unresolved traumas, losses, and memories underlying maladaptive responses to the loss (e.g., childhood-based attachment memories).

Initial EMDR Therapy Targets

Note: In Table 10.1 this is under 3A.

Moment of Shock/Realization

Conceptualizing the loss as a traumatic event (Rando, 2000; Solomon & Rando, 2007, 2012, 2015), EMDR memory processing can begin at 'ground 0': *the initial impact or moment the death* event started for the client. This is usually the most acutely felt moment or intrusive memory or the point when the death became 'real'. If clients were present at the time of the death, the moment of impact may be the death scene. This can be the moment the loved one died (e.g., 'my wife taking her last breath'), memories of suffering, seeing the body, or funeral scenes. If clients were not present when the loved one died, this moment of initial shock or realization is often getting the news of the death (e.g., the police officer knocking at the door to deliver a death notification). In some instances, the initial moment of shock or realization may be *before the loved one died*. This may be the memory of a physician saying, 'There is nothing more that can be done', the last conversation with the loved one, or an earlier scene, as one man later described, 'Three weeks before my father died, I saw him in the hospital bed and I knew we were going to lose him.' The moment of impact/realization may be *after the death*. For example, 1 month after her husband was killed in car crash, the wife saw the car and thought, 'No one could have survived.' It was at this moment when she really knew her husband had indeed died. Other relevant moments may also be *negative events leading up to the death* (e.g., loved one's suffering, distressing hospital scenes) and *after the death* (e.g., funeral scenes, other people's reactions, and dealing with the administrative or legal issues).

Case Example 1 (Getting the News): Gary's father died of a heart attack. Although he spent time with his father's body, and in that way said, 'Goodbye', Gary felt guilty that he was unable to make it to the hospital before his father died. His worst moment was hearing the news from his brother by telephone, which became the initial target for EMDR processing. During processing, the time he spent saying goodbye after his father died came up and he experienced it as a peaceful and comforting moment.

Case Example 2 (Getting the News): Doreen, the mother of a teenager killed in an accident, requested EMDR therapy 5 months following her daughter's death. The initial target was, 'the knock at the door at 3 am', with a policeman and a chaplain there to deliver the death notification. The reprocessing session was intense, but at the end of the session, the loss felt more real, as something that did happen.

Case Example 3 (Before the Death): Teresa's mother died of heart failure. Her worst moment was 8 months before, during a previous hospitalization. There was a moment when she saw her mother 'truly suffering' and said, 'I knew it was the beginning of the end.' This was the initial target for EMDR therapy.

Case Example 4 (After the Death): Franco's wife died in an auto accident. Franco went to the hospital with his brother, identified his wife, and then went home where family members and friends were gathering. The funeral was 8 days later. The day after the funeral, Franco automatically found himself calling his wife at lunch time, as he had every day since they started dating. After the phone rang and the automatic message answered, it struck him that his wife was really dead and not coming back. When Franco received EMDR treatment eight months later, this was the most intrusive and distressing memory, and was the initial target for EMDR processing.

Other Distressing Memories (Images of Suffering, Funeral Scenes, and Other Disturbing Moments)

Case Example 5 (Getting the News and Other Intrusive Images): Doreen, described above in Case Example 2, was also haunted by images of her deceased daughter in the hospital, and saying goodbye to her at the funeral. These memories were subsequently reprocessed with EMDR therapy.

Case Example 6 (Hospital Mortuary Scene): EMDR therapy was provided 7 months after Kelly's father died in an accident. Following her father's death, the family went to the hospital mortuary to identify the body. The worst moment for her was when her mother threw herself on top of the body, crying. Along with her siblings, she comforted the

> *mother. In taking care of her mother, Kelly did not have a moment to say goodbye to her father. The memory of her mother on top of her father's body was the starting point for EMDR therapy. Processing this memory resulted in Kelly's being able to imagine saying goodbye to him in the mortuary.*

Nightmares, Flashback Scenes Related to the Death, and Vicarious Negative Images

Mourners may have nightmares pertaining to the death, flashbacks of distressing moments, or imagined vicarious (constructed) negative images (e.g., imagined scenes of the loved one suffering) which can be quite distressing and intrusive. After targeting past distressing moments of shock and/or realization situations involving hearing about the loss, or the moment or realization, these dreams, flashbacks, or vicarious imagery can be targeted. However, if such phenomena are very intrusive and dominating the clinical picture (e.g., mourners cannot think of the loved one without being plagued by the images), they can be targeted first.

> *Case Example 7 (Nightmare): Roger's father died 2 years after his mother died. For the first 2 months following his father's death, he was numb, with occasional bursts of sadness when the death of his father felt 'real'. Four months after the death, he dreamt that his mother had told him to come quickly because his father was ill. In the dream Roger went home and he found his father dead in bed. He turned to his mother and saw she was dead at which point he woke up very distressed. This dream was targeted as part of an overall treatment plan (after targeting the memory of being present when the father died). The session was very emotional, resulting in Roger's feeling a deeper sense that the loss was real and permanent. It then became easier to adapt to the death of his parents.*

> *Case Example 8 (Intrusive Image): Vera's sister died. Vera was preoccupied with a distressing image of her sister in pain that would intrude on her not only when she was thinking of her sister, but, as Vera described, 'at the oddest moments when I would be engaged in activities or thinking about something far removed from my sister'. Because this image dominated the clinical picture, it was the first EMDR target for Vera when she came to treatment 9 weeks following the loss.*

Often, mourners who were not present at the death will construct vicarious negative images of their loved one suffering (imagining what it must have looked like or what their loved one felt). Overidentification or an obsession with the loved one's suffering can be traumatizing. The author has found EMDR therapy to be quite helpful and efficient with these situations, as the outcome leads to the realization that the suffering is over and the loved one is at peace.

Case Example 9 (Vicarious Negative Image): A 9-month-old infant was killed in the Oklahoma City bombing. The mother, Loretta, was told that the baby had died of a head wound. For the next 2 months, the image of her baby with a severe head wound was all she could imagine. She appeared to have no access to other memories. In addition, this negative image was easily triggered, and disrupted her ability to function. During EMDR therapy, the negative vicarious/constructed image of the baby was targeted. After the first set of eye movements, a memory of the baby with her husband came to mind, with many memories of her child emerging, ending with the memory of handing her baby over to a daycare worker as she said, 'Goodbye' and 'I love you.' Loretta then felt a sense of peace, and this final memory was then installed by pairing bilateral stimulation while focusing on the positive image and feelings that had emerged during reprocessing.

This case illustrates that there are times when a vicarious or constructed image is so powerful and emotional, it becomes the target in and of itself. The traumatic circumstances, along with being unable to view the body of her baby, resulted in intrusive, negative, vicarious imagery that blocked access to other memories. Reprocessing the vicarious image allowed spontaneous access to these other memories. resulting in a sense of peace. This illustrates how EMDR therapy can give rise to an adaptive inner representation, facilitating the transformation of the relationship. However, it must be understood that reprocessing the trauma of the loss is only the beginning of the mourning process. Treatment with the mother continued and EMDR therapy was again utilized to help work through the rage she felt toward the perpetrator of the bombing.

Secondary Losses

Secondary losses also need to be identified and processed, which is the third subprocess of the *react to the Separation process*. These are the losses that occur as a result of the primary loss of the loved one, and need to be dealt with. EMDR therapy can target a key moment where the secondary loss was experienced.

Case Example 10 (Secondary Loss): Coleen's husband died in a car crash. Coleen, 38 years old, with two children, came in for treatment 6 months later. What compounded the loss of her husband was losing her dancing partner. She and her husband went dancing every weekend, were members of a dance club, and took part in dancing contests. Initially, the trauma of his unexpected, sudden death was processed, focusing on the moment of getting the news. At the next session, a moment of acute distress was targeted when Coleen was listening to their favourite dance song and felt the pain of losing a dance partner as well as a husband. During reprocessing, after experiencing deep pain, positive heartfelt memories of past dance experiences with her husband arose. The processing was incomplete and ended with safe place imagery and her embracing the positive memories that emerged during the session. The following week, processing of the memory continued. What evolved for Coleen was an acceptance that her dancing life was over. She said, 'Dancing would never be the same ... Although that part of my life is over, I can still engage in meaningful activities.' Over the next 4 months, sessions continued to focus on present situations that triggered feelings of loss. Coleen became more engaged in her children's school and community activities and felt balanced and involved in life.

This example illustrates how secondary losses compound the burden of grief and need to be dealt with as well. Losing a loved one can also mean losing other important aspects of one's life and a separate grief and mourning process may be needed for each loss.

Memories Pertaining to the Deceased (E.g., Unfinished Business, Conflicts, and Earlier Memories Involving the Deceased)

Remembering and re-experiencing the deceased and the relationship are an important parts of mourning. This is the third 'R' process. As previously noted, during the processing of grief-related memories, intense emotions are experienced, followed by the linking in of adaptive information. This commonly involves the emergence of memories of the deceased. These memories provide a link between the world with and the world without the loved one.

Quite often these are positive, meaningful memories which provide a sense of connection and start to build an adaptive inner representation. Moving from 'I cannot connect', to 'I can connect', through these memories transforms the relationship (a continuing bond).

The mourner has to *remember realistically* and *experience the emotions that accompany the memory* (the subprocesses of the third 'R' process). Remembering realistically includes dealing with the negative or conflictual memories. Unfinished business can continue to haunt mourners. Painful or conflictual memories do not go away with the death, they need to be faced, dealt with, and integrated to provide a realistic inner representation that the mourner will continue to interact with whenever there is a reminder.

EMDR targets include conflictual memories, painful memories, and memories representing unresolved issues.

Case Example 11 (Conflictual Memory): Carl sought treatment 3 months after his wife died from cancer. They had been married 17 years. He described how fulfilling their marriage had been for the past 8 years, even though they experienced a problematic beginning. Early in their marriage, Carl had an affair and moved out when his wife was pregnant with their son. The marital issues did resolve over time as he and his wife overcame their difficulties. After his wife's death, Carl's past behaviour haunted him. The initial treatment focused on dealing with his guilt over the affair and his leaving before the birth of his son. With four sessions of EMDR reprocessing, Carl faced his guilt, accepted that his role in his marital difficulties, and expressed the sorrow and remorse he felt about his actions. The marital issues did resolve over time as he and his wife overcame their difficulties. Through positive, heartfelt memories, he was finally able to realize and articulate that their last years together had been fulfilling.

This above example illustrates that EMDR therapy does not eliminate appropriate guilt. Instead, EMDR leads to taking appropriate responsibility and a wider perspective of one's actions. When Carl was able to experience and express his guilt and sorrow, he was also able to take a broader view of his marriage that included resolving their problems and enjoying their last years together.

Case Example 12 (Painful Memory): Beatricia had an argument with her husband on Mother's Day. Later that evening, contrary to her husband's desire, she did not want to make love. However, they did spend some time cuddling. The next day, Beatricia's

> *husband was killed in an accident. Even after months and having worked on many is-sues related to the loss, she was still haunted by the memory of their last night together. She felt guilty and wished that she had been more physically intimate with her husband. EMDR therapy was utilized to target and reprocess the most painful moment when she declined to have sex with her husband. It was an emotional session, filled with sadness and guilt. During the reprocessing, Beatricia spontaneously re-experienced how good their cuddling had actually felt. Upon completion of the session, the memory of the sen-sations and feelings associated with their time cuddling were predominant, and the memory now brought up a sense of intimacy and closeness.*

Painful memories that continue to intrude upon mourners can compli-cate the mourning and need to be reprocessed. Sometimes, the reprocessing of painful memories provides the opportunity to realize formerly unrecog-nized aspects of the situation that may give it new meaning. The results of EMDR therapy are ecologically adaptive and appropriate to the situation. Beatricia still regretted not making love that evening. However, she was able to re-experience an aspect not previously acknowledged (i.e., the pleasure and intimacy of the cuddling). Re-experiencing this intimate event provided a balance to her former painful memory, enabling her to recognize the pow-erful intimate connection she shared with her husband that night. This also illustrates what makes EMDR so potent—it can go places words do not go. For Beatricia, resolution did not come from a new cognitive perspective. It came from re-experiencing emotions and sensations associated with the memory. The association of the feeling/sensation aspects of the memory, which pro-vided the basis for new meaning, is quite commonly the basis for resolution of a painful memory.

Some people may have 'unfinished business' with the deceased. Sometimes, there are issues were never dealt with, were put off until another day, or may remain in other ways unresolved. With the death of the deceased, such unre-solved issues can surface, adding to pain and guilt. These can be targeted by focusing on specific past situations associated with the unresolved problems.

> *Case Example 13 (Unresolved Arguments): Throughout their marriage, John and Peggy had many arguments about financial priorities. Then, John died suddenly from a heart attack. Two years later, Peggy was still greatly concerned about their fights. Following several sessions of history-taking and exploration, representative memories of their disagreements were targeted for intervention with EMDR. After reprocessing three*

memories over the course of three sessions, Peggy realized that there was much more to their marriage than their argument, and memories emerged of positive interactions and the positive aspects of their marriage. Peggy felt assured that her husband did love her and that their frequent arguments did not define their feelings for each other, or their marriage. As she put it, 'I can take the bad with the good, and that is what makes life.'

This case illustrates how reprocessing unresolved issues enabled the client to view her conflicts from a global perspective. Rather than feeling weighted down by their unresolved conflict, she found a place to put their conflicts within a whole life context that allowed for both 'good' and 'bad'.

If Processing Is Blocked or Reactions Are Complicated

Memories Underlying Client's Reactions to the Loss

When EMDR processing is blocked and/or grief symptoms persist (e.g., after 6 months the client meets criteria for Prolonged Grief Disorder), then clinicians need to take a comprehensive approach to treatment. The AIP model states that present problems result from memories that are maladaptively stored. Attachment theory describes how child-caregiver interactions lead to the development of attachment styles, that influence a person's grief reactions. Clinicians can assess and treat previous trauma, loss, and attachment and developmentally related maladaptively stored memories that are being triggered or aggravated by the loss, and/or underlie blocked processing.

Previous Trauma and/or Losses

There are times a past trauma or loss is triggered and interfering with processing the current loss. It then becomes important to process the earlier loss.

Case Example 14 (Previous Loss): Robert's brother was murdered. Robert (aged 32 years) began treatment 14 months later because he was continually haunted by his brother's death. He felt sad and helpless, with alternating feelings of agitation and numbness. The fact that there was nothing he could do was upsetting. His history revealed that his father had died of cancer 16 years before. While it had been a sad time, he felt he dealt with the loss of his father and had been doing okay. After two sessions of history-taking and preparation and stabilization (e.g., safe/calm place), EMDR reprocessing targeted the moment of getting the news of his brother's death. Reprocessing became stuck, with Robert feeling tension that would not abate. Through the Affect Scan, earlier experiences of the tension we explored. Robert remembered the feelings of powerlessness he experienced when his father died of cancer. As a teenager, Robert avoided dealing with the anguish and feelings of helplessness that there was nothing he could do. Reprocessing continued with the focus on the death of his father. After two more sessions targeting issues related to his father's death, Robert was able to process the death of his brother (starting with 'getting the news'). Treatment continued for another four months focusing on issues pertaining to both childhood and adapting to his brother's death.

In AIP terms, the death of Robert's brother triggered unresolved feelings of guilt stemming from his father's death. Dealing with the father's death first enabled Robert to then process the trauma of his brother's death and proceed through the mourning process.

Attachment-Related and Other Developmental Memories

There may be times when first reprocessing childhood attachment memories is appropriate. For example, someone who is very anxious may have childhood experiences related to a lack of safety. Someone who feels guilty and readily blames oneself may have a history of 'It's my fault', beliefs originating from distressing interactions with a parent. When these memories are dominant and intrusive, clients may receive greater benefit from reprocessing these childhood memories before approaching the present loss. Similarly, if reprocessing more recent loss-related memories becomes blocked then targeting earlier memories may be helpful.

Case Example 15 (Attachment-Related Child Memories): 6 years after her mother died of cancer, Sonja, aged 47 years, was still feeling guilty and depressed over her mother's death. She felt she should have taken better care of and been more supportive of her mother. Her worst memory was being with her mother when the doctor told them at a check-up that further treatment would not help. On the way home from the appointment, they stopped at a restaurant and talked casually. Sonja wished she had talked more openly with her mother about what the doctor said and encouraged her mother to speak more openly to her, allowing them to share a moment of closeness rather than avoidance. Sonja, who demonstrated an anxious attachment style, described a history of growing up with an alcoholic father who was critical, and a mother who tried to be supportive but was often overwhelmed by the father's behaviour. EMDR reprocessing of this worst memory (avoiding talking about the doctor's prognosis) became stuck.

When an Affect Scan was used (following the negative feelings back in time) a memory came to mind of her father being very critical of her, with her mother visibly upset about her husband's treatment of their daughter. In the session, Sonja recognized as a child that she was not only distressed about what the father said, but also felt guilty that her mother was so upset. Over the next three sessions, this memory, and other memories (e.g., moments where she felt alone or experienced helplessness) were reprocessed. There was a generalization effect from processing the past memories, with her worst memory (at the restaurant with her mother) spontaneously resolving. Sonja then could experience heartfelt memories of her mother and was able to feel a positive connection with no more guilt. Reprocessing distressing childhood memories enabled her to integrate the loss of her mother.

In this example, when reprocessing of the client's worst felt memory became stuck, an Affect Scan revealed a distressing feeder memory. After processing this attachment-related memory and other similar memories there was treatment generalization and the client's grief issues resolved.

Pervasive childhood attachment difficulties, which underlie complex trauma (see Chapter 19), impact self-esteem, affect regulation, and relationships, and interfere with adapting to trauma and loss. Therefore, the treatment plan needs to include the following:

- Appropriate stabilization—according to the needs of the client.
- Treatment of earlier experiences underlying current difficulties in functioning.
- Assistance in adapting to the loss.
- Processing both present triggers and future templates for each trigger.

Case Example 16 (Affect Regulation Difficulties):Danny's son, who had experienced significant medical issues, died at age 12 years. It had been a difficult journey for the whole family. After his son's death, Danny felt alone and withdrew from his family, often seeking a place to be alone to cry. While in family therapy, he was referred for individual therapy. His history revealed that Danny's parents divorced when he was young, and he lived primarily with his mother. Often, he felt alone and scared. His mother seemed to get upset when he was upset, so Danny would find a place to be alone when he was frightened or distressed, and did his best to hide his emotions from his mother.

Focusing on the moment his son died, while the family was at the bedside, Danny described the image and verbalized his negative and positive cognitions ('I am powerless, I am a bad father for not being able to do more/I did all I could for my son, I am a good father') but it was difficult for him to describe his emotions. While he could de-scribe the physical tension he was experiencing, Danny was unable to put what he was feeling into words. After several sessions that interspersed affect regulation and resourcing with history-taking, he was able to connect with childhood memories where he felt alone and frightened, and would hide in the closet of his room. Over the next 4 months, memories from childhood, starting with a memory of being alone on his sixth birthday (feeling abandoned and frightened) were reprocessed. Only then was Danny able to experience and describe the emotional impact of the death of his son. The loss was reprocessed with EMDR therapy. Therapy continued for another 14 months dealing with (a) distressing childhood and later memories related to present problems; (b) present triggers, including situations where he experienced significant emotional pain about his son; and (c) future templates for each trigger.

The above example illustrates how treatment of loss may need to proceed with comprehensive treatment to deal with the client's broader emotional difficulties as well as issues related to the death.

Some mourners may strive to keep the good memories while avoiding the negative memories and aspects of the relationship. Similarly, if the relationship was negative, some mourners strive to avoid the positive memories, experiencing ambivalence about having positive feelings for the person who was cruel, neglectful, or abusive. Such avoidance of memories can block processing and needs to be dealt with.

Mourners need to understand that all relationships have positive and negative aspects. The loving parent may have been neglectful or overly punitive at times. The abusive parent may have also been helpful at times. The ambivalence can block the reprocessing and mourners may need to be helped to take an objective stance that there are positive memories and feelings along with negative memories, and both are important aspects of the relationship.

Case Example 17 (Avoiding Negative Memories): Silvio's father died of an illness. Silvio, aged 38 years, came in for treatment 7 months following the death. He reported that his mother was very abusive while his father had been a source of safety. However, there were times when his father left the family for weeks at a time with no explanation, and many occasions when his father would do nothing while his mother was acting in a cruel way towards Silvio and his siblings. Further, Silvio and his siblings witnessed their mother being emotionally abusive towards the father. Silvio was conflicted because he wanted to maintain the good memories of his father and not ruin his image of him as a source of safety and someone who cared about him in an otherwise scary atmosphere. Treatment started with reprocessing the distress of the father's death, focusing on the expression of his face when he died. In reprocessing of this memory, Silvio's ambivalence surfaced. He felt anger towards his father but did not want to acknowledge it and spoil the good memories he wanted to keep. Through a cognitive interweave, the clinician offered a different perspective, explaining that both aspects, positive and negative, were valid, and that both perspectives were important aspects of his relationship with his father. In subsequent sessions, negative memories involving his father were reprocessed. After several sessions, Silvio gained insight into his father's personal problems, and the negative and conflictual marital relationship. He was able to see him more as a whole person, not just a father who made him feel safe. With further reprocessing of negative memories, positive memories of his father began to surface. Ultimately Silvio could acknowledge the good and the bad, with the negative aspects of the relationship not taking away from the positive aspects.

Case Example 18 (Avoiding Positive Memories): 8 months after Lilly's father died of an illness, she sought treatment. Lilly (aged 44 years) was one of her father's caretakers, along with her siblings, when he was sick,. Children caring for their ageing parent was a valued part of her family culture. During his last few months of life, Lilly and her father had gotten along well, and he was grateful for her care. Lilly wanted to think of her father as being a good father, but the reality was her father had been abusive and frightening. Because of his abusive behaviour when they were young, Lilly and her brother were frightened by him when they were young, would hide when he came home from work and would not bring friends home from school because of their father's abusive behaviour. Reprocessing started with a childhood memory of her father telling her he should have thrown her in the river after she was born. After more negative memories emerged, positive memories started arising. The family was poor, but the father bought her a dress she liked. There were times there was little to eat, but the father was always able to provide food for the children. Lilly remembered a time he went to a neighbour and brought home eggs for dinner. The session ended with Lilly recognizing that despite all the negative, there were some positive memories and bright spots in her childhood.

The first example illustrates a client who was reluctant to acknowledge the negative aspects of the relationship with her father. The second example illustrates a client who wanted to think positively about her father despite having only negative memories. With both clients, treatment involved processing distressing childhood memories involving the parent. This resulted in both positive and negative memories emerging, allowing for a more balanced, and realistic inner representation.

Memories Related to Responsibility, Safety (Mortality), Control, and Connection/Belonging

These clinical themes are the basis of negative and positive cognitions, and can also be utilized to conceptualize clients' problems and serve as a guide to treating the issues underlying complicated grief and mourning. Further, these themes help clinicians determine the issues causing blocked reprocessing, can guide cognitive interweaves, and be the basis of the Floatback and Affect Scan procedures to identify earlier memories 'feeding' (underlying) the block.

The examples described in this book could also be categorized according to clinical themes. These themes not only may be manifested in the mourner's current reactions to loss, but also have a core, developmental component. In terms of Attachment Theory and the AIP model, as a result of negative child-caregiver interactions (which result in insecure or disorganized attachment styles), core themes develop such as, 'I am not good enough' (responsibility), 'I am not safe' (safety), 'I am powerless' (control), and 'I don't belong' (connection/belonging). With complicated grief, these themes can guide clinicians to identifying underlying core memories that need to be reprocessed.

Negative and Positive Cognitions will be further discussed in the next chapter. Below are some examples of how the clinical themes can underlie clients' response to loss, and guide clinicians towards identifying relevant memories that need to be reprocessed. Each case example illustrates complicated grief where core memories related to the clinical theme needed to be treated.

RESPONSIBILITY

This theme involves self-defectiveness, where the attribution of the problem is oneself. This can involve issues revolving around self-worth (e.g., I am bad/ I am unlovable/I am not good enough/I don't matter) or action/guilt ('It's my fault/I should have done something [more] … ').

Case Example 19 (Responsibility): Rhonda's daughter (aged 7 years) died as a result a severe disease after 6 months. Reprocessing the trauma of the loss was helpful, but still the theme of 'I am a bad mother', and 'It's my fault', dominated the clinical picture. Childhood memories of a critical mother who would alternatively scold Rhonda for mistakes or not talk to her resulted in Rhonda having a negative self-belief of, 'I am bad/ I am inadequate.' Reprocessing these core memories, along with present triggers and future templates for each trigger, resulted in clinical improvement.

SAFETY (MORTALITY)

This theme involves not feeling safe in the present.

Case Example 20 (Safety/mortality): Ken's wife (aged 44 years) died of COVID-19, after 4 weeks of illness. The circumstances of her death, traumatic in and of itself, aggravated feelings of isolation, and feeling unsafe that were already being felt because of COVID-19 restrictions. Ken had been coping with COVID-19 restrictions, but with the death of his wife, his sense of isolation and lack of safety were exacerbated. Particularly acute was his realization that he also could die. He had known this at an intellectual level but experienced this fear at a deep emotional level. History-taking revealed, he felt anxious as a child. His mother was addicted to pain medication and often left Ken and his two siblings (Ken was a middle child) on their own. As a result, Ken was often anxious and fearful, particularly when he saw his mother high on the pain medication. After several sessions of history-taking and stabilization (safe/calm place, resource installation, and stress reduction strategies), EMDR sessions focused on treating the trauma of his wife's death (e.g., when she got sick, when she was hospitalized, saying goodbye to her, and when she died). Ken's own issues of mortality arose during these sessions. He experienced symptom relief with accepting the fact that he indeed was vulnerable and could die, and that was part of the human condition. He sorely missed his wife, and felt unsafe without her. She had been a steady support for him. Consequent sessions focused on a combination of resource installation (focusing on enhancing memories where he experienced competence and confidence), strategies to keep socially engaged with family and friends, and reprocessing attachment-related memories (e.g., mother being high on medication and unavailable) related to his lack of safety. Present triggers and future templates for each trigger were also provided. Ken increasingly experienced a felt sense of safety within himself and which facilitated adaptive coping with the loss of his wife.

Note: Another choice would have been to begin memory reprocessing with past memories involving Ken's mother, and then distressing memories related to his wife's death, which I believe would also have led to successful results. The starting point is largely determined by what is most intrusive and pressing for the client, which is why I began with the distressing memories related to his wife's death.

CONTROL

This theme has to do with feeling powerless, no control, or helpless. In the example below, improving the client's sense of efficacy and self-confidence preceded treatment to increase her integrative capacity and ability to function.

> *Case Example 21 (Control): Linda's father died after a stroke. Linda (aged 23 years) felt helpless because she could not help him. She sought treatment 7 months later because feelings of helplessness persisted. In growing up, and in her adult life, her father was her major source of support. She had depended on him to help her when there was a problem, and though she became increasingly self-reliant as she got older, she had always believed that she could not handle things on her own. Exploration of this theme revealed that her parents, particularly her father, tended to coddle and do things for her. This embedded the belief that she was not capable to deal with problems on her own. The treatment plan started out with Resource Development and Installation (Korn & Leeds, 2002) to increase her sense of self-efficacy and confidence. Then treatment focused on childhood memories where she felt incapable, for example, when her parents would do something for her, which resulted in her feeling she could not do it herself. After several sessions of reprocessing such childhood memories, her feelings of helplessness decreased, and her feelings of competence increased. Present triggers, with future templates for each trigger were also provided. Then EMDR memory processing sessions focused on the worst memories related to her father's death (i.e., when he had the stroke, hospital scenes, and when he died). After 5 months, treatment goals of feeling confident in herself, and coping adaptively with her father's death were met.*

CONNECTION/BELONGING

This theme was added to the EMDR Institute Basic Training (EMDR Institute Training Manuals, 2021). This theme describes clients who have internalized negative social or interpersonal treatment from others resulting in feeling alienated and disconnected from others. Feeling alone, isolated, and the separation distress that results from a death can be particularly acute with the loss of connection resulting from a death.

> *Case Example 22 (Connection/Belonging): Lucia, a gay woman, was married to another woman for 30 years. Her wife died of cancer. The trauma of the multiple losses was compounded by the restrictions of Covid-19, which increased her feelings of being alone and isolated. Seven months after her wife, died Lucia sought treatment. Treatment initially focused on the trauma of the death. As the trauma of the death was being reprocessed, Lucia became afraid that she would lose the felt connection to her wife. After cognitive interweaves that she would not lose anything that she needed, reprocessing continued, resulting in positive memories emerging. Lucia felt a sense of connection to her wife. The next session the trauma of the loss felt somewhat resolved.*

However, she still felt a profound sense of aloneness, and was afraid of giving up her pain out of fear of losing the connection. Further exploring her theme of losing connection and being alone revealed that in childhood, Lucia felt alone and scared about being gay. There was no one to talk to, and she was afraid to talk to parents or friends because of the social stigma. As an adult she became comfortable with being gay, and enjoyed a happy marriage to her wife. After the death, the feelings of being isolated and scared were triggered. Treatment then focused on childhood memories with the theme of, 'I don't belong', and her lack of connection. With the processing of present triggers and future templates, Lucia increasingly became able to adapt by engaging in more life activities, which eased her depression and social isolation.

Summary

In summary, the first prong of the three-pronged protocol is past memories. Conceptualizing the loss as a traumatic event, when the client meets readiness criteria, the initial EMDR targets can be the moment of initial shock or realization. Other important memories to target are distressing moments inf forms such images of suffering, hospital scenes, funeral memoires, and the like. Nightmare and flashback scenes and vicarious (constructed) images of the deceased (or what was imagined they experienced) can also be targeted. Moments that encapsulate secondary loss are also relevant targets for EMDR therapy. It is also important to identify and reprocess negative memories of the deceased, such as unfinished business, conflicts, and other negative memories involving the deceased. If processing is blocked, earlier unresolved traumas, losses, or attachment-related memories that underlie the block need to be identified and reprocessed. Memories related to the clinical themes of responsibility, safety, control, and connection/belonging can also impact grief reactions and need to be reprocessed. Though EMDR memory reprocessing usually starts with the moment of shock or realization, the memories that underlie difficulties in coping can be processed first.

12

Three-Pronged Protocol

Second and Third Prongs—Present Triggers and Future Templates

The discussion second and third prongs of the three-pronged protocol will illustrate how the different models of grief can integrate into the Adaptive Information Processing (AIP) model and guide case conceptualization and treatment planning.

The second prong of the three-pronged protocol is reprocessing present triggers. These are the situations, places, and people that evoke distress and pose challenges to adaptation.

Present Triggers

Note: In Table 10.1, present triggers are 3B.

Triggers That Evoke Separation Distress

After a loss, present triggers can be the painful reminders that the loved one is dead and not coming back. Difficult moments having to do with Dual Process model's Loss Orientation (LO) such as the deceased's birthday, an anniversary, hearing a song associated with the deceased, or participating in an activity that reminds the mourner of the deceased are examples of present triggers that can be reprocessed. Understanding and accepting the implications of the loss does not come with one EMDR therapy session but takes place over time. Mourners think about or are reminded of the loved one ('This is the day Janet makes fresh bread.') and are struck again by separation distress when they realize that their loved one is dead. In Appendix 2, there is the example of Sharon (case example 2), a mother of a 16-year-old son who was killed in a car crash. When she would try to imagine her son's 'beautiful smiling face', she

EMDR Therapy Treatment for Grief and Mourning. Roger M. Solomon, Oxford University Press. © Roger M. Solomon 2024.
DOI: 10.1093/oso/9780198881360.003.0013

would become overwhelmed with the realization that he was dead, and feel she was losing him again. Such moments, present triggers, that evoke separation distress, need to be reprocessed.

Triggers That Evoke Difficulty in Adapting to the Loss

Present triggers can also be the situations that pose challenges to adaption to life without the deceased. These difficult moments having to do with Dual Process model's Restoration Orientation (RO), (e.g., 'It is so difficult to think of myself as single.'/'It is difficult to go to a party alone.') can be processed, enabling the mourner to better oscillate between LO and RO. However, in conjunction with the processing of present triggers, clients may need to have psychosocial education and skill building to deal with current stressors and anticipated difficulties.

Rando's fourth through sixth 'R' processes, specifically, are helpful when addressing the second and third prongs of the three-pronged protocol; the death of a loved one forces the mourner into a new world that is not wanted. Letting go of the old world to move into the new can be an arduous journey filled with fear and resistance. The mourner needs to Relinquish *the Old Attachments to the Deceased and Old Assumptive World* (fourth 'R' process) that are no longer valid because of the death, in order to *readjust to move adaptively into the new world without forgetting the old* (fifth 'R' process). Complications occur when there are difficulties in letting go of attachments that have been rendered obsolete by the death. Relevant to the fourth 'R' process EMDR therapy can target situations, *present triggers*, in terms of the AIP model, where mourners experience difficulties in letting go or in severing the ties to the deceased and the old assumptive world. Reprocessing these moments facilitates a transformation in the attachment to the deceased and a revision in the assumptive world. This enables mourners to move adaptively into the new world without forgetting the old (fifth 'R' process). The subprocesses here are the following:

1. Mourners revising their assumptive world.
2. Developing a new relationship with the deceased.
3. Adapting new ways of being in the world.
4. Forming a new identity.

Indeed, processing situations that represent difficulties in letting go of the old world/attachment naturally seems to segue into adaption into the new world and transformation of the relationship from loving in presence to loving in absence. This sets the stage for the client to re-engage in life (Rando's sixth R process of 'reinvest').

Situations That Represent Obstacles: Stuck Points to Re-engaging in Life

The death of a loved one can tear apart one's world, produce a significant void in one's identity, and create fear and uncertainty where before there was stability and security. As described above, EMDR therapy can focus on the difficulties in relinquishing attachments and assumptions that are no longer valid because of the death to facilitate adaptation to the new world without the deceased and without forgetting the old. With revision of the assumptive world and transformation of the relationship, mourners can again engage (reinvest) in life. Post-traumatic growth (Tedeschi & Calhoun, 2004) takes place, with mourners developing new understanding of themselves and the world. Values may change and life may no longer be taken for granted. As one mourner put it, 'I've always stopped to smell the roses, now I just linger a little longer.'

No one can replace the loved one who died, but life can still be meaningful and purposeful. Life goes on. There can be obstacles to getting back into life. Mourners' areas of difficulty can be dealt with through exploring and identifying what prevents an adaptive adjustment. Clinicians can assess whether there are past memories that interfere with present functioning, pinpoint present triggers, and identify what new skills clients may need. Part of treatment is providing appropriate education and coaching for learning new skills and dealing with novel situations. In terms of the Dual Process Model, EMDR therapy can target current obstacles (present triggers) that impede adaptation to the new world, and so facilitate RO. Examples include the moments of fear or anxiety about engaging in new activities, pursuits, relationships, and/or resuming one's life (e.g., 'I met someone I want to date, but I feel I'm cheating on my deceased husband.' Or 'I want to go back to college, but I'm afraid.').

Future Template

Note: In Table 10.1, future template is 3C. In the third prong of EMDR therapy, a future template is provided for adaptive functioning: following successful reprocessing of each present trigger, clients are asked to imagine responding in an adaptive way when the same or a similar triggering situation occurs in the future. This one-two punch of processing a present trigger, immediately followed by providing a future template for dealing adaptively with the same (or similar) situation provides a more powerful resolution of the issue. Future templates serve to bridge the treatment results from the therapy room to real life by identifying and reprocessing anticipatory anxieties, clarifying what skills are needed, enhancing adaptive responses to difficult situations, and preparing clients for potential challenges, such as returning to daily life situations (RO). Hence, installing future templates enhances the clients' ability to oscillate between LO and RO.

Note: As described above, it is crucial that mourners have the knowledge and skills to deal with obstacles, stuck points, and challenging situations. An important part of comprehensive therapy is teaching and coaching clients on adaptive life skills and practices relevant to the problem.

Case Examples

The case examples below illustrate how processing a stuck point or obstacle in relinquishing the old world/attachment (fourth 'R') segues into moving into the new world without forgetting the old (fifth 'R'). Then, case examples relevant to re-engaging in life (sixth 'R' of reinvestment) will be presented to illustrate how processing stuck points and obstacles can help mourners move forward in life.

The fourth 'R' process is to *relinquish* the old attachments to the deceased and the old assumptive world. Present triggers can be situations and moments when mourners want to recapture the old world (i.e., the way the world was understood before the death) and not go into the new.

Examples of targets are the following:

- Situations and moments when mourners want to recapture the old world (i.e., the way the world was understood before the death) and not go into the new (e.g., 'The world is different, I do not like it, and I do not want to live in it.').
- Situations where life difficulties demonstrate how much mourners long for things to be the way they were when the loved one was alive (e.g., 'When I was cleaning up after dinner, it hit me how difficult things are now . . . I want my old life back.'
- Moments when it is realized that the loved one is no longer able to fulfil a need, (i.e., 'My brother is no longer here for me to discuss problems with.').

> *Case Example 1 (The Fourth 'R': Difficulty Relinquishing the Old World/Attachment): Sam's wife, a first responder, was killed 11 September 2001 while responding to the World Trade Center. Sam had a lot of support from friends and family and remained successful in his job. However, he experienced mild to moderate anxiety and depression. Especially without his wife, he had a felt sense that the world had changed and was no longer predictable. Thirteen months after her death, Sam began treatment with EMDR therapy.*
>
> *For Sam, 11 September was traumatic on many levels. His assumption of a stable, predictable world was no longer valid, and he was left feeling depressed and unsafe. After three sessions of history-taking, discussing the circumstances of his wife's death, and developing a safe/calm place, reprocessing began with the moment he was told his wife had been killed. Reprocessing involved not only the death of his wife, but the horror and gravity of the terrorist attack. An additional four sessions focused on other painful memories and difficult moments pertaining to the sudden death of his wife, the realization that the world had changed with the attack, and his resulting feelings of powerlessness and disillusionment.*
>
> *One session involved reprocessing a recent painful moment of disillusionment when he experienced his changed world as 'just too much'. He had been tending the garden, something he often did with his wife, 'and now she is not there'. The negative cognition was, 'I can't manage', and positive cognition was, 'I can manage.' During the reprocessing, he concluded, 'The world has not changed, it is the same . . . my world has changed, and it is me who has to adapt.' After this session, he felt more able to go on without her. Gardening became a positive, meaningful way to remember his wife. Imagining gardening with the positive feelings was provided as a future template.*

In this case, Sam was suffering from the trauma of the 11 September terrorist attacks as well as the death of his wife. He believed the world had changed, and he no longer could fathom how to adapt or where he fit in. The ties to the old world that are specifically based upon the loved one's existence have to be revised (e.g., gardening with his wife), as well as the more global assumptive world elements that have been invalidated or impacted by the death (e.g., one's belief in fairness or expectation that the world is safe). During reprocessing of a present trigger, Sam became aware that bad things do indeed happen. He realized it was his circumstances and not the world that had changed. For Sam, this provided a perspective from which he could see a way to adapt, helping him to relinquish his old assumptive world and adapt to the new world without his wife. This was enhanced by providing a future template of gardening as a way to meaningful engage in the new world without forgetting the old.

The fifth R process is to *readjust*, to move adaptively into the new world without forgetting the old. This involves four subprocesses:

1. Revise the assumptive world.
2. Develop a new relationship with the deceased.
3. Adopt new ways of being in the world.
4. Form a new identity.

Revise the Assumptive World

Adaptation to the new world means that world assumptions have to be revised. Expectations, goals, values, and meaning have to take into the world is now different without the loved one.

> Case Example 2 (Revising the Assumptive World): Giorgio came in for treatment 11 months after his wife died of cancer. Initially, EMDR was utilized to reprocess moments when she suffered, the moment she died (he was at her bedside), and the funeral. His most painful present trigger was walking his dog, an activity he and his wife shared. As Giorgio put it, 'Walking the dog reminds me she is dead and it's hard to give her up.' He had lost his companion and life seemed empty and he felt that he was just going through the motions without her. A recent experience of walking his dog was targeted, with the negative and positive cognitions being, 'I can't go forward— I can go forward.' During reprocessing, he realized the depth of his loss, how he had assumed his wife would always be in his life, and how many day-to-day, mundane activities involved her (e.g., washing the dishes after a meal, talking about what to watch on television). Giorgio could then connect with meaningful moments of being with her and with how much he enjoyed her felt presence even when doing nothing. By the end of reprocessing the recent trigger of walking the dog, he could experience the positive connection with her, and wanted to carry on with what they enjoyed together. A future template of walking the dog while holding in mind the sense of connection with his wife, was successfully installed.

Reprocessing these distinct moments—present triggers—that encapsulate the anxiety associated with relinquishing a tie to the 'old world' and providing future templates for each trigger paves the way for adaptation to the new world without the deceased, but without forgetting the old. In the case of Giorgio described above, walking the dog evolved from being a painful reminder of his wife's death and how much of his world he had lost to being an affirmation of the connection to her and a way to adapt to his new world. The transition occurred through the emergence of heartfelt memories, forming an adaptive inner representation. In this way EMDR therapy assists in reprocessing the obstacles to revising the assumptive world and makes room for mourners to form (in the fifth 'R' process) new attachments to the loved one that are appropriate to the new world without the deceased.

Developing a New Relationship with the Deceased

Commonly mourners, yearning for the loved one, experience the anguish that goes with the absence of connection. Life that promised to be fulfilling with the deceased is now shattered, with mourners having to go on with a new life that was neither wanted nor anticipated. Reprocessing these painful moments, which are maladaptively stored in the brain, results in linkages to adaptive information. A broader perspective emerges. Commonly positive memories of the deceased come to mind that are meaningful, heartfelt, and provide a sense of connection that mourners can take with into the future. Sometimes the connection to the deceased is through the pain, with mourners fearing that losing the pain results in losing the connection. EMDR therapy will not take away appropriate emotion or what is true. The pain of missing someone who was an intricate part of one's life cannot be processed away. However, the processing of painful moments can help mourners develop a sense of connection to the loved one and enhance the courage and motivation to adapt to current circumstances.

- Situations and moments when mourners are stuck in making the transition from loving in presence to loving in absence; it is too much to accept that the loved one is truly gone (e.g., 'I know my wife died, but I don't want her to be gone.').
- Moments when it is realized that the loved one is no longer able to fulfil a need (e.g., 'It's too much to think my father is no longer here to help me with car problems.').
- Moments that represent the pain, fear, and anxiety associated with losing the connection (e.g., 'I can't live without him/her.'), as illustrated in Case Example 3.

Case Example 3 (Fear of Losing the Connection): Rifca's husband died. As the first anniversary of the death approached, Rifca requested treatment. She usually experienced distress throughout the day, but mostly when coming home to an empty house. After several sessions of history-taking and preparation for EMDR memory processing, the hospital scene when he died was targeted. Processing became blocked with Rifca fearing, 'If I lose the pain, I will really lose my husband.' In a cognitive interweave, the therapist suggested that she would not lose anything that she needed and that most likely reprocessing the pain will allow her to experience positive, meaningful memories that will give her a positive sense of connection. Rifca agreed to continue sets of bilateral stimulation. With continued reprocessing of the pain, heartfelt memories did, indeed, arise, and, Rifca exclaimed, 'He will always be with me and will continue to be part of my life.' The therapist provided another interweave to focus on the sense of connection: 'Is there any way this feeling could ever leave?' Rifka replied, 'Never', and further bilateral stimulation was added to enhance the positive feeling. The next two sessions focused on present triggers, the most painful of which was coming home to an empty house. The sadness of being without her husband was intense, but resulted in Rifca feeling lighter and more balanced because she had people and meaningful activities in her life. Future templates first focused on enjoying the company of a close friend and family members, and pursuing her hobbies. This resulted in her feeling more hope. Then, in a later session, a future template focusing on her coming home to her 'empty' house, with a positive cognition of 'I still have a life, and a feeling of hope and balance, was provided.'

This example illustrates a connection to the loved one through the pain, with the fear that losing the pain will result in losing the connection. With the therapist using an interweave that she would not lose anything that she needed and that her sense of connection would be enhanced, Rifka continued processing. The positive memories that emerged indeed gave Rifka a connection through love that was enhanced by further sets of bilateral stimulation. Another interweave, that the author has found useful with mourners: 'Is there any way this feeling could ever leave?' was also helpful in enhancing the sense of positive connection. The reprocessing of present triggers, such as coming home to an empty house, were targeted, with future templates provided for each trigger to enhance adaptation.

Adopting New Ways of Being in the World

Adaptation to a loss requires finding new ways to meet the needs and fulfil the roles that were taken care of by the deceased. Navigating life without the loved one is a challenge requiring mourners to engage in life in new ways. Present triggers to be targeted include:

- Situations/moments that evoke guilt/ambivalence/resistance/fear/anger about assuming new roles and behaviours or having to adapt to a new life (e.g., 'I feel uneasy when I start watering the plants; that is what Leslie used to do, it's not supposed to be me doing this.') This is illustrated in Case Example 4.

- Moments where mourners resist making changes in order to deny the implications of the loss (e.g., mourners find it difficult to engage in new activities or assume new roles to avoid accepting the death as real or permanent). This is illustrated in Case Example 5.
- Moments where mourners are reluctant to assume new behaviours because of a belief that the old behaviours are the sole ties remaining to the loved one.

Case Example 4 (Anger and Sadness at Having to Adapt to a New Life): Janet came into treatment 6 months after her husband died of cancer. Toward the end of his life, he experienced a great deal of pain. She was flooded by images of his suffering and even felt discomfort breathing, just as her husband had experienced. Symptoms mimicking the experiences of the deceased are not uncommon in bereavement. Janet was angry with her husband for dying and leaving her with two children in high school and college. As she put it, 'I did not marry him to raise my children alone. This should not be happening ... he should be here.'

After four sessions of history-taking and preparation and stabilization, the most distressing memory, her husband experiencing significant pain while she felt very helpless, was reprocessed. After reprocessing she was able to think of her husband at peace, with memories of when he was 'robust'. At the next session, her feelings of abandonment were targeted, along with her felt sense that he should not have left her with two children. This was accomplished by focusing on a moment, 2 weeks before, when she was making breakfast for the children before school. Initially, anger and sadness were experienced. She expressed that this was not the world she wanted, and it should not have happened. With further sets of BLS, she experienced intense emotion and said, 'He has died, and he is not here for us anymore.' In the next sets of bilateral stimulation, present-day information began to link in. Janet stated that although the children had their struggles, they were doing okay in school were still actively engaged with their friends and were helping with chores. She realized how the children had greatly benefitted from their father during his lifetime and that they had a solid foundation because of their relationship with him. She found it comforting that she could see her husband's presence in her children. She also had hope for the future and that her children would always have the base their father gave them. Later sessions focused on processing present triggers such as situations where she felt alone and resentful. Examples included cooking dinner for her children alone and having to do the chores her husband did. Future templates for each trigger were provided, such as cooking, with a positive cognition of, 'I can cope' and feeling calm and competent. She gradually adapted to her role *as a single parent. Further, she expanded her social network of friends and family who could provide concrete help when needed.*

In the above example, Janet was understandably distressed at having to adapt to the world without her husband. Treatment first focused on the trauma of the death. The intrusive imagery of her husband's suffering made it difficult for her to deal with issues related to the loss, particularly having to raise her children without her husband. As is typical with EMDR therapy, the raw felt emotion (i.e., anger and sadness) was followed by the linking in of adaptive information creating a wider perspective where she could see that her daughters were coping and continued to benefit from their father. This gave her hope for the future. The adaptive inner representation that arose during EMDR processing took the form of memories of her husband when he was robust and of seeing her husband's presence in her children. This enabled her to move into the new world without forgetting the old. After processing the trauma of the loss, it was possible to target a recent moments encapsulating her difficulties in relinquishing the old world (e.g., making breakfast for the children without her husband), and enhance her adaptation with a future template for each trigger. The processing of present triggers and providing future templates further enabled her progress and adaptation.

Case Example 5 (Resistance to Adapting to the New World): Dorothy entered treatment a year after her husband was killed in an auto accident. They had been married for more than 20 years. A competent professional, Dorothy relied on her husband's encouragement and support to succeed. With his death, she felt incompetent and unable to take care of herself. Fearing failure, she avoided taking on new projects. Her history revealed she had been very insecure while growing up due to an overly critical mother. Her husband had been supportive of her and had helped her work through her insecurities. The first EMDR session focused on hearing the news of his death. After the shock of this moment was processed, Dorothy described how her husband had been the greatest resource of encouragement in her life and had helped her overcome her self-image problems. With his support, she had developed a strong sense of competence and self-esteem and was successful academically and professionally. With more sets of bilateral stimulation, a new awareness emerged. She was afraid to be competent because it meant she did not need him and would have to let him go. Hence, feeling incompetent and not able to care for herself was a way of keeping a connection with her husband. After this realization, she was able to appreciate the meaning their relationship, how much she had grown with him, and how frightened she was of letting him go. With more sets, and further realization about how her insecurity linked to her fear of letting go, she was able to say, 'Taking care of myself does not mean letting him go', and with further sets: 'I can take care of myself.' This was installed as a positive cognition. Further sessions focused on attachment issues related to her mother as well as on her grief. Sessions processing present triggers and installing future templates related to taking on new projects and self-care were also targeted. For example, she had felt insecure in taking on a new project at work. A recent moment when she was asked to participate in a project that interested her, but felt incapable, was targeted, followed by a future template of taking on the new project, with a positive cognition, of 'I am competent' and a feeling of competence.

In this example, Dorothy's husband had been the major source of encouragement and self-esteem in her life. Dorothy's insecurity and difficulty in functioning after his death was a manifestation of her fear of letting go of her husband. She could still need him and maintain the attachment by being insecure, not taking care of herself, and not going forward at work. After reprocessing the trauma of the loss and underlying memories relating to her insecurities, as well as associated present triggers and future templates, she came to realize how not taking care of herself and needing him was her attempt to stay connected. With this awareness and processing underlying attachment, trauma-related memories, and present triggers with a future template for each trigger, she was able to go forward in life, both personally and professionally. This example also illustrates how past attachment-related issues can again be triggered by new losses. The death of her husband triggered unprocessed memories pertaining to her critical mother. Reprocessing the memories underlying current problems were essential to adapting to the loss.

Forming a New Identity

Relinquishing the old world and transitioning to the new requires a shift in one's identity. The deceased may have been the mirror that reflected back who one is and affirmed one's identity. With the mirror shattered, mourners may not know whom they are, and the challenge is to redefine oneself without the deceased.

Here, relevant targets can include:

- Moments where individuals are wondering who they are in this world without the loved one. As one mother of a 10-year-old expressed, 'I was the mother of a 10-year-old, and now I am not and no longer know where

I fit it', or, as one man whose wife died put it, 'I am now a widower, which feels so different than who I am.' This is also illustrated in Case Example 6.

- Situations that exemplify complications in forming a new identity without the deceased such as difficulties in going from a 'we' to an 'I' (e.g., 'When I went to the party by myself, I realized I don't know who I am without him.')
- Situations/moments that evoke fear/guilt/ambivalence/resistance about engaging in the new world (e.g., 'My world has changed, and I don't know who I am now.').

Case Example 6 (Loss of Identity): Susan's husband was a police officer who was killed in the line of duty. They had been married five years. Susan had been aged 16 years when they had met and started dating. She described that she had been 'crazy in love' as only a teenager could be, and her world centred on him. They married when she was 18 years old. After his death, Susan felt lost. She had good relationships with her immediate family, good friends, and a satisfying professional career, but her husband had been her focus in life. She described how he had been the main part of her identity, and that without him she did not know who she was. She coped with his death through her religious faith, exercise, and maintaining contact with significant others. Nevertheless, Susan was depressed and living in a world with little meaning. One year after her husband's death, she came in for treatment.

After several sessions of history taking, establishing a safe place, and doing resource installation, EMDR memory reprocessing began. Targets included the moment Susan had heard about her husband's death and the overwhelming hospital scene. After two sessions of targeting these traumatic moments, Susan's feelings of loss of identity were still quite strong. A recent painful moment when these feelings were particularly acute (i.e., hiking to their favourite place) was targeted with EMDR. Initially, much pain and grief came up. Susan did not know who she was without her husband and did not know how to live in a world without him. With further reprocessing, she remembered life before she met her husband and of 'who she was' prior to her marriage. She got in touch with her previous goals and ideals and no longer felt disconnected from herself. Memories with her husband, where she felt like a 'firmly rooted person', also emerged. With further processing, Susan felt her usual sense of self, something she had not felt in long time. Over the next two sessions, Susan decided to go back to college and pursue the educational and vocational interests she had had prior to meeting her husband. An example of a present trigger that was targeted was receiving the application to enrol at the university, followed by a future template of filling out the application. Therapy continued for another three months with periodic 'tune-up' sessions over the next 3 years.

Assumptive world elements specifically based upon the loved one's existence always must be let go. In this case, Susan's deep attachment to and identification with her husband and the world they had lived in together resulted in her feeling a significant void and loss of identity after she became widowed. After reprocessing the trauma of his murder, recent moments where she felt lost and out of touch with the world were targeted. The mind finds a way and she got in touch with previous memories that rooted her in her premarriage identity. This enabled her to feel grounded and to transition from the world with her husband to the world without him.

Situations That Represent Obstacles and Stuck Points to Re-engaging in Life

The cliché 'life goes on' does not articulate that adaptation involves emotionally investing in life, engaging in a life that has meaning, fulfilment, and even joy.

The first two case examples come from my work with a group of police widows whose husbands were killed in the line of duty. We met as a group once a year, and individually on an as needed basis. Around 3 years after the deaths of their husbands, several of the women were ready to date, but were reluctant because of fears of forgetting their husband or of being disloyal. The third example illustrates more general problems in re-entering life and illustrates how treatment needs to involve dealing with the trauma of the loss, past memories contributing to present problems, present triggers that interfere with functioning, support in learning new skills, and installing future templates.

Case Example 7 (Fear of a New Relationship): 3 years after her husband was killed, a widow was ready to engage in a new relationship, but felt this would mean she was forgetting her husband. A recent moment (present trigger) when she experienced anxiety about dating and forgetting her husband was targeted (i.e., watching a television show where a couple was on a date). During reprocessing, a childhood memory came to mind where the family dog died. Several months later, the family got a new dog. She loved the new dog and realized that loving the new dog did not take away her love of her previous dog. Then she realized she could have a new relationship without forgetting her husband. After processing this recent memory, a future template of going on a date was provided.

Case Example 8 (Fear of A New Relationship): Similarly, another widow felt guilty about entering a new relationship. Focusing on a specific moment when she felt this guilt, resulted in her realization, 'My husband was the love of my past, Joe (i.e., the new boyfriend) is the love of my present.' A future template of comfortably being with Joe was provided.

Case Example 9 (Comprehensive Treatment Needed in Going Forward): Maria, another police widow, took 6 months off work following the death of her husband who was killed in a helicopter crash. Four months after her loss, she sought treatment. Maria had been off work since her husband's death and had planned to start work within a month. After two sessions of history taking and teaching the safe/calm place, the trauma of her husband's death was reprocessed (e.g., when she heard about the death, seeing his body at the hospital, and a funeral memory). Present triggers (i.e., going to bed alone at night and other moments when she missed him) were reprocessed. Upon returning to work, she found that she had difficulty completing her usual workload because of decreased ability to concentrate, and being more easily fatigued. It is not unusual to experience a mental fog after a traumatic experience (Brico, 2018). Her drop in efficacy caused anxiety and feelings of incompetence and inadequacy. Further, she never paid the bills before; this was something her husband took care of. This also fuelled anxiety about the future. Maria's feelings of anxiety and inadequacy made her miss her husband even more. Treatment focused on arranging a paced return to work with a new schedule, more realistic expectations (e.g., working less hours with fewer projects), and stress management strategies. A plan to learn how to deal with paying her bills (e.g., monitoring bank accounts, scheduling payments, keeping records) started with contacting her bank to go over the family bank accounts and set up procedures for paying bills. Resource Development and Installation, where she accessed past moments of confidence and competence, was utilized to enhance her ability to deal with current stressors. Getting in touch with these positive memories felt grounding to Maria and motivated her to continue working at a more realistic pace. Recent situations at work (present triggers) where she felt particularly incompetent were also targeted, with future templates installed for each trigger. Another example of targeting a present trigger was dealing with finances. A recent memory where she felt lost and incapable when paying her bills was targeted, with a future template of being able to implement her financial plan as provided.

Once Maria's work situation was stabilized, childhood memories related to feeling inadequate were also identified and reprocessed. Maria's energy level gradually increased and within five months she was functioning at her previous capacity. She began to do more activities with friends and family and married 5 years later.

Consistent with the Dual Process model, this last example illustrates that dealing with stressors interfering with adaptation (RO) must go hand in hand with dealing with the traumatic impact of loss (LO). Some sessions focused on reprocessing the trauma of the loss while other sessions focused on dealing with new challenges (e.g., adaptation to work and learning how to deal with her finances). This included learning new skills as well as targeting recent distressing moments (present triggers) and providing future templates for each trigger. It was also important to target past memories underlying her current insecurities, along with present triggers and providing future templates.

When Processing Is Blocked or Reactions are Complicated

Complicated grief and mourning or blocked processing, may result from previous trauma, losses, and/or attachment or developmentally related memories. Difficulties can be due to personal issues, necessitating identification and reprocessing of previous trauma, losses of attachment and developmentally related memories, along with reprocessing present triggers and installing future templates. Treatment needs to be more comprehensive than just treating grief, focusing broader personal issues.

Case Example 10 (Difficulty in Going Forward Because of Attachment-Related Issues): Cloe was aged 32 years, with two children, when her husband, a soldier, was killed in combat. A year later, Cloe entered treatment. She was mildly depressed and described how she seldom engaged in hobbies or visited with friends and families. She was working and taking care of her children with help from her family. Her life felt bland and colorless, with her days feeling the same no matter what she was doing. After three sessions for history taking and providing affect regulation strategies (safe/calm place, breathing exercises), reprocessing the moment she received the news was initiated and successfully resolved. In a later session, a present trigger when she felt life had lost its meaning was reprocessed. The target was a moment when she was doing laundry while reflecting on her empty life. Her negative cognition was, 'I can never be happy', and positive cognition, 'I can be happy again.' Reprocessing became stuck with her continuing to feel sad and believing that, 'I can never be happy.' A floatback was provided: 'Close your eyes, notice the thought, 'I can never be happy', and the sensations, and float back in time to an earlier memory where you may have had similar thoughts and feelings.' A childhood memory emerged when her mother was depressed and harshly telling her children to quiet down when they were playing. She became aware of her blocking belief, 'If mother was not happy, no one could be happy.' This new target was incompletely processed and in the following session reprocessing resumed. After fully reprocessing the childhood memory, Cloe was able to return to the original target of feeling her life was empty (doing the laundry). Her positive cognition evolved to, 'I can be happy in the future.' A future template was provided where she imagined the present trigger (doing the laundry) with the positive cognition 'I can be happy', and feeling capable. Treatment continued with reprocessing additional childhood memories and present triggers of difficulty engaging in life, with a future template installed immediately following the resolution of any present trigger. Her outlook broadened to a felt sense of, 'There is a lot to life.'

This example illustrates how a person can adapt to life following a significant loss but lose their sense of meaning, no longer experiencing joy. When EMDR reprocessing of a recent memory that included Cloe's belief of, 'I can't be happy', stalled, a floatback brought her back to attachment-based memories. When these memories were processed, and the processing of present triggers and providing future templates. Cloe was able to reinvest in life with a sense of 'There is a lot to life.'

Below is an example of a client who could not adapt to the 'new world' because of underlying trauma and attachment-based memories.

Case Example 11 (Trauma and Attachment-related Memories): Wendy was aged 46 years when her husband of 22 years died of cancer. One year later, she was going to a restaurant for a college reunion, and when she arrived there was no place for her to sit. She went home. Her reaction to this was, 'I can't do this life.' She came to treatment because of her difficulty in adjusting to living without her husband. The oldest of five children, her early childhood was difficult due to poverty, and an alcoholic father, who was emotionally and physically abusive. Her mother was caring, but also victimized by the father. During their life together her husband was a source of safety. With his death, she felt insecure, and as she put it, 'I don't have a place ... I don't know how to fit in.'

Treatment started with teaching stabilization skills (safe/calm place, resourcing, problem-solving skills) and focusing on spending time with friends, her siblings, and joining a grief support group. After 2 months, EMDR therapy first focused on reprocessing the trauma of her husband's death (the death scene in the hospital). Then the present trigger of the restaurant was targeted, with the Negative Cognition of, 'I don't have a place', and a Positive Cognition of, 'I do have a place.' Reprocessing got stuck, with her experiencing agitation and tension. Discussing what she was feeling brought her back to distressing childhood memories of her father's scary behavior when he was drinking.

Treatment shifted to reprocessing distressing childhood sessions. After 14 sessions, the present trigger at the restaurant experience was again targeted. The Negative Cognition and Positive Cognition were, 'I don't have a place', and 'I can find my place', and the target and beliefs were successfully reprocessed. This positive cognition was used to install her future template, where she imagined a similar situation, but this time she made arrangements to sit down, and 'find my place'.

This example illustrates how past traumas and losses can interfere with adaption to the new world without the deceased. Not finding a seat at the restaurant seemed an insurmountable challenge. It exacerbated her growing perception that, 'I can't do this life', resulting from unprocessed experiences of the loss of her husband (her source of safety) and childhood trauma. Processing the trauma of her loss, earlier traumas and attachment-based memories were essential to adapting to life without her husband. And resolving long standing personal issues.

Summary

Present triggers are the situations, places, and people that evoke distress. When mourners think or are reminded of the loved one, powerful separation distress can be experienced. Targeting these triggers, along with installing a future template, facilitates further integration of the loss.

Future templates help mourners deal with their fear of the future, identify skills that need to be learned, and facilitate the implementation the therapeutic gains in the office into real life. Present triggers and future templates are a 'one-two punch' to build resilience, with future templates being installed for each present trigger.

SECTION 4
EIGHT PHASES OF EMDR THERAPY

A significant loss may indeed be traumatic when an important person is gone forever. Life will be different, but it is not over, and it can be meaningful again. Reprocessing the trauma of the loss enables mourners to go through the processes necessary for adaptation. Eye movement desensitization and reprocessing (EMDR) therapy can help transform the separation distress through enabling a sense of connection through the formation of an adaptive inner representation of the loved one, as in the Continuing Bonds model. Reprocessing present triggers of the obstacles to going through the mourning process, and installing future templates for each present trigger enables a person to reinvest in life. When grief and mourning are complicated or processing is blocked, identifying and targeting unresolved trauma, losses, and developmental memories underlying present problems are important. EMDR therapy is imbedded in an overall framework, providing affect regulation and resource installation strategies as needed, psychosocial education, skill-building, and problem-solving, with therapists providing a secure and collaborative relationship and accompanying clients through this difficult journey. This section will discuss each phase of EMDR therapy.

13

Phase 1

History-Taking and Treatment Planning

Introduction

Some approaches to grief therapy recommend a careful and systematic assessment of the client before beginning treatment (Pearlman et al., 2014), while others, including eye movement desensitization and reprocessing (EMDR) therapy, believe that treatment begins when the client first walks through the door, and history-taking is part of the treatment process. The initial clinical interview is not a discrete and separate process preceding therapy; it is part of building safety in the therapeutic relationship as well as the client feeling understood by the therapist. Kosminsky and Jordan (2016) point out that gathering history can evolve in parallel with the growth of the therapeutic alliance that builds a safe base. In the immediate aftermath of a death, history-taking needs to be integrated with psychological first aid (see Appendix 3).

History-taking includes identifying the following:

1. *Past Memories*—past experiences that underlie clients' present problems.
2. *Present Triggers*—situations, reminders, and people that trigger symptoms in the present.
3. *Future Templates*—future goals and skills that are needed for effective coping in the future.

Past experiences not only include distressing moments pertaining to the death (e.g., getting the news, hospital scenes, or funeral moments), but also past trauma and losses and unresolved past experiences with the deceased. Present triggers include situations where symptoms are experienced, and future templates for adaptive functioning are developed for each present trigger.

It is important that history-taking be sensitive to the needs of clients. Asking for details can be too much for some clients, flooding them with emotion. However, some clients may need the therapist to bear witness to their story as they relate what happened 'frame by frame'. The pacing of history-taking and

EMDR Therapy Treatment for Grief and Mourning. Roger M. Solomon, Oxford University Press. © Roger M. Solomon 2024.
DOI: 10.1093/oso/9780198881360.003.0014

gathering of information pertaining to current functioning and problems are conducted according to the needs of the client, slowing the pace when emotions get too much, respecting silences when clients are contemplating and 'going inside', and helping to draw out clients when they do not know how to begin or to tell their story.

In EMDR therapy, assessing client readiness for reprocessing is also an aspect of history-taking. As the history is taken, therapists can assess:

- Emotional stability, including affect tolerance.
- Ability to deal with emotional content and maintain dual awareness.
- Ability to utilize self-control techniques (e.g., safe/calm place).
- Ability to implement coping strategies to deal with difficulties that arise.
- Handling of emotional material and symptoms that arise between sessions.
- Stability of the social environment (e.g., life pressures, life supports that are available and utilized (or not)) (Shapiro, 1995, 2001, 2018).

Therapists should always take a psychosocial history. The following are some suggested topics for discussion that would augment the usual history-taking, and not an ordered sequence of questioning. History-taking with an understanding and empathic response builds therapeutic rapport. The following information can be gathered according to the client's pace and readiness. These topics may need to be explored over the course of several sessions.

Cultural Issues

Throughout history-taking, as well as the other phases of EMDR treatment, clinicians should be cognizant of cultural issues. Though beyond the scope of this book to discuss, mourners' cultural, social, religious or spiritual identity, and family heritage can impact all aspects of life, including beliefs about death and mourning practices. Clinicians must have the utmost respect and sensitivity to cultural issues throughout the treatment process.

Issues Related to the Death

Circumstances of Death

When it comes to how the death occurred, important questions to ask include:

- What were the circumstances of the death, including the events that led up to and followed it? Was the client somehow involved in or a witness to the death?
- If not, how did the client get the news about what happened?
- What happened afterwards?
- In the initial aftermath of the loss, what did the client do, who did the client communicate with, who offered comfort, and how did the client cope?
- What was the planning and experience of the funeral or remembrance event like?

Talking about what happened, before, during, and after the loss provides the therapeutic experience of clients telling their story and is helpful in building a trusting therapeutic relationship.

High-Risk Factors for Complicated Grief

It is important to assess any risk factors that could be problematic over the course of clients' mourning. Risk factors (see Chapter 4) such as suddenness and lack of anticipation of the death, violence, human-caused event, suffering of the loved one prior to the death, unnaturalness, preventability, intent of responsible agents, randomness, multiple deaths, untimeliness, and loss of a child increase the likelihood for complicated grief and are important for clinicians to identify to be well-informed.

Nature of the Loss and the Meaning and Personal Impact to Clients

Clinicians can assess the nature of the attachment with the deceased person, strength of the relationship, security, conflicts, and unresolved issues. Risk factors associated with the premorbid relationships include marked anger, ambivalence, and/or dependence, and these may impact how clients go through the mourning process. For example, one woman never felt accepted by her mother. When her mother died, the realization that she would never get the acceptance she always wanted resulted in a secondary loss that complicated the grief.

Cognitive, Emotional, Physiological, and Behavioural Reactions to the Death

See Chapter 2 for a description of reactions.

It is important to ask about medical problems and current physical symptoms. Clients should consult a physician if physical symptoms or medical conditions have worsened.

How Is the Grief Manifested and Impacting Daily Life?

Another important question to ask is, 'To what extent are reactions interfering with daily living and functioning?' Assess how the client is functioning in regard to (see Chapter 2 for elaboration):

- Family life.
- Work life.
- Structures of daily life (attending to daily life obligations) and dealing with changes brought about by the death (secondary stressors, e.g., going from husband to widower, dealing with financial changes).
- Religious or spiritual community.
- Criminal Justice/legal system (if a crime or other legal issues are involved).

Ask about the clients' coping skills:

- What coping strategies do you use? Are they successful?
- What coping strategies have you used in the past to deal with tragedy?
- How do you feel about how you have been doing?
- How do you anticipate you will be coping in the future?
- What difficulties do you expect? What coping strategies will you need to deal with these challenges

Changes in the Client's Life Since the Death

Many things in clients' lives and perspectives may have changed. This can include mourners' living and occupational situation, attitudes towards life (and death), relationships with family, friends, and others, and more.

Ask the following types of questions:

- What feels comfortable about the changes?
- What is difficult?
- What are the continuing challenges in adapting to the changes?

How the Client Is Dealing with Bereavement-Specific Issues

It is important to ask about how the client is dealing with bereavement issues such as managing the deceased's belongings, any business related to the death, and coping with holidays and important dates such as anniversaries or birthdays.

Ability to Regulate Affect and Ability to Maintain Dual Awareness

EMDR memory processing requires one foot in the past and one foot in the present. Powerful, distressing affect can arise during EMDR processing, so evaluation of the client's capacity to maintain dual awareness is essential. Questions to ask your client include:

- How do you respond in times where you experience strong emotions?
- Can you maintain contact or regain connection with your own inner experience and with external situations while experiencing strong emotions?
- Do you have effective strategies to use when you are upset (e.g., safe/calm place, breathing strategies, and resources)?
- Are there coping strategies that have been problematic for you (e.g., drinking, compulsive eating, or isolating)?

Oscillation Between a Loss Orientation and Restoration Orientation

According to the Dual Process model (see Chapter 7), adaptation to loss involves the dialectical oscillation between loss orientation ((LO) clients' ability to experience, feel, and reflect on the loss) and restoration orientation

((RO) being able to put grief aside to cope with secondary stressors and meet the new demands resulting from the death). Assess clients' ability to balance and move between these two orientations.

Reactions of Others in the Client's Life and Degree of Support Received

The quality of support for clients is especially important. Many friends and relatives do not want to hear about the loss, or insensitively say the mourner should be, 'over it', and should 'move on'. Other people in the support system may be inconsistent or uncomfortable around the mourner. Perception of lack of support is a risk factor for complicated grief.

Issues of Trauma, Loss, and Attachment, and Psychological Issues

Past Experiences: Trauma and Loss History

Current loss can trigger previous unresolved losses and traumas; understanding clients' history of prior losses and trauma is essential. Usually, treatment addresses the primary loss first, followed by other losses or traumatic events that contribute to clients' current experience. However, not uncommonly, a previous loss or trauma may need to be addressed before dealing with the primary loss, depending on what is most prominent in the clinical picture.

History of Relationships with Close Attachment Figures

As previously elaborated, it is particularly important to assess clients' attachment history with the deceased since a loss can be compounded and complicated by unresolved attachment issues and conflicts (Kosminsky & Jordan, 2016). For example, a client may feel lost and helpless without the loved one, and this can be due to childhood experiences involving feelings of helplessness. Attachment style, determined by the myriad of child-caregiver interactions, significantly impacts how trauma and loss are dealt with. Significant past memories that underlie insecure attachment can be identified and targeted for treatment.

Psychological Problems Clients Experienced Prior to the Loss and How These Issues are Impacting Clients Now

Not uncommonly, clients will come in with depression or anxiety symptoms that they do not recognize as linked with an earlier loss. Similarly, a previous loss that clients believe they had accepted may be unrecognized because of present dysfunction. For example, one man came into treatment to deal with his increasing anxiety after an automobile accident. The fear and helplessness experienced during the accident was connected to the death of his brother when he was 8 years old. Once this was processed, his fear significantly abated, allowing the auto accident to be targeted successfully.

Present Triggers and Future Template

Present Triggers and Reactions to Reminders
Identify what are the present situations, places, people, or circumstances where clients get triggered. In addition to the questions mentioned previously, ask:

- How do you react when reminded of your loved one? With sadness and tears? With feelings of helplessness? With anger? Do you feel numb?
- Are you trying to avoid thoughts and feelings about the deceased to minimize the pain of the realization of the loss?
- How do you cope with these reactions? Are your coping strategies effective?

Future Goals or Templates for Adaptive Functioning
For each presenting problem and present triggers, a goal for adaptive future functioning (a future template) should be discussed.

Case Conceptualization and Treatment Planning: Putting It All Together

The following framework (adapted from EMDR Institute, Weekend 2 manual) is a way to organize the information gathered during history-taking.

Presenting Problems, Symptoms, and Issues

Presenting Problem
The presenting problem is the specific problem(s) that brought the client to treatment, the 'Why now?' In the context of this book, it is the loss of a loved one. Does the client experience problems in daily living in the areas of affect regulation, self-esteem, relationships, and other stressors?

Acute Symptoms

Symptoms acute because of the situation (e.g., the loss), and chronic (long-standing) need to be identified.

Underlying Issues

Issues underlying the presenting problem need to be identified and prioritized in order of urgency and importance. There may be issues pertaining to self-esteem, safety, affect management, control (lack of control or overly controlled or controlling), or lack of connection and belonging. Other examples of presenting issues may include issues of unresolved grief, relationship issues, and abandonment issues owing to an early attachment loss, and more.

Treatment Goals

Treatment goals are discussed in collaboration with the client based on the client's presenting problems, symptoms, and underlying issues.

Clinical Themes of Responsibility, Safety, Control, and Connection and Belonging

Inadequately processed memories are stored without access to information needed for resolution, resulting in distortions leading to core clinical themes. Each theme may have a situational component as well as a core, developmental aspect.

Responsibility

Responsibility includes both self-defectiveness (shame) and/or action or inaction (guilt). Mourners may blame themselves, and/or perceive themselves to be defective for what they did, or did not do (whether real or perceived). Example of negative and positive cognitions are the following:

- *It's my fault, I should have done more/I did my best.*
- *I don't deserve love/I deserve love.*
- *I am inadequate/I'm okay as I am.*

Safety

Safety includes not only a person's sense of basic safety, but trusting one's emotions, thoughts, and choices. Examples of negative and positive cognitions are the following:

- *I'm not safe/I am safe.*
- *I am in danger/I survived.*
- *I can't trust myself (emotions/feelings)/I can(can learn) to trust myself (emotions/feelings).*

Control/Choices

Control/Choices pertain to feelings of helplessness, powerlessness, and confusion about what was and what was not under one's control (internal versus external control). Examples of negative and positive cognitions include:

- *I am helpless/I have choices.*
- *I have no control/I have some control.*
- *I can't go on/I can go on.*
- *I cannot trust myself (or my judgment)/I can (learn) to trust myself (my judgment).*

Connection and Belonging

Connection and belonging pertains to a sense of belonging or connection to others versus feeling isolated, alone, or different. This can be a pervasive theme in persons' lives, especially after a loss. Further, the loss of connection to the deceased can leave persons feeling alone and isolated, with their life having no meaning. Early losses and attachment history can lead to mourners not being able to recognize or accept the support and connection that is available to them currently. Consequently, the negative cognition and positive cognitions can be the following:

- *I can't connect (to others) /I can connect (to others).*
- *I don't belong (My life has no meaning)/I do belong (My life does (or can have) meaning.*
- *I am alone/I can be with others.*

Pertinent to the theme of connection is the felt sense of being alone and isolated after the death of a loved one. As stated previously, EMDR therapy often results in a felt sense of connection to the loved one through emerging heart felt memories giving clients a felt sense connection to the deceased which facilitates adaptation.

Adaptive Memory Networks

Clients' resources, both internal and external, are identified during history-taking and strengthened and enhanced, based upon clients' needs and situation, during the Preparation & Stabilization phase and throughout treatment. Successfully processed earlier losses, traumas, or challenges are part of adaptive memory networks and can contribute to resiliency and hope. If additional resources are needed, they can be developed through resource development procedures (Korn & Leeds, 2002) and/or teaching clients affect management and coping strategies. These resources and strategies may be useful to assist clients during history-taking and all phases of treatment as needed.

Case Conceptualization

Case conceptualization is an overall view of client presentation and guides treatment planning. Clinicians take into account clients' presenting symptoms, stability, current resources, coping ability, skill deficits, contributory experiences, and additional relevant information to formulate treatment priorities and plan the sequence of interventions and targets for reprocessing. Attention is given to client goals and priorities, with a mutual decision made about the optimal order of interventions.

Stability and Resources

Clients' needs for stabilization, affect regulation, or other skills to prepare them for memory reprocessing are identified. Does the client have the capacity to handle intense emotion? Do clients have sufficient affect regulation skills to deal with their grief reactions? Do the clients have sufficient healthy coping strategies to deal with the challenges that come with adaptation to a loss? If not, such skills and strategies can be taught during the Preparation & Stabilization phase and as needed throughout the course of treatment. All clients should also be evaluated for dissociative symptoms and the presence of a dissociative disorder.

Three-Pronged Approach (Past, Present, and Future)

Memories are identified for reprocessing including experiential contributors, present triggers, and client desired response to life's challenges (future template for each trigger). Presenting problems are informed by maladaptively stored memories. Treatment usually proceeds with the sequence of past, present, and future. For grief and mourning issues, the past includes memories related to the death (e.g. 'getting the news') and, if clinically relevant (e.g. complex presentations), earlier memories underlying current symptoms (e.g., previous trauma, loss, and attachment-related memories). It is important to identify present triggers and goals for future desired outcomes for adaptive functioning of each trigger.

Treatment Planning

The entire clinical picture is evaluated. Relevant memories to be reprocessed, treatment priority, and the order of memories to be reprocessed is identified as determined by clients readiness for reprocessing, need for symptom relief, time constraints, and current life challenges. The sequence of interventions, including the order of memories to be reprocessed, can be planned in accordance with client readiness and treatment goals. Treatment priorities may be symptom reduction, focusing solely on the trauma of the loss. For others, a more comprehensive approach to deal with long-standing issues that complicate their grief may be appropriate. For many people focusing on present symptoms (e.g., the immediate impact of the trauma of the loss) naturally segues into more comprehensive treatment (e.g., memories underlying current issues). Clients who do not meet readiness for full reprocessing may benefit from focused reprocessing, such as eye movement desensitization.

Below are brief examples of case conceptualization and treatment planning.

Case Conceptualization and Treatment Planning Examples

> Case Example 1, Sharon: The following example illustrates a case where the trauma of a death was the main focus of treatment. Sharon's son, Joe, was killed in an auto accident. Sharon is married with two children, Joe (who was killed) and a daughter, 2 years younger than Joe. Sharon and her husband were going to grief counselling at the time she requested EMDR therapy to deal with the trauma of the loss.

Presenting Problems and Issues

Presenting Problem

Sharon, a 42-year-old woman, was referred for EMDR treatment 12 months following the death of her 16-year-old son Joe, who was killed in an auto accident. Sharon and her husband were attending grief counselling, and she was referred for EMDR therapy by her grief counsellor.

Acute Symptoms

Sharon was very distraught, crying as she talked about her son. She experienced flashbacks of getting the news of her son and seeing his body at the hospital. When thinking of her son, or reminded, Sharon would become overwhelmed. Seeing other boys the same age as her son, driving past his school, and hearing about car accidents triggered significant distress. Life had lost much of its meaning, and Sharon felt disengaged. However, she was motivated to carry on in order to care for her husband and 14-year-old daughter. She had hobbies of quilting, playing cards with her friends once a week, and enjoyed cooking, but had become more withdrawn, seldom engaging in these activities. Sharon had a stable employment history working as a nurse. Though not as productive as she was prior to her son's death, she was managing at work.

Underlying Issues

Sharon, the second of three children, grew up in a middle-class family with both parents working. Her father was stern, but usually caring and attentive. Her mother was often tired after coming home from work and could not always attend to Sharon, resulting in Sharon's sometimes feeling alone and anxious. However, overall, her parents could be counted on in times of distress. Sharon appeared to have a relatively secure attachment style.

Treatment Goals

1. Manage her grief reactions.
2. Resolve the trauma of her son's death.
3. No longer be overwhelmed by reminders of the loss, including being able to cope with seeing boys around the same age as her son, driving past his school, hearing about car accidents, and having confidence in the future.
4. Restore a sense of meaning and re-engagement in life (including engaging in her hobbies and seeing her friends).

Clinical Themes of Responsibility, Safety, Control, and Connection and Belonging

With Sharon's deeply missing her son, she felt disconnected from life (connection and belonging theme). Further, life has lost much of its meaning, which gave Sharon a sense of futility and powerlessness (control and choices).

Adaptive Memory Networks

Sharon has hobbies of quilting, playing cards with her friends once a week, and enjoys cooking, though lately she has been more withdrawn and seldom engaged in these activities. Her relationship with her husband was stable, and they had been sharing their grief with each other through grief counselling. Sharon also had a good relationship with her daughter. Sharon had a stable employment history as a nurse.

Case Conceptualization

Stability and Resources

Sharon appeared to be suffering moderate to severe grief symptoms following the death of her son. She was functioning well before the death, and her symptoms appeared to be related to the sudden and unexpected loss of her son. She had a good support system, and had been coping actively (e.g., involved in grief counselling).

Three-Pronged Protocol (Past, Present, and Future)
PAST

Memories related to the death:

1. The police coming to her home at night and giving her the news of Joe's death.
2. Seeing her son in the morgue at the hospital.
3. Funeral scene of the coffin being lowered in the ground.

Memories prior to the loss:

1. At age 5 years, feeling alone and anxious when her mother said she was too busy to play with her.
2. At age 6 years, seeing her father leave for work before breakfast (after a new job required him to start early, missing breakfast with the family).

PRESENT TRIGGERS

1. Thinking or being reminded of her son.
2. Seeing other boys the same age as her son.
3. Driving past his school.
4. Hearing about car accidents trigger significant distress.

FUTURE TEMPLATE

1. Able to think of her son with love and a sense of connection.
2. Able to go places and engage in activities that remind her of her son (e.g., driving by his school, sitting down at dinner, or bedtime).
3. Able to cope with hearing about accidents recalling her son with love.
4. Engage in life activities with a sense of positive meaning, such as her hobbies and being with friends.

Treatment Planning

Sharon had a stable family situation, and was utilizing her support system of friends, was participating in grief counselling with her husband, and had hobbies she enjoyed prior to the death of her son. Therefore, Sharon had minimal stabilization needs and appeared ready for EMDR therapy targeting the trauma of her loss.

1. Initial EMDR preparation & stabilization, providing psychosocial information about EMDR therapy and grief, and teaching affect regulation strategies (safe/calm place; resourcing).
2. EMDR therapy can target memories related her son's death, then targeting present triggers followed by future templates after resolution of each trigger.
3. If needed, or reprocessing gets stuck, childhood memories related to being alone and anxious can be targeted.

> *Case Example 2, Betsy: This case represents a client with complicated grief who benefited from comprehensive treatment. Beginning sessions focused on affect management, followed by reprocessing childhood memories related to current symptoms, and then reprocessing loss-related memories related to her deceased mother.*

Presenting Problems, Symptoms, and Issues

Presenting Problem
Betsy a 48-year-old married woman, came in for treatment 18 months after her mother died of cancer.

Symptoms
Betsy experienced sadness and despair and felt guilty that she could not do more for her mother. These symptoms were particularly acute on her mother's birthday and on the anniversary of her mother's death. She also experienced significant feelings of inadequacy and powerlessness, especially if people were angry with her. For example, she felt very inadequate when her supervisor pointed out mistakes or gave her negative feedback on her performance. Her relationship with her husband was basically stable, but she felt powerless and inadequate during their arguments over financial issues. She found it difficult to complete everyday tasks, had withdrawn from family and friends, and her work performance suffered.

Underlying Present Issues
Betsy's underlying issues had to do with problematic childhood attachments. Betsy's father, who died of health complications seven years earlier, suffered from alcoholism and was often angry, yelling at both Betsy and her mother. As a child and into adulthood, she witnessed numerous arguments between her parents, the most distressing being occasions when her father yelled at her mother, and her mother would just be quiet. She was very worried about her mother during these instances. The mother was the parent Betsy felt safe with and went to when there was a problem. She described her mother as introverted and intimidated by the father's temper. Betsy often felt the need to be a comfort to her mother, even though she needed comforting herself.

Treatment Goals

1. Become free of feelings of distress and guilt over her mother's death.
2. Resolve the trauma of her mother's death.
3. Increase her sense of self-esteem and confidence in herself.
4. Manage conflictual situations (e.g., with her husband, supervisor, and colleagues) in a more constructive way.
5. Re-engage in life (e.g., example, continue gardening, and spending time with friends).

Clinical Themes of Responsibility, Safety, Control, and Connection and Belonging

Betsy's themes included responsibility (guilt over not doing more for her mother, self-defectiveness with feelings of inadequacy) and control (feelings of powerlessness).

Adaptive Memory Networks

Betsy had hobbies of gardening and reading, and a small circle of friends with whom she enjoyed spending time. She had a stable marriage and though there were some conflicts, she felt safe with her husband.

Case Conceptualization

Stability and Resources
Betsy appeared overwhelmed by her mother's death, with underlying issues from childhood complicating the clinical presentation. She would benefit from sessions focusing on affect management and increasing integrative capacity to help her reach criteria for memory reprocessing (e.g., safe/calm place, resource development and installation, and stress management strategies).

Three-Pronged Protocol (Past, Present, and Future)
PAST

Memories related to the death:

1. Being at her mother's bedside when she died.
2. Memories of her mother's suffering.
3. Doctor telling her and her mother there was no more hope.

Memories prior to the loss:

1. Age 5 years: Childhood memories of feeling unsafe when she saw her mother upset. Similar memories throughout childhood and adolescence.

2. Age 5 years: Feeling guilty for not being able to help her mother. Similar memories throughout childhood and adolescence.
3. Age 7 years: Seeing her father yell at her mother; her mother being scared and quiet; and being worried about the mother. Similar memories were noted throughout childhood and adolescence.
4. Age 8 years: her father being angry that she did not clean her room well, with similar memories noted throughout childhood and adolescence.

PRESENT TRIGGERS

1. Sadness and guilt when reminded of her mother, particularly at her mother's birthday and anniversary of her death.
2. Hearing about other people who have cancer.
3. Conversations with colleagues, supervisors, or her husband where their voices were raised, or they were angry at her for something. Recent examples included:
   A. A disagreement with a colleague at work.
   B. A supervisor annoyed with her for being late with an assignment.
   C. An argument with her husband about paying the bills.

FUTURE TEMPLATE FOR EACH TRIGGER

1. To be able to think of her mother with love when reminded of her, particularly at her mother's birthday and anniversary of her death.
2. To feel compassion for people who have cancer, and to remember that her mother is now at peace and not suffering.
3. To feel grounded and empowered when there is a disagreement (specifically in relation to the same or similar disagreement with her colleague, supervisor, or husband).

Treatment Planning

After providing stabilization in the Preparation & Stabilization phase, the clinical priority is treating the issues complicating the grief, such as targeting attachment-related childhood memories pertaining to her feelings of inadequacy and powerlessness. Then treatment can focus on the trauma of her mother's death, present triggers, and future templates for each trigger. This plan would change if memories pertaining to the mother's death intruded or predominated her symptom presentation.

Summary

This chapter presented a guide for history-taking relevant to grief and mourning. Issues related to the death include the circumstances, risk factors for complicated grief, nature of the loss and its meaning and personal impact on the client, reactions to the death, manifestation of grief in daily life, changes since the death, dealing with bereavement-specific issues, oscillation between RO and LO, reactions of others, and the ability to regulate affect and maintain dual awareness. History-taking should also include identifying past trauma and losses, history of relationships with close attachment figures, and psychological problems prior to the loss and their impact on the client now. Present triggers and future goals and a template for adaptive functioning also need to be identified.

Case conceptualization and treatment planning was also discussed. This includes (1) identifying present problems, symptoms, and presenting issues; (2) clinical themes; (3) adaptive memory networks; (4) constructing a case conceptualization, based on an all the information gathered, that guides treatment; and (5) treatment planning that maps out stabilization needs, memories to be reprocessed, and their sequencing, based on client readiness, need for symptom relief, time constraints, and current life challenges.

14

Phase 2

Preparation & Stabilization

The Preparation & Stabilization phase of eye movement desensitization and reprocessing (EMDR) therapy involves preparing the client for memory processing. This includes providing affect regulation and coping strategies as needed, establishing a therapeutic alliance (which begins when the client first comes in the door), and providing education regarding grief, mourning, and EMDR therapy treatment. This phase should be integrated with the history phase to help provide stabilization, coping strategies, and information on grief and mourning, as needed.

Affect Regulation and Coping Strategies

How much preparation or affect regulation does a client need before memory processing? This is not so much a question of time, but rather a question of the client's readiness. See Table 14.1 for a list of the criteria for client readiness (i.e., to a "good enough level") in terms of EMDR therapy.

In a nutshell, clients need to be able to have one foot in the past (i.e., experiencing the memory and related affect) and one foot in the safe present while going through EMDR processing.

Therapeutic Relationship

The therapeutic relationship must provide the emotional safety, safe base, and safe haven for clients to explore the painful emotions and reactions to loss and explore new ways of adapting to life without the deceased. There must be sufficient trust for clients to engage in the EMDR therapy process which can be intense. A large part of supporting client maintenance of dual awareness comes from the therapist-client relationship, with therapists being able

EMDR Therapy Treatment for Grief and Mourning. Roger M. Solomon, Oxford University Press. © Roger M. Solomon 2024.
DOI: 10.1093/oso/9780198881360.003.0015

Table 14.1 Criteria for Client Readiness

Ability to:
- Access the experience and stay present (i.e., maintain dual awareness between past experience and present situation).
- Observe the experience and reflect on it, rather than be completely absorbed in it.
- Tolerate distress for a short period without becoming overwhelmed (i.e., hyperarousal) or shutting down (i.e., hypoarousal).
- Shift emotional states (e.g., from distress to calm) and access positive experiences and resource states.
- Practice self-soothing, containment, and adaptive coping strategies and skills in between sessions as needed.
- Create a stable (and safe) social environment
- Experience sufficient trust and safety in the therapeutic relationship.

to pace the processing and help clients stay present. Some clients can feel safe with the therapist and ready to process relatively quickly in the treatment process, while other clients need more time to develop a sense of safety.

Issues of Attachment

Attachment history has a lot to do with client readiness. The death of an attachment figure (or, in the case of parents, the recipient of their caregiving) can threaten one's sense of control and safety. We are wired to attach to caregivers for safety. After a loss, mourners may react to threatening interpersonal experiences (e.g., therapy) in a learned attachment style (e.g., anxious, avoidant) that evolved as a protection from interpersonal threat. Given that attachment style underlies how clients grieve, clinicians must be able to adapt to clients' attachment orientation and adjust the pace of therapy.

Attachment Styles and Effect on Therapeutic Alliance
Clients with a secure attachment often can present with distressing emotions and describe it in a coherent fashion. They can more easily trust the therapist and engage in the therapeutic process. They are better able to oscillate between loss orientation (LO) and restoration orientation (RO). However, trauma can interfere with the oscillation in a manner similar to those with insecure attachments (Stroebe et al., 2005).

The client with an *avoidant style* may tend to deny emotional distress and, thereby, avoid the activation of the attachment system (Mikulincer & Shaver, 2014). Clients may be overly focused on RO, where the intensity of grief is actively avoided through keeping busy through the safety of avoiding contact with others. In contrast to the anxiously attached person, avoidant individuals operate on the principle that negative emotions are something to be managed without the help of others. Consequently, clinicians may initially need to go slowly in exploring the relationship with the lost loved one and clients' emotional reactions to the loss.

Anxiously attached individuals, on the other hand, may tend to sustain or even exaggerate negative emotions in order to attract and maintain the attention and care of attachment figures (Kosminsky & Jordan, 2016; Mikulincer & Shaver, 2014). This strategy, which involves *over*activation of the attachment system, is seen in mourners' tendency to ruminate on painful memories, be preoccupied with the deceased, and exaggerate their inability to cope with current life difficulties. Further, there may be difficulty accepting that the loved one is truly gone and not coming back (i.e., it may be too much to realize). Affect regulation strategies may need to be blended in while exploring the impact of the loss in order to prevent clients from being overwhelmed.

People with *disorganized attachment* will have difficulty tolerating and managing emotion. It may be more difficult for them to trust therapists, making it important for therapists to spend more time building a collaborate therapeutic alliance. Further, an extended Preparation & Stabilization phase may be needed to build integrative capacity and enable clients to meet criteria for memory processing. Phase-Oriented Therapy is recommended (Van her Hart et al., 2010), where first there is (1) stabilization (e.g., learning how to calm, getting to know the personality system, and obtain some degree of cooperation and collaboration among the "parts" of the personality), (2) memory work (including EMDR memory processing protocols), and finally a third phase of (3) personality (re)integration and rehabilitation to enable the client to engage life in new, adaptive ways (see Chapter 19).

Psychoeducation

Providing Information on Grief and Mourning

Principles of psychological first aid (Appendix 3) should be remembered when dealing with the newly bereaved. In initial sessions, psychosocial education on common reactions and coping strategies may be useful since acute grief can be quite frightening, and clients do not necessarily understand their reactions or why they are experiencing them. Often the newly bereaved need reassurance that the distressing feelings and reactions are normal responses to an intense situation. Clients sometimes feel a strong sense of presence of the loved one, have conversations with the loved one, see signs of the loved one, mistake other people as the loved one, find it hard to concentrate or find themselves crying for no apparent reasons (although on reflection there are very good reasons), and may think, "I am going crazy." Clients should be assured that this is not the case. There are many resources, such as books, online tools, and social media websites that provide useful information on grief and mourning.

Balance Between Loss Orientation and Restoration Orientation

It is important to help clients achieve a balance between LO, with its focus on coping with the emotional aspects of the loss, and RO, with its focus on dealing with the changes that result from the death. For clients with an anxious attachment overly focused on LO, introducing problem-solving strategies and affect regulation methods may help them better deal with the challenges and changes posed by the death, and balance the back and forth shifting between LO and RO. Clients with an avoidant attachment, overly focused on RO, may also benefit from affect regulation strategies to deal with emotions and gradually approach exploring emotions at their own pace.

General strategies for coping, specific to attachment style, are presented in Table 14.2.

This is by no means an exhaustive list, but it is hoped, gives clinicians some helpful suggestions for helping clients cope with their pain.

Preparing for EMDR Therapy

Calm/safe state exercise or *Resource Development and Installation* (Korn and Leeds, 2002) can be a benign way to introduce EMDR therapy. These methods provide an opportunity to both understand bilateral stimulation and experience what happens and gives clinicians information on clients' response to EMDR and predicts how clients will respond to EMDR memory processing. If clients can hold the safe/calm state and resource in mind and it enhances with bilateral stimulation, this is indicative of sufficient capacity to begin processing. If upsetting or intrusive material emerges, then further stabilization and assessment may be needed, as this response predicts that negative material may be quick to surface or intrude. If there is no movement, or nothing is happening, further assessment as to underlying factors such as avoidant attachment style, dissociation, or even misunderstanding directions can help determine what is needed to assist clients in recognizing and staying present with emotions.

Table 14.2 Coping Strategies

For Clients with Anxious Attachment:
- Safe/calm place.
- Resource development and installation.
- Breathing exercises to lower physiological arousal.
- Container imagery (e.g., being able to put distressing emotions in a "bank vault" or other container at the end of the session).
- Focusing on the physical sensations that accompany emotions (e.g., rapid breathing, tension in the chest, and tightness in the neck), and reporting the sensations to oneself without attaching meaning to them.
- Pendulation—focusing on a tense part of the body and then focusing on a neutral place (e.g., the knee, an elbow), and alternate or "pendulate" back and forth.
- Noticing one's surroundings, getting specific about what is seen, heard, smelled, tasted, and felt (i.e., sensations) to keep externally focused.
- Grounding exercises (e.g., standing tall, imagining one's legs go to the center of the earth so one is centered and grounded).
- Clients may also need guidance in problem-solving life challenges that have to be dealt with, planning balanced daily life routines (e.g., meals, exercise, getting enough rest/sleep).
- To achieve a balance between LO and RO, help clients problem-solve current challenges and learn the skills needed to cope with life changes.
- Taking a break from grief. Help clients understand that this is okay and even healthy (oscillate from LO to RO), and can be achieved not only by attending to everyday activities but also having "breaks," watching a favorite television show, going to a movie, planning a social activity with a friend with whom one is comfortable, and so on.

Clients Who Are Avoidant, and Stuck in RO, May Benefit from:
- Understanding that avoidance of feelings was a survival strategy in childhood. Perhaps the best strategy in a family where asking for help or showing distress/expressing needs was ignored, criticized, or even punished was to shut down feelings and/or not ask for help.
- Identifying people the client knows and trusts (e.g., friends, family, physician, or clergy) who can be resource persons to talk to or ask for something.
- Suggesting clients allow space in themselves for feelings to exist. Feelings are important information about what is going on inside. Notice what feelings are experienced during the week, and "what you say to yourself about them."
- Suggesting clients have compassion for themselves and their feelings, rather than treating emotions as enemy intruders. Emotions are normal, particularly under the sad, distressing circumstances.
- Teaching mindfulness techniques of noticing what they are feeling emotionally and physically, without judging.
- Bringing in photos, videos, and other mementos to the session that may help clients start to deal with the emotional impact.
- Interventions that promote connection may be effective, given the importance of establishing a sense of connection with the deceased (continuing bond). These might include talking about the deceased, going over photographs or videos of the deceased, visiting the gravesite, writing letters to the deceased, or visiting places where the deceased used to go. These interventions counteract the tendency for the avoidant mourner to defensively orient their attention away from the loved one and serve to facilitate the process of dealing with the loss. However, such interventions should be done at mourners' emotional pace with attention to their readiness to deal with the emotions that may arise.

Table 14.3 Highlights of EMDR Therapy with Grief and Mourning

- Distressing moments and situations can become maladaptively stored in the brain because it is "too much" to process, and continue to be triggered when there is a reminder of the deceased loved one or their death. These moments are painful and can interfere with understanding and coping with the loss.
- EMDR therapy can process these moments, and reduce distressing images, thoughts and feelings related to the trauma of the loss.
- EMDR therapy will not take anything away anything people needs. By processing difficult moments and obstacles, EMDR therapy enables a people to adaptively engage in the mourning process.
- Often mourners are very distressed, and it is difficult to access positive memories and feelings regarding the deceased—there is often a sense of, "I can't connect." EMDR therapy helps process the trauma of the loss which enables people to have heartfelt memories and a sense of connection, "I can connect." This helps people go through the mourning process.
- Processing the disturbing moments can be very intense. Integration is realizing something that one may not want to realize—the loved one is dead and not coming back. However, processing these emotions sets the stage for finding meaning through the heartfelt memories and the sense of connection that results.
- Clients are in control of the process, and the pace of processing can go according to their needs. Clients have a stop sign, can ask for the bilateral stimulation to go slower or faster or come closer or go farther away, or tell the therapist whatever is needed.
- Explain the EMDR procedures to clients. It is especially important to explain that clients should notice what is happening, report it to the therapist, and let whatever happens happen, without trying to steer the process.
- Discuss the treatment plan, including stabilization and affect regulation methods, and the memories that can be processed and in what order, leaving room for flexible modification, as necessary.

A safe/calm state exercise where the imagery has special significance to and memories of their loved one (e.g., their house, a special place they visited) may increase the feelings of loss or being alone, or in other ways be unhelpful. In the history-taking and case conceptualization, it is worth exploring other places and times they have felt calm or safe, which are not intrinsically linked to memories of their loved one.

It is also important to explain EMDR therapy in the context of grief and mourning and what clients can expect, which is illustrated in Table 14.3.

These points need not necessarily be explained in the order presented and should be adapted to clients' levels of understanding and current situation.

SUMMARY

The Preparation & Stabilization phase of EMDR therapy prepares clients for the reprocessing of disturbing experiences. Clients should meet readiness criteria and be provided with affect regulation strategies as needed. The therapeutic alliance is particularly important to provide the trust and safety for the reprocessing of intense, disturbing memories. Specific education on grief and mourning, coping strategies, and the EMDR therapy process needs to be provided to clients.

15
Introduction to Reprocessing Phases

When to Start

In the previous chapter, readiness criteria for memory reprocessing were discussed. Depending on clients' responses and readiness, eye movement desensitization and reprocessing (EMDR) therapy can begin within the days and weeks following a tragedy. Several EMDR therapy protocols have been developed for the processing of recent traumatic events (Jarero, Artigas, & Luber, 2011; Shapiro, 1995, 2001, 2018; Shapiro & Laub, 2008, 2013) and can be helpful in the immediate aftermath of a traumatic event.

EMDR Therapy for Recent Events

The Recent Event Protocol

Brief descriptions and examples of recent event protocols are provided below. It is beyond the scope of this book to thoroughly discuss the different protocols for utilization of EMDR therapy for recent events and readers are invited to read further about these useful protocols.

The recent event protocol is used within the first several months of an incident/event when there has not been sufficient time for the distressing memory to consolidate (Shapiro, 1995, 2001, 2018). A memory may have more than one moment of disturbance. For example, the death of a loved one can involve the death notification, the ride to the hospital, and the identification of the body. The structure of how the recent event protocol unfolds is the following:

1. *Targeted Memories*—each distressing moment can be treated as a distinct memory, starting with the worst moment, and then reprocessing the moments, as needed, in chronological order (except for Body Scan).

EMDR Therapy Treatment for Grief and Mourning. Roger M. Solomon, Oxford University Press. © Roger M. Solomon 2024.
DOI: 10.1093/oso/9780198881360.003.0016

2. *Run a Movie*—after reprocessing these moments, a movie of the event is mentally run to check if there are other disturbing moments, which can then be reprocessed.
3. *Positive Cognition + Movie*—an overall positive cognition is then identified, and clients are asked to run the movie of the event with the positive cognition in mind.
4. *Body Scan*—an overall body scan can then be implemented.
5. *Present Triggers*—present triggers are processed, and future templates for each trigger are installed.
6. *Future Template*—a future template is provided for each present trigger.

It should be noted that the recent event protocol can be helpful for symptom relief and can be implemented shortly after an upsetting event. It may take several sessions to reprocess each point. Also, it is crucial clinicians have knowledge of the history of their clients, including previous trauma and losses. Reprocessing a memory can evoke unresolved trauma and losses that may be beyond the client's integrative capacity. Further, clients should be taught containment and affect management exercises (e.g., breathing methods, safe/calm place and resource). At a later time, when clients are ready, the full standard protocol on the memory can be implemented to ensure complete reprocessing.

Example 1 (Recent Event Protocol): 2 weeks following the death of his wife to cancer, Gregory sought treatment to deal with the suffering his wife experienced during her last day of life. The recent event protocol was utilized. Targets identified were (a) the moment she took a turn for the worst as seen by her labored breathing, (b) her difficulty breathing with rasping noises, (c) the look on her face as she experienced pain, and (d) her last breath and going limp.

The worst moment was her last breath, which was reprocessed. Then the other moments were targeted in chronological order. After reprocessing this memory, targets (a) and (b), he felt calm, with treatment effects generalizing to target 3 (Positive Cognition + Movie), which was neutral and did not need to be targeted separately. After installation of an overall cognition was installed, "I did the best I could, I was there the whole time," and running the movie of the event with the positive cognition in mind, Gregory felt significant relief. It was still upsetting, but he could now cope. This session took 2 hours. Treatment continued, with the full standard protocol utilized in future sessions to reprocess disturbing memories, reprocessing of present triggers, and installation of future templates for each trigger.

Eye Movement Desensitization

Eye movement desensitization (EMD) (Shapiro, 1989, 1995, 2001, 2018) may be helpful in relieving distressing images and moments to provide symptom relief and increase stability when clients are not ready for full processing. In EMD, after each set of bilateral stimulation, clinicians take clients back to the image and negative cognition and ask for another SUD scale point (i.e., "How disturbing on a 0 to 10 scale, where 0 = calm or no disturbance and 10 = the highest disturbance, is it now?") When the SUD lowers as far as it can go ecologically (SUD may not go to 0), the installation phase is implemented. There is no body scan. EMD is appropriate when the processing needs to be contained to avoid opening emotional material that may be too much returning to target, after each set, provides such containment and may prevent other channels of association from emerging.

> *Example 2 (EMD): Following a quarrel, Sally's husband committed suicide by shooting himself. She witnessed the act. She was exposed to extreme sensory stimulation through what she saw, heard, touched, and smelled. She had blood and brain matter on her hands and clothes. Her mother brought her to the clinician's office 2 days later. She was unable to function in her daily tasks and constantly experienced intense and repetitive intrusive images from the suicide. In a session lasting 2.5 hours, Sally first gave a detailed account of what had taken place, and some background information about the relationship. She had no previous history of mental problems but was experiencing symptoms of acute stress disorder. The therapist's usual approach was to encourage the client to go over what happened, and to provide normalizing information about common after-reactions, and then wait for natural reactions to decline before doing further direct therapeutic work on reactions. However, because of the extent and intensity of the intrusive material, and given Sally's functional incapacity, it was decided to try EMD at this first meeting. EMD was used for each of the sensory systems separately—first focusing on the visual image until that no longer bothered her when she brought it up, and then continuing with the auditory, kinesthetic, and olfactory impressions in the same manner. Within 1 hour, the intrusive imagery in all senses was desensitized. The client was no longer in shock and was able to function in an adaptive way. Treatment continued for another 9 months.*

> *Example 3 (EMD):EMD was utilized for Gregory's 13-year-old son from example #1, who felt guilty because he never told his mother "I love you." He would come to the hospital every day, and when the visit was over, he would tell her goodbye and he would see her tomorrow. The day came when she died, and there was no tomorrow with her. Using EMD, where the focus was on the last time he saw her and said "Goodbye," wishing he said, "I love you." Within 5 minutes of reprocessing he said, "Every time I told her goodbye, see you tomorrow, I was telling her I loved her," and his distress reduced considerably.*
>
> EMD can also be applied more flexibly. If the client's response after a set is adaptive and/or positive, sets of BLS can continue, rather than going back to target after each set. But if other emotional material starts to come up then the client is brought back to target for structure and containment. Such flexibility is incorporated in the recent event protocols authored by Shapiro and Laub (2013) and Jarero, Artigas, and Luber (2011).

Two other protocols that have been utilized for recent events are (1) The EMDR Protocol for Recent Critical Incidents and Ongoing Traumatic Stress ((EMDR-PRECI) Jarero, Artigas, & Luber, 2011) and (2) The EMDR Recent Traumatic Episode Protocol ((R-TEP0, Shapiro & Laub, 2013).

It is beyond the scope of this book to have a thorough discussion of these important protocols, but they are briefly introduced in Appendix 4.

Be Cautious

It cannot be emphasized enough how important it is to do assessment for readiness, dissociation, and whether the current reaction is being fueled by past trauma and losses.

> *Example 4 (Be Cautious): Veronica sought help 2 weeks following the death of her husband in a motorcycle accident. She was experiencing distress at the image of his bloody body at the hospital. The client denied any trauma history but did say she had no clear memories before the age of 8 years. The clinician attempted a calm/safe state exercise, but the client could not come up with a safe place. No other self-soothing methods were attempted. The clinician, wanting to provide symptom relief, targeted the image of the husband in the hospital. When this was done, past memories of physical abuse surfaced accompanied by intense emotion. Veronica was destabilized for the next month, but did stay in treatment. The clinician focused on teaching Veronica calming strategies,*

> *dealing with daily living stressors, and provided resource installation. Treatment then proceeded in a manner appropriate for complex trauma and dissociation (see Chapter 19).*

In this example the inability to access a safe place or utilize any self-soothing techniques should have been a clue to proceed cautiously. Further, not having childhood memories is also a red flag for deferring memory processing, and indicates the importance for further assessment, particularly for Dissociative Disorder (Van der Hart, Nijenhuis, & Steele, 2006).

It is strongly cautioned against using EMDR therapy in the aftermath of a loss when numbness, denial, or dissociative symptoms are being experienced. These psychological defenses indicate there is an overwhelming reality to cope with that is "too much" for mourners, and this needs to be respected. Processing memories prematurely can be an intrusion on clients that may stimulate overwhelming emotions that they are not ready to deal with, or nothing may happen because the emotional impact has yet to be felt. Psychological First (Appendix 4), support from friends and family, and "tender loving care" are needed at this point (Solomon, 2008; Solomon & Rando, 2007). At some point, once the emotional impact is felt, and clients meet readiness criteria, EMDR memory processing can begin. Not uncommonly, people can experience numbness or not feel ready to process distressing memories for several months. Other people are ready within days or weeks.

When the Client Meets Readiness Criteria

The decision of when to begin processing of the loss is guided by clients' meeting readiness criteria. As described in Chapter 14 on the Preparation & Stabilization phase, the basic criteria (to a "good enough" level) for EMDR memory processing readiness, includes ability to stay present with the emotions, maintain dual awareness with one foot in the past and one foot in the present, self soothe and lower arousal, and articulate and reflect on the impact of the loss, and there is a sufficiently stable external environment. Especially when there is complicated or chronic grief, with affect dysregulation impacting the clinical picture, the adage "slower is faster," or "make haste slowly," can be sage advice. Clinicians should take the time to help clients understand, articulate, and express the emotional impact and meaning of the loss before doing EMDR therapy (Solomon & Rando, 2007, 2012, 2015).

Example 5 (Client Readiness): Two police officers were killed in a car crash. After 4 months had passed, one of the wives was emotionally ready to target "getting the news" and the trauma of the loss. The other wife alternated between numbness and anxiety and did not feel ready to deal with the trauma of the loss for 9 months. Providing affect regulation strategies (e.g., calm/safe place, RDI), supportive psychotherapy and helping her link current feelings of anxiety to past insecurity in childhood (e.g., mother and father argued a lot in front of her and were inconsistent in providing support to her) preceded the processing of the trauma of the loss.

Start with A Specific Memory

In memory processing, it is best to start with a specific memory whenever possible, rather than only focusing on emotions, sensations, or a vague sense of something. If much emotional material arises or associations go to many places, clients can always return to target for containment and structure. One clinician who specialized in grief reported that using EMDR therapy was very helpful for clients. However, emotions usually kept coming up, and they were difficult to contain. It turned out this clinician was focusing only on the emotion clients were experiencing. When this clinician started identifying a specific memory and going through each component of the target assessment phase, the reprocessing was reported by the clinician to be "organized, more efficient, and contained."

Starting with a specific memory provides a specific moment to return to when the client (a) goes outside the window of tolerance, (b) time is running out, (c) associations are going far away from the target, and/or, (d) no further associations are coming up (which can be the "end of a channel," or a blockage). Going back to the memory the reprocessing started with identifies the next channel of association to be processed and provides structure and containment. This will be further elaborated on in the Chapter 16.

Allow Sufficient Time

The author has had many EMDR sessions related to grief and mourning where the usual 60-minute session has worked out well. However, many clients may need more time. Sessions can be quite intense, and a 90-minute or 2-hour session is not uncommon. Once the emotional impact hits, it is helpful for therapists to accompany clients through integration or until emotions subside. Francine Shapiro, in her early trainings, said that the typical period of intense emotion lasts 20 to 30 minutes. I have found this to be, for the most part, accurate—*regarding the most intense part.* However, sessions can commonly last 90 minutes to 2 hours, or more, given the time before the emergence of emotion and time needed to continue reprocessing through the next phases, or if incomplete, to have time for grounding and closure.

What If I Only Have an Hour?

Many clinicians can only provide the usual hour-long session. It can be helpful to plan the session and do the Phase 3 Target Assessment in one session, and process the memory the next session. What can help EMDR therapy be efficient is:

1. Be sure clients have sufficient affect regulation skills.
2. Explain the session may be emotional, but that their containment skills can be used to close the session, if needed, and at home, if disturbance continues.
3. Have a safety plan in regard to getting home after the session.
4. Promote self-care or support after the session.
5. Be aware that incomplete sessions are common (i.e., Subjective Units of Disturbance is above 0, and the Validity of Cognition is below 7, or Body Scan not clear, and the level of tension is more than being ecologically appropriate or adaptive).
6. Attempt to stop or start closing down at a moment where clients are experiencing some relief, understanding, resolution, or a calm moment, or whatever seems to be a natural moment to pause.
7. Going back to target more often, or using EMD to limit associations, may keep the processing more focused and contained.
8. Know what stabilization strategy works best for clients so you can utilize it as necessary.
9. Check in with clients after the session of an emotional and incomplete session (e.g., later the same day or the next via text, email, or phone call).

How do therapists plan the length of a session? There is no substitute for knowing your clients. Therapists should have a good indication how clients process from taking the history and doing a safe/calm place or resource exercise, and from how clients express themselves in the session.

Summary

Memory reprocessing should start when clients meet readiness criteria. However, in the immediate aftermath of a traumatic event, including a death, recent event protocols can be used for symptom relief. Clinicians should always take a history and assess for dissociation and readiness for reprocessing to avoid any undue upset. Stabilization or psychological first aid is appropriate if clients are showing dissociative symptoms, numbness, or denial. Further, when doing memory reprocessing, starting with a specific memory offers structure and containment. Reprocessing a loss-related memory can be very intense: consequently, making sure to have sufficient time (90–120 minutes) is important.

16

Phase 3

Target Assessment

Accessing and activating the memory as it is currently stored in the brain is essential for clinicians, prior to the initiation of memory reprocessing. This is accomplished in the target assessment phase. Table 16.1 outlines the specific components of the targeted memory.

Elements of the Assessment Phase

There is a therapeutic flow going from the image representing the worst part, to the cognitive components (e.g., negative cognition and positive cognition), to the emotional, and felt sense of the memory. This is an essential part of eye movement desensitization and reprocessing (EMDR) therapy, and, in and of itself, it is therapeutic and promotes integration. Consequently, clinicians should take the time that is needed in identifying the components of the target assessment phase.

The bulk of this chapter will discuss negative and positive cognitions, which can be challenging, but is perhaps the most important part of this phase. Negative cognition expresses the meaning of the dysfunctionally stored affect that pervades people when they think of the traumatic event. Positive cognition points the way to an adaptive resolution: that is, it provides a therapeutic goal.

Image

EMDR reprocessing flows more efficiently and productively when the focus is on a readily available and distressing moment. Clients are asked to identify the worst part of the memory which grounds the memory in a specific moment in time. The image can be in any sensory modality (e.g., visual image, a sound or conversation, sensation, taste, or smell).

EMDR Therapy Treatment for Grief and Mourning. Roger M. Solomon, Oxford University Press. © Roger M. Solomon 2024.
DOI: 10.1093/oso/9780198881360.003.0017

Table 16.1 Elements of the Target Assessment Phase

Image	Image or picture that currently represents the worst part of the identified memory.
Negative cognition	A negative irrational, self-referencing belief, affectively laden, generalizable, and currently associated with the targeted memory. *Examples*: 'I am not good enough.' 'I am vulnerable.' 'I am powerless.'
Positive cognition	A preferred, positive cognition (or positive, adaptive belief), triggering positive affect, generalizable identified to ascertain and verbalize the client's desired outcome. *Examples*: 'I am good enough.' 'I am safe now.' 'I have some control/choices.'
Validity of cognition	How true the PC feels *now* in relation to the memory on a scale of 1 to 7 scale, where 1 is totally false and 7 is total true.
Emotion(s)	The current emotion(s) associated with the experience.
Subjective units of disturbance	How disturbing the memory now feels on a scale of 0 to 10, with 0 = being calm or no disturbance and 10 = being the highest disturbance the client can imagine.
Body sensations	The location of the associated body sensations.

Negative Cognition

Negative cognition, or negative irrational self-belief, represents the meaning of the image and memory to the client's self (e.g., 'I am powerless.'), and elicits the associated affect that clients experience when thinking of the memory. Understanding the impact and meaning of the event, in relation to self, is integrative in and of itself (Niemeyer & Sands, 2015). Unlike the image or picture that may stand out like a flashbulb moment and can be relatively easy to obtain, eliciting negative cognition (i.e., the verbalization of the stored affect and meaning of the event to the self) can be a more challenging therapeutic task.

In many instances, therapists engage in a therapeutic conversation to help clients explore and expand upon the meaning to the self that resonates with currently experienced affect. For example, clients may initially respond with, 'I should have been there for him.' Therapists can further explore what this means to clients about themselves and deepen its meaning by asking, 'What does that say about you?' Or further explore clients' responses, such as, 'Tell me more about how the death impacts you.' Such discussion can facilitate the identification of negative cognitions like, 'I'm unworthy' or 'I am a bad person.'

Positive Cognition

Positive cognition is a positive, adaptive belief that points the way to an adaptive way of thinking, and it can be conceptualized as a therapeutic goal (i.e., the belief clients would rather have in contrast to the negative cognition). Positive cognition is self-referencing and reinforces clients' feelings of self-worth and enhances self-efficacy, current safety, or current connection and belonging. It is usually a 180-degree shift from the negative cognition (e.g., 'I'm not good enough' to 'I am good enough.'). It is important the positive cognition initially be somewhat acceptable (e.g., 'I *can* be good enough.'). The positive cognition accesses the adaptive information stored in clients' brains that has been inaccessible and is necessary to link to the memory network(s). Discussing the positive cognition is also a way to assess whether clients have sufficient adaptive information available, and if not, for therapists to provide appropriate information. For example, clients may wrongly believe a loved one's death was foreseeable or predictable (e.g., 'I should have known that' or 'I should have seen it coming.'). Such second-guessing is a common reaction (i.e., a psychological attempt to have a sense of control) to a traumatic death or unexpected loss, and provides an opportunity to discuss the feeling of powerlessness and/or provide accurate information. Realistic information may need to be presented if clients have incorrect information (e.g., 'CPR always works.') or unrealistic expectations (e.g., 'My CPR should have worked.') For instance, physicians or emergency medical technicians can provide credible and realistic information that can help mourners realize the reality that there was nothing that could have been done. Situations where mourners had a role in the death, where there is some responsibility will be dealt with later in this chapter.

Validity of Cognition (VoC)

The VoC provides clinicians and clients a baseline or pretreatment measurement of the strength and believability of clients' positive cognitions in relation to the target memory.

Informational (Clinical) Plateaus: Responsibility, Safety, Control, and Connection and Belonging

Negative cognition (i.e., the meaning to the self that verbalizes the stored affect) and positive cognition (i.e., a therapeutic goal) are the nuts and bolts of the target assessment phase. Memories that are inadequately processed result in negative, irrational beliefs about the self. These are not only themes of negative and positive cognitions, but as discussed in Chapter 0, can offer a clinical direction towards exploring factors that complicate the grief or block memory reprocessing. The themes of responsibility, safety, control and choice, and connection and belonging are outlined below.

Responsibility

This theme of responsibility reflects two important aspects:

1. *Action*—action or guilt over what I did or did not do.
2. *Self-defectiveness*—believing oneself to be defective.

Mourners may have an irrational self-attribution of blame; that is, they take responsibility and feel guilty for events or factors that were beyond their control (e.g., 'I did something wrong.') and/or believe oneself to be defective, and experience shame (e.g., 'I am something wrong. I am defective.').

Mourners can feel guilty for a death (e.g., not being able to do more, not foreseeing an unpredictable event: 'I should have made sure he took his medicine that day.'). Exploring negative cognition pertaining to guilt (e.g., 'It's my fault.') with follow-up questions (e.g., 'What does that say about you? What does that mean about you?') often identifies negative cognition related to defectiveness (e.g., 'I am a bad person. I am inadequate/weak/stupid.') Guilt or self-blame can be the price clients pay to feel a distorted sense of control. A common line of thinking is, 'Because of what I did or did not do, this is what happened. If I had done something differently, it would not have happened.' The presupposition is that there was some control, which may be psychologically more comfortable than realizing that bad events can happen outside of their control.

In terms of positive cognition, a self-enhancing belief can be, 'It's not my fault/It was beyond my control.' Or 'I did the best I could.' Or 'What I could do, I did do.' Or 'I'm good enough/I'm okay as I am.' And such cognition sis a positive direction towards adaptive resolution.

Table 16.2 provides complimentary examples of negative and positive cognitions for the theme of *responsibility*.

There are times when clients have some responsibility and cannot say, 'I did the best I could.' In fact, in these situations, clients contributed to the death of the loved one either through neglect, a mistake, an oversight, or poor decision-making. Situations such as driving while intoxicated, speeding in a

Table 16.2 Examples of Positive and Negative Cognitions for Theme of Responsibility

Negative Cognitions	Positive Cognitions
Action/guilt	
It's my fault/I should have done more . . . I am unforgivable.	I did my best/I did the best I could/I can forgive myself.
I am horrible (I made a mistake).	I am okay in spite of my mistake/I can go (despite my mistake).
Self-worth/shame	
I am bad.	I am good/I'm innocent.
I am unlovable.	I am lovable.
I'm not good enough.	I am good enough.
I am incompetent/inadequate	I am competent /adequate
I don't matter.	I do matter.
I don't deserve to love (or have happiness).	I deserve to love/can have love (or have happiness).

vehicle resulting in a crash that kills the loved one, or making decisions that result in the death or injury of others (which happens with first responders and in the military). EMDR therapy does not take away appropriate responsibility, but rather EMDR can facilitate a realistic appraisal of what is and what is not their responsibility. The negative cognition may be, 'I am a terrible person.' The therapeutic direction is, 'I can learn from this . . . I can make amends . . . I can strive to be a better person . . . I am a good person who made a terrible mistake.'

Case Example 1 (Responsibility): Michael, aged 22 years, came in for treatment 18 months after an automobile accident in which his brother was killed. Michael and his brother were driving home after drinking at a party. He was speeding when the car went out of control and crashed into a tree. While Michael did not have serious injuries, his brother was killed. He was experiencing agitated depression symptoms, difficulty concentrating, physical agitation, difficulty sleeping, and deep feelings of guilt and shame. After six sessions of history-taking and teaching affect regulation strategies, EMDR reprocessing of the accident began. The initial memory was the crash and seeing his brother's body. His negative cognition was, 'I am a terrible person', and the positive, was 'I am a good person who made a terrible mistake.' Reprocessing was very painful, with Michael experiencing the horror of the accident, the reaction of his parents, and his own guilt and self-reproach for 'doing something utterly stupid'. At the close of the 90-minute session, with the reprocessing being incomplete, affect regulation strategies were used for closure and stabilization. At the beginning of the next session, Michael reported that

> while it was easier to think about the accident, he still felt guilty. Reprocessing resumed, with him recognizing that they were having fun, but he was 'stupid and wrong' for discounting the risk he had taken that night. At the end of the session Michael reported feeling less disturbance, saying, calmly, 'I did it, I was wrong, and that cannot be changed.' This session of incomplete memory reprocessing was closed with affect regulation strategies. The next week, Michael reported he was able to think of his brother more easily, but he still experienced deep sorrow. Reprocessing resumed, and he had an imaginary dialogue in which he apologized profusely to his brother and asked his forgiveness, acknowledging to this brother that he was wrong to drink, drive, and speed. This led to a spontaneous insight that they did it together, they had fun, and while what he did was wrong, it did not make him less of a brother or define their relationship or make him evil. The next associations were memories where Michael and his brother had good times together. The session ended with a SUDs of 3, which was felt to be ecological for the moment. The positive cognition of 'I am not evil, and I can go on with my life', was installed. Treatment continued for another eight sessions, with some sessions devoted to continued reprocessing of the accident, and other sessions processing present triggers and developing future templates. At termination, the accident had a SUDs of 1, and with the positive cognition 'I am a good person who made a terrible mistake, and I can go on with my life', with a VOC of 7. Quoting an old adage, Michael said, 'I'm sadder but wiser, with life not taken for granted, and a commitment to live in a responsible manner.' He felt awful about his brother's death and his role in it, but could acknowledge his pain, and know, 'I still can go on.'

Safety/Mortality

A death can trigger feelings of vulnerability and lack of safety. The death of a loved one triggers the ultimate vulnerability in all of us—we can die. This can be particularly true if the death was traumatic (e.g., sudden, unexpected, or violent) and a person wonders, 'There for the grace of God, go I'. Negative cognitions of 'I'm unsafe/I'm vulnerable' and positive cognitions of 'I'm safe (or I'm safe today)' reflect the maladaptive to adaptive continuum. Facing one's own mortality is not easy. A therapeutic direction for a negative theme of 'I am vulnerable/I can die (and cannot face it)' may be 'I am vulnerable (can die), and that is part of the human condition/I can cope with my mortality/I can die but I can be fully alive now.'

Table 16.3 provides complimentary examples of negative and positive cognitions for the theme of *safety*.

Table 16.3 Examples of Positive and Negative Cognitions for Theme of Safety

Negative Cognitions	Positive Cognitions
I am not safe/I am going to die.	I am safe now/I can move beyond it.
I am vulnerable/I can't handle my vulnerability.	I can learn to handle my vulnerability.
I can't trust anyone.	I can choose whom to trust to protect myself.
I can't protect myself.	I can protect myself (or learn to protect myself or cope with uncertainty).

Control: Choices

Clients may feel helpless or powerless watching a loved one suffer and die, not being able to do more or prevent what happened (e.g., 'I'm helpless/I'm powerless.') or believe that they cannot trust themselves (e.g., 'I can't trust myself/I can't trust my choices.'). Positive cognitions can be, 'I have some control/choices.' Or 'I can control what I can.' Or 'I can handle it.' Positive cognitions can help attain a more adaptive and realistic perspective relating to what was in their control then versus their current choices and ability to handle the future. Although positive cognitions are usually about the self rather than the situation, and are present-tense rather than past-tense, a common adaptive positive cognition that provides a positive and realistic perspective is, 'I can trust myself/my judgment.' Or 'I can learn to trust myself.' Variations are, 'It was beyond my control/I did what I could do' or 'What I could do, I did do,' which can reflect the belief 'I have some control (or choices).' Other negative beliefs for grieving clients may relate to their ability to cope or go in life without the deceased or face the possibility of future loss (e.g., 'I can't go on living. I can't handle it. I cannot/will not love again.') Positive cognitions need to reflect an adaptive coping response such as, 'I can go on living.' 'Life can have meaning.' 'There is hope for the future.' 'I can handle it.' Or 'I can experience love now (or in the future).'

Table 16.4 provides complimentary examples of negative and positive cognitions for the theme of *control*.

Connection and Belonging

The theme of *connection and belonging* puts a spotlight on the need for human connection and social belonging and the fundamental need for attachment, which result in a felt sense of safety and belonging. The focus

Table 16.4 Examples of Positive and Negative Cognitions for Theme of Control

Negative Cognitions	Positive Cognitions
I am helpless/powerless.	I now have choices/I can cope.
I am not in control.	I am now in control/I have some control.
I can't handle it.	I can handle it.
I have no life/I have no future/can't go on.	I can have a life/a future/I can go on.
I can't trust myself (or my judgement).	I can (learn) to trust myself (or my judgement).

of this theme is the interpersonal and relational aspect between self and other people, as opposed to only the self as in the other themes. Negative social and interpersonal treatment by others—whether from their caregivers, or on a broader social level (e.g., exclusion from a group, racism, or sexism)—results in a sense of isolation, exclusion, stigmatization, and alienation. In relation to loss, this theme describes the feelings of isolation, being alone, or feeling unsafe that comes from the loss of a loved one to whom they felt a close connection. There is considerable overlap between this theme, and the other themes given that, 'I don't belong,' can result in self-blame and beliefs of inadequacy, lack of safety, and powerlessness. In relation to grief, there is not only the very real loss of connection to the loved one, but a sustained belief that they can't meaningfully connect now and in the future. There can be a sense of 'I don't fit in or belong', when a partner dies and mourners feel separate or different in relation to their married friends, or a child dies and the parent finds it difficult to be among other parents. A pervasive sense that 'I am alone', can interfere with mourners experiencing the connection and support that is, in fact, available to them.

An important clinical dynamic with loss (as previously described) is the transformation from, 'I can't connect' to 'I can connect.' The 'I cannot connect' reflects the sense of being alone, isolated, and perhaps unsafe because of the loss of a loved one (an attachment figure). The felt sense that 'I can connect' or 'I can still experience my connection (to the loved one)' describes a positive adaptive direction that comes with the experiencing of positive, heartfelt, meaningful memories of the loved one—the building blocks of an adaptive inner representation that often emerges with EMDR therapy. Other negative and positive cognitions that reflect this theme include 'I am alone/I can be with others' and 'I cannot be happy/I can have a happy (or meaningful) life.'

Table 16.5 provides complimentary examples of negative and positive cognitions for the theme of connection/belonging.

Table 16.5 Examples of Positive and Negative Cognitions for Theme of Connection and Belonging

Negative Cognitions	Positive Cognitions
I can't connect.	I can connect/I am connected (to others).
I don't belong/I'm not (or can't be) part of life.	I do belong/I can be part of life.
I am alone.	I am not alone/I can be with others.
I have no future/I have no life.	I have a future/I can have a life.

Challenges in Identifying Negative Cognition

Sometimes negative cognition may not be a readily apparent. There may not be a clear sense of guilt, loss of self-esteem, or lack of personal safety, control, or connection. In these cases, Phyllis Strauss (personal communication ()), a psychologist in Israel, suggested asking mourners what they miss the most. For example, one woman, after the death of her husband, could not identify a negative cognition. When asked what she missed the most, she said, 'his companionship', and with further exploration came up with 'There will never be any more happiness— I can never be happy.' This was used as a negative cognition and, consequently, her positive cognition was 'I can find happiness in life.' Further, one can ask mourners 'What did you lose with the death?' One client answered 'My life.' The negative and positive cognitions were 'I can't have a life' and 'I can have a life.'

Nevertheless, sometimes it can be difficult to find a negative cognition despite this gentle exploration. After the Oklahoma City bombing in 1995, the author worked with a man whose daughter was killed. After discussion about negative cognitions, the father said, 'I know it's not my fault, I know I am safe, and I know I am not helpless (and in a loud, sad, and angry voice) I lost my daughter God damn it!' At this point, we started reprocessing his experience of hearing the news about his daughter, with the father expressing intense sadness and anger. Eventually, he experienced and expressed his love for his daughter (adaptive inner representation). It is not uncommon for clients who are experiencing intense emotion to find it difficult to come up with a negative cognition. Clinicians should use their clinical judgement to evaluate whether to continue an exploration about negative cognitions or not. It can be helpful to focus on the emotional pain, and begin reprocessing, especially If there is a risk of misattunement in the therapeutic relationship. In such cases, clinicians can gather information on the image, emotion, subjective units of disturbance (SUD) and location of sensations and proceed with reprocessing.

Issues Concerning the Validity of Cognition

Clients are asked to rate how true the positive cognition feels on a 1–7 scale, where 1 = totally false and 7 = totally true. Francine Shapiro (1995, 20021, 2018) described how this rating provided a baseline measure, and allowed clients to see how far they have come at the end of the treatment session (with the goal a VoC = 7). A low rating (e.g., a VoC of 1) can sometimes indicate that the positive cognition may be unsuitable or perceived as too far a reach for clients. Discussing the reasons for a VoC = 1 can help fine tune the positive cognition (e.g., 'I have the potential to be happy again', can be perceived as more attainable than, 'I can be happy.').

Going Deeper: Emotions, Subjective Units of Disturbance, and Body Sensations

In the Phase 3 assessment, the emotions, level of disturbance, and location of bodily sensations are the next components identified. The inclusion of these aspects enables clients to access the maladaptively stored information at a deeper, somatic level while also providing a baseline measurement. Just as the meaning of the memory deepens when clients' name the negative cognition associated with it, exploring and focusing on the emotions and the level of disturbance (SUD) helps clients to go to a deeper, *felt sense* of the disturbance.

Emotions

Clinicians direct clients to bring up the image and hold it in mind with the negative cognition, and ask 'What emotions do you feel now?' The pairing of the image (or worst part of the memory) with the negative cognition stimulates the maladaptively stored material to a greater intensity than either of these components alone, providing deeper access into the memory network.

Subjective Units of Disturbance

The SUD rating is a rating of the disturbance of the entire memory, not of each separate emotion. The SUD provides a baseline reading for both clinicians and clients. Even if the disturbing memory is not fully reprocessed at the end of session, there generally is a decrease. As Shapiro (2018) said, 'This can give the client a sense of accomplishment, which is one of the goals of every therapy session' (p. 130).

Body Sensations

Following the SUD measurement clients are asked where the disturbance is felt in the body. The sensations are the purist indication of the existence and strength of the maladaptively stored information and, once appropriately accessed, readies clients for the active memory reprocessing.

Summary

The Phase 3 target assessment phase activates the memory as it is currently stored, and is an essential step before engaging the adaptive information processing system in reprocessing. From an initial image or worst part; to the meaning of the event to the self (negative cognition); to a therapeutic direction (positive cognition) and a rating of how true it feels (VoC); to the emotions, the intensity of the disturbance; and, finally, to the location of the felt disturbance in the body, this phase not only optimally accesses and activates the memory for reprocessing, but is good therapy in and of itself. With the memory being activated as it is currently stored, desensitization (Phase 4) should immediately begin.

17
Phase 4

Desensitization

The desensitization phase begins with clients focusing on the image, negative cognition, and physical sensations associated with the disturbing memory while simultaneously engaging in sets of bilateral stimulation. If there is a change after a set, clinicians stay out of the way by simply saying, 'Go with that' or 'Notice that', to facilitate clients' natural processing. When there are no changes for two consecutive sets (the end of a 'channel'), clinicians guide clients back to target. After returning to target, clients report that it is positive or neutral for two consecutive sets, the subjective units of disturbance (SUD) is obtained. Processing continues with the goal of a SUD = 0, or whatever is ecologically adaptive. Then the next phase, installation of the positive cognition, can be implemented.

Dealing with Intense Emotion

The desensitization phase can be emotionally intense. Clients realize and experience now what was 'too much' at the time of the distressing event. Experiencing and processing the emotional pain resulting from the absence of the deceased sets the stage for the transformation of the relationship with the deceased through the emergence of the heartfelt memories, and it is an important step to adapting to the new world without the deceased. Examples of dealing with intense emotions are presented in transcripts in the Appendix 2. Though words cannot do justice to the emotional intensity experienced by clients (or seen in videos of clients), it is hoped the reader will get a good idea of how to interact with clients during an intense session and keep clients within the window of tolerance.

Because of the intensity, clients may become *hyperaroused* (i.e., anxious, overwhelmed) or *hypoaroused* (i.e., numb, emotionally flat, shutdown). Also, blocked processing is often evidenced by headaches or body aches that

EMDR Therapy Treatment for Grief and Mourning. Roger M. Solomon, Oxford University Press. © Roger M. Solomon 2024.
DOI: 10.1093/oso/9780198881360.003.0018

intensify with continued bilateral stimulation. There are several choices to bring clients back into the window of tolerance:

- *Alter the length and speed of bilateral stimulation*—Slower and shorter sets (e.g., 4–8 passes) can also help clients get through intense processing moments. These sets may help clients stay more present and avoid being swept away by emotion. On the other hand, when emotion is intense, and clients can stay present, clinicians can do longer sets. Shapiro (1995, 2001, 2018) offered the metaphor to demonstrate the fastest way to get a car through a tunnel is to keep your foot on the accelerator. Up and down (vertical) movements can be soothing, and help when clients are experiencing uncomfortable physical sensations such as a headache. Shapiro (2018) pointed out that the vertical bilateral stimulation may help lower arousal, but is not usually used for reprocessing.
- *Nurture the client through*—During sets with intense emotion, clinicians, in low, soothing tones, can encourage clients to go through the process. Two ways to nurture clients through are to help clients *get distance* from the material and for clinicians to *join* clients on their emotional journey. To help get some distance from the material, clinicians can say, 'Just notice the scenery passing by.' This is again a reference to Shapiro's train metaphor (i.e., being on a train and watching the scenery pass by; 1995, 2001, 2018). Joining with clients is also important, letting clients know they are understood and not going through this process—you are there with them. Clinicians can also offer soothing words to join with clients, such as, 'I know it hurts, I know it's very painful.' 'I'm here with you.' Further, it is helpful if clinicians maintain a compassionate expression. The author has been told by some clients that a concerned expression and open, accepting posture help clients get through the intense moments. Clinicians join clients in the journey, and if clients go through hell, clinicians accompany clients through hell, and to the other side.
- *Relaxing or soothing imagery*—Therapists can assist clients in accessing a previously established safe/calm state or resource states (e.g., spiritual figure, symbol of strength and courage), or doing some relaxation breathing in between sets can also be helpful to clients experiencing 'too much'.
- *Increase talking between sets*—Talking more in between sets can also help during emotional processing. Encouraging clients to describe more

about what is happening and engaging in a therapeutic dialogue may help clients stay more present and slow down the pace of processing.

- *Returning to target more frequently provides structure and containment, and may limit the opening up distressing information.*
- *Eye movement desensitization (EMD)* (Shapiro, 1989, 2018)—EMD is a procedure where clients are brought back to the target image and negative cognition, and a SUD is taken after every set. This strategy, keeping the focus on a specific moment, can be containing, preventing other material from opening up.
- *Focused processing*: The EMDR Institute training manual (2021) describes focused processing, with clinicians taking clients back to target frequently can be containing, prevent other associations form arising. and keep the focus on the target. If the emotional material that is arising goes beyond the client's integrative capacity, returning to target more often can provide structure and containment. This is similar to EMD, but the client is not necessarily brought back to target after each set of BLS.
- *Think of the loved one (elicit inner representation)*—It is common that intense, raw felt motion is experienced during processing. Usually after the processing of this emotional pain, adaptive information may start to link in, often in the form of heartfelt memories. There have been many occasions when clients are experiencing painful emotions that do not seem to be resolving. It is helpful, in most instances, to have clients think of the loved one as this often leads to positive, meaningful memories arising, which are helpful to clients. The reason this may happen is that the emergence of such memories is the natural pattern of resolution when reprocessing the emotional pain of loss. After reprocessing a sufficient amount of the emotional pain, thinking of the loved one will stimulate positive memories, which facilitates integration of the loss. Then, clients can return to the target and resume processing. There have been times, this author has observed, that asking clients to think of the loved one results in the continuing of emotional pain. This occurs when there are more painful emotions or distressing memories that need to be reprocessed. Indeed, there are many clients who continue to experience significant pain when thinking of the loved one. As described in earlier chapters, it is important to assess and process earlier memories of loss, trauma, negative memories involving the deceased, or early child attachment memories that may underlie the current pain. This can be helpful when processing is blocked and will be illustrated below.

Blocked Processing or When Processing Gets Stuck

Blocked processing is evidenced by clients' looping (i.e., going around and around in the same memory network with no new information or perspective linking in). Clients may be experiencing distress at an emotional and a somatic level (e.g., headaches, stomach aches) or there is no feeling at all (i.e., numbing). Continued BLS may not lead to a shift or may intensify the distress. Inquiring about what is being experienced when the processing is stuck or going back to target and exploring what is there, often clarifies the cause of the blocked processing.

Processing may be blocked for many reasons:

1. *Feeder memories*—these are earlier memories) related to previous trauma, loss or attachment-related memories (feeder memories) are being triggered as described in Chapter 10.
2. *Emotional impact*—the emotional impact may be too much, such as, it is too much to realize the loved one is dead and not coming back
3. *Blocking beliefs*—these are negative beliefs which block progress, such as the fear of losing connection.

Feeder Memories

Reprocessing can be stalled or blocked because earlier trauma, losses, or attachment and developmentally related memories are being evoked. Shapiro (1995, 2001, 2018) called these 'feeder' memories, earlier memories that contribute to the current dysfunction and block processing. Doing a 'floatback' (clients focus on the negative thought, feelings, and sensations and float back to an earlier time) or affect scan procedure (clients focus on the negative sensations and scan back to an earlier time) may reveal the feeder memory. After reprocessing the underlying memory, often the target memory has lost its emotional charge, and reprocessing can be completed.

Example 1(Feeder Memory): Michelle became stuck when processing the death of her sister. A floatback procedure with, 'I am all alone', went to a memory of her mother coming late to pick her up from the baby sitter (a frequent occurrnce). Reprocessing continued focusing on this memory. Then the original target involving her sister was successfully processed.

Often identifying the memories underlying the blocked processing has a 'delinking' effect: that is, it disconnects the underlying memories from the target memory, allowing the reprocessing of the target to continue to reprocess (Laliotis, 2020). With Pierre, described in a case example above, an option would have been to explain that the childhood memories were being triggered and blocking the processing. Saying something to the effect, 'These are important memories that are coming up. For now, let's put them aside, understanding we will come back to them later.' Then going back to the target memory may have resulted in continued reprocessing. This is illustrated in the case example presented below.

Example 2 (Delinking): Emanuela's sister died of cancer. Emanuela, a physician, thought she should have been able to do more for her sister. For the next year, Emanuela was angry and argumentative with people. She recognized there was not more that could be done, but still felt guilty about not being able to do more for her sister. As children, the parents worked long hours and Emanuela often took care of her sister. When processing a scene of her sister suffering just before her death, the processing became stuck. The clinician inquired what was coming up. Emanuela described her guilt for not being able to do more for sister, especially being a physician. A brief discussion connected this concern to childhood, with Emanuela understanding the connection. The clinician said this issue and underlying memories regarding childhood were important, but for now, they could be put to the side for another time. With Emanuela's agreement, she was guided by the clinician back to the target memory, which then she could fully process.

Blocking Beliefs

Typical examples of beliefs that can block the process are the following: 'I deserved this tragedy.' 'It is always my fault.' And/or 'I can't live without him/her.' Blocking beliefs result from memory networks containing maladaptively stored memories that are triggered by a tragic event/s and may be evoked during memory processing. For example, if there is a belief regarding helplessness, powerlessness, or lack of safety, explore the past memories underlying these beliefs. As previously discussed, attachment-related memories may underlie such beliefs, and the distressing memories triggered by the loss need to be identified and processed. For example, people who believe it is all their fault (when the loss is indeed not their fault) may have difficulty accepting that bad things can happen beyond their control, or believe they have to do everything right (e.g., be perfect), or that they could have or should have done more. It may be too difficult to handle the feelings of helplessness that may accompany the reality that there was nothing more that could be done. The past memories underlying such beliefs needs to be explored and processed.

Example 3 (Blocking Belief): An army unit was ambushed in Afghanistan and was able to repel the enemy. The medic needed to help two of his buddies who were hurt badly, and he had to choose which one to help first. He knew the injuries from one of his buddies were going to be fatal, whereas the other buddy, though badly hurt, could make it. The medic chose to help the soldier who could live. He said to the other soldier, who seemed unconscious, that he would be right back, he was just going to attend to the other solider. This soldier, with his eyes closed, grunted, letting the medic know he heard him. By the time the medic could attend to this soldier, he was dead. The medic felt very guilty that he could not have done more, despite his fellow soldiers, superiors, and knowledgeable medical staff telling him he did a great job and that nothing could have been done for his friend. Three years later, he received EMDR therapy. The processing got blocked with him looping on his guilt for not being able to save both his friends. The clinician explored the block and the client realized he had a blocking belief, 'I have to be perfect.' In discussing this, and how during childhood to be perfect to please the parents was an important survival strategy, he said, 'My father never told me he loved me, and I tried so hard to be loved.' This was the root of the believe of having to be perfect to be loved. After some discussion and highlighting the importance of this insight and putting it aside for later, processing the target memory resumed. The memory was successfully processed, with the positive cognition, 'I made a good decision and did the best I could.' He ended with a validity of cognition (VOC) of 7. Further treatment focused on processing childhood attachment (trauma) memories.

Example 4 (Blocked Processing): Pierre's son, aged 17 years, died in an auto accident. He was in the hospital for 8 days before he died. Seven months after the death, Pierre sought EMDR treatment for the trauma of the death that included the police doing the death notification, images of his son in the hospital, including the moment when his son passed. When processing the moment his son died, Pierre got stuck at the moment he tried to talk to his son, and he could not answer. When asked What was the worst part of that? he replied, 'I failed him.' Cognitive interweaves regarding his responsibility (e.g., what was under his control what was beyond his control) did not help. Then the origins of 'I am a failure' were explored. This brought up memories of his mother scolding him as a child, saying, 'Can't you ever do things right' with a tone of anger and disgust in her voice. After processing, several childhood memories over the next two sessions, he was able to return to the scene of his son's dying and process through it.

Emotional Impact Is Overwhelming

EMDR processing, as described above, can evoke the raw, felt emotion that comes with the realization that the death is real and a loved one is never coming back. The world as the client knows it is shattered, and it is too much to take in, and this causes processing to get blocked. Parents are losing the object of their caregiving and love. This can be devastating. Clients with an anxious attachment style may feel frightened and power-less, imagining life without the loved one, and experience hyperarousal. Clients with avoidant attachment style may shut down, experiencing hypoarousal, because emotions are starting to surface. In these instances, the strategies described above for *dealing with intense emotion* can be implemented. Further, it is important to pace therapy according to clients' ability to stay present. Alternating sessions of memory reprocessing, stabi-lization (e.g., safe/calm place, resourcing), supportive listening, teaching skills, problem-solving, and the like can be provided according to clients' needs and readiness.

Fear That Processing the Emotional Pain Will Lead to the Loss of Connection

Clients may feel connected to the deceased loved one through their pain, and fear that EMDR reprocessing may lead to decreasing the pain and result in forgetting about the deceased, or mean they do not love the deceased. Pain becomes the attachment to the deceased and may be the expression of love that has been lost when the loved one died. Losing the pain means losing the connection and leaving the loved one behind. Clinicians can explain during the Preparation & Stabilization phase and again, as a cognitive interweave, the following points (as appropriate for their clients):

1. *EMDR as a natural process*—explain that EMDR is a natural process and clients will not lose what is important, needed, or what is true.
2. *Connect to positive memories*—clinical experience and research (Sprang, 2001) have shown that EMDR results in the emergence of meaningful, positive memories that provide a sense of connection through love.

3. *Transformation of pain*—processing the pain is not letting go of the loved one, it is the transformation of the relationship from connection through pain to connection through love experienced through heart felt memories.

A case example was presented in Chapter 12, Developing a New Relationship with the Deceased with Rifca, Case Example 3. Another example follows:

Example 5 (Connection Through Pain): Anne's baby died when he was 2 weeks old. Twelve years later, the trauma of this loss was still present, despite seeing several therapists over the years. She had been told to 'find the meaning', but this was not helpful. During EMDR processing, intense emotion arose, and continued for around 30 minutes. The therapist then asked her to think of her baby (as explained above in 'Think of the Loved One' in the Dealing with Intense Emotion section). Positive memories arose such as holding her baby, and feeding her baby. However, she suddenly felt 'a crush' of pain. This was explored and she said that she believed that if she lost the pain (the crush), she would lose her connection to the baby. For Anne, the crush was her connection. First, the therapist explained that she would not lose anything that she needs. Next, the therapist asked her to try an experiment focusing on both the positive images and feelings that had arisen, and the crush, and see what happens, and we could evaluate the results. Focusing on both the positive feelings and the crush led to more positive feelings and memories coming up. She realized she was still a mother to her baby. Though she initially found it was confusing how she could have a relationship with a dead person, she did feel a connection through the heart felt emotions that accompanied her memories. The transcript of this session is in appendix 2.

Cognitive Interweaves

In terms of the Adaptive Information Processing (AIP) model, processing involves the linking in of adaptively stored information into memory networks which hold maladaptively stored information. When the processing is blocked and no new associations are developing after several sets, it can be assumed that adaptive information is not linking in. A cognitive interweave involves making a suggestion, offering information, or asking something that will evoke the next level of information the client needs to process the memory. Interweaves can be used when the client is *looping* (i.e., going 'round and round' the same memory network with no substantial change taking place), when *emotional distress is too much*, to *increase generalization* through the memory work, and to help *close an incomplete session*. Below, the themes that guide cognitive interweaves will be discussed. These are the same themes used for negative and positive cognitions: responsibility/self-defectiveness, safety, control/choices, and attachment/belonging.

RESPONSIBILITY/SELF-DEFECTIVENESS
Clients may be stuck in a feeling of guilt over not being present at the death or not being a 'good enough' child/spouse/parent. Indeed, guilt can be the price one pays to feel in control and realizing, 'It's not my fault', and can precipitate a confrontation of the human condition of vulnerability and lack of control over tragedy. Cognitive interweaves can be helpful in restoring a balance between knowing what was under one's control and what was beyond one's control.

> *Example 6 (It's My Fault): One client, Rita, got stuck when processing the death of her husband who had died by heart attack. He had mild chest pains before leaving for work, but neither she nor the husband believed it was serious as these pains were not unusual. She was stuck on the thought, 'It's my fault (I should have known better)/I am a bad wife.' Asking her, 'What was going on in your mind at the time?' And following up with: 'And, did it make sense then?' helped Rita understand that her actions/decisions were reasonable given her and her husband's frames of mind (e.g., what was known) at the time.*

It is not uncommon that there is a great deal of guilt experienced for giving permission to take a loved one off of life support. Clients can think, 'It's my fault/I'm bad/I killed my father/mother.' An interweave pertaining to the origin of the decision/on whose recommendation was life support turned off, can be helpful.

> *Example 7 (Responsibility: 'I Caused My Mother to Die'): Based on the physician's saying there was no more hope, Marion made the decision to turn off life support for her unconscious mother who had deteriorated significantly with cancer. Though Marian knew this is what her mother would have wanted, Marian felt guilty because ultimately, 'It was my decision for my mother to die ... I was the one who ended her life.' During processing, focusing on the moment she made the decision, associations pertaining to events leading up to the mother's hospitalization, including the moment when she had to be put on life support, she got stuck on, 'I made the decision, she died because of me.' When asked the basis of this decision, she replied, 'The doctor said there was no hope, and I sensed this as well.' With further processing, the client could accept the situation, 'It was inevitable, and the people who loved her were with her when she died.'*

Example 8 (Responsibility: 'I Am a Murderer'): In a similar situation, Josephina's husband was murdered during a robbery. She made a decision to turn off life support, given he was braindead and the physician said there was no hope. When Josephina got stuck on feeling like a murderer herself, she was asked, 'What was the basis of your decision?' which helped her gain a more objective perspective, that she could only respond to the situation, she did not cause it, and, 'I made the right decision, but I don't have to like it.' This enabled processing to complete with a SUD equal to 2 (i.e., which was deemed ecologically appropriate because it was indeed a distressing situation), a positive cognition of, 'I did what I had to do', and a VOC equal to 7. This example, with the session ending with a SUD of 2 also illustrates EMDR does not take away appropriate emotion.

The client may feel guilty for not being able to prevent the death or do more (i.e., sense of helplessness). Interweaves to help clients gain a realistic perspective regarding what can or cannot be controlled or what is foreseeable or unforeseeable can be helpful.

Example 9 (Responsibility: 'I Should Have Prevented It'): Michele was the father of a police officer. Prior to going to work, the son was working at Michele's gas station before going on duty, something he routinely did. He told Michele he needed to go to his police job a little early. The son left and was killed several hours later. Michele felt guilty for not keeping him working at the gas station, and became stuck, as he put it, 'I could have prevented it by asking him to stay longer.' The clinician used a pattern that is very helpful in cases where the client is overtaking responsibility (i.e., taking responsibility for things beyond one's control) and which can result in guilt and/or helplessness: 'Who had control over what happened to your son.' Michele realizing the circumstances were beyond his control, experienced a deeper level of pain that comes with the realization his son died and he could not help. After going through this painful session, Michele had a balanced perspective that something awful happened that he could not foresee or prevent. Further EMDR sessions to deal with the loss enabled an adaptive inner representation composed of loving memories of working together. At the end of treatment, eight sessions in all, Michele reflected that this was the worst thing that had ever happened to him, but it does not take away from what his son meant to him or what they shared together, which enabled him to carry on and go forward.

SAFETY

Issues of safety, including awareness of one's mortality, may arise when the client's own vulnerability gets triggered.

> *Example 10 (Safety: Vulnerability/Mortality Is Triggered): Alberto felt an acute sense of vulnerability after his father died. When reprocessing the moment he received the news, he got stuck when he realized, 'It's going to happen to me too. I'm going to die.' The interweave that worked was, 'Yes, we all do, it was your father's turn now.' The client could then respond, 'It's not my turn yet, but some day it will be. I know I have to deal with that.' This got him through processing the memory. Further sessions dealt with his childhood memories of fear and lack of safety, which had been triggered by his father's death.*

A person can also feel vulnerable and insecure in functioning without the loved one. The loved one may have been the person whom the mourner depended on for security and it may be difficult to feel safe now that the loved one is gone. Fear about being alone or coping without the loved one can evoke more fear and vulnerability. Interweaves evoking strengths, resources that have been previously established, present abilities, or capability to learn how to deal with issues can be helpful. As the above example illustrates, previous memories (e.g., losses, trauma or attachment-related) underlying a sense of vulnerability need to be identified and reprocessed.

CONTROL/CHOICES

Mourners can get stuck in the powerlessness and lack of control experienced when nothing could be done to save their loved one or prevent the death. 'Is there anything more that you realistically could have done?' or 'Is there any realistic way you could have known about . . .' or 'What was under your control and what was beyond your control?' As illustrated above, these interweaves are helpful when dealing with issues of guilt that arise from overwhelming responsibility. Clinicians can also help clients realize that they are not always in control or have that kind of power (e.g., 'It can be hard to take in that there are times we are helpless and vulnerable.'). Along these lines, it is useful to say (especially with first responders), when a client is feeling helpless, 'You have found the boundary where being a human being ends and God begins. Some things are not possible for human beings to do or change.' Another strategy is to remind clients about what was done to deal with the situation or ask them to describe their response to the situation, moment by moment.

> *Example 11 (Control: Stuck on Feeling Helpless): Joan, aged 38 years, watched her father die a painful death over time. She felt helpless and had awful images of her father's suffering. The processing became stuck with her feeling of helplessness as she watched him suffer. When asked what she did when she saw her father suffer, she described how she would talk to him, hold his hand, and try to ascertain if there was anything he*

needed. This interweave enabled her to realize her caring attitude and behaviours were indeed something and a way of showing her love.

Example 12 (Control: Stuck on Feeling Helpless): Richard, aged 15 years, attempted CPR and heart massage when his father had a heart attack. Unfortunately, his father died in the ambulance. Richard felt guilty, believing the death may have been due to his inexperience and from his using a wrong technique. He did receive valid information from physicians that the heart attack was quite massive and even the most experienced person applying CPR/heart massage would not have changed the outcome. During the EMDR processing on doing CPR, Richard became stuck on his powerlessness (i.e., 'I felt so helpless, nothing I did was working.') The interweave utilized with him involved going over the actions and decisions he made moment by moment as soon as his father collapsed (e.g., calling emergency services, immediately starting resuscitation procedures). Further, the clinician asked, 'Did you give up?' to which Richard replied, 'No.' With these interweaves, his sense of helplessness lifted.

CONNECTION AND BELONGING

When clients are experiencing intense emotional pain which is looping, asking them to think of the loved one may evoke positive, meaningful memories of the deceased. The positive memories can then be enhanced. This was illustrated with Anne, in Case number 5. Issues of attachment and belonging can be manifested in populations that are marginalized and be experienced as, 'I don't belong' or 'I cannot connect.' Reprocessing memories related to these issues can help people reach positive cognitions of, 'I do belong (I deserve to belong), or I am (or can be) connected to others.

Example 13 (Connection: 'I Cannot Connect'): Atsa's father died of Covid-19. Atsa, a Native American entered treatment 8 months later. He was divorced, with two teenage children. He had grown up in a big city, away from his tribe. The father had always taken pride in his heritage. Atsa, having little contact with the tribe had always had a sense of being different, and not belonging. Treatment first focused on the acute trauma of the father's death, occurring 7 weeks following onset of symptoms. After reprocessing their last conversation, he had with his father (online before his father went on ventilation), Atsa became more aware of the isolation he had felt his whole life. He had friends and a good relationship with his children, but

> the death of his father left him feeling empty and remembering how he felt different when growing up, and this feeling was felt more strongly now. It was decided to focus on this issue by reprocessing child memories central to his belief, 'I am different.' EMDR treatment targeted a memory when he was 8 years old, watching a movie about Native Americans. When reprocessing this memory, other memories came up where he felt different (e.g., different from classmates in school, and in the church he belonged to). When the processing became stuck on a feeling of isolation (no change after two sets), the clinician provided a cognitive interweave by asking what his father might tell him about his ancestry and heritage. Atsa then remembered a conversation with his father during adolescence where his father told him of his own father and grandfather, and other relatives, and how they had come to where they are today. Atsa remembered his father's pride in telling him this, and now Ralph looked at this conversation in a new way—he did have a heritage as a Native American, and he did have a place in his current life now. This realization helped fully reprocess the target memory with a positive cognition of, 'I do have a place and a heritage.' Further meaningful memories with his father arose giving him a deeper sense of connection to his father, which were enhanced with further sets of bilateral stimulation (see Chapter 18).

This example illustrates how a loss can evoke issues stemming from the past. Relevant memories need to be identified and reprocessed as seen in the example above. Atsa had felt isolated due to his heritage, and these issues were evoked by the death of his father. When processing a childhood memory became stuck, an interweave involving his father elicited meaningful memories that helped Atsa feel a sense of connection and belonging. Though beyond the scope of this book to fully discuss, it must be noted that many people are negatively impacted by macro- and microaggression, which can complicate grief and mourning.

'What Do You Want to Keep? What Do You Want to Let Go of?'

If processing is blocked, asking clients, 'What do you want to keep?' And/or 'What do you want to let go of,' can be helpful (Lazrove, cited in Shapiro & Forrest, 1997) may help clients get in touch with a positive sense of connection. Clients may answer, they want to keep the happy memories and feelings and let go of the distress, nightmares, for example. Then clinicians can say, 'Think of that' and provide further sets of bilateral stimulation. Getting in touch with what they 'want to keep/let go of' can put clients in touch with positive emotions and memories, and differentiate it from the pain of loss and negative reactions.

> *Case Example 14 ('What do you want to keep... ?'): Della's teenage daughter died of complications from surgery. Reprocessing the trauma of the death a year later (the doctor telling her the news) was a tearful experience. When Della reported she felt 'stuck in my tears', she was asked, 'What do you want to keep?' Della replied, 'the love, the memory of brushing her hair while she was in the hospital, and memories of being home laughing together when watching their favourite television show.' When asked, 'What do you want to let go?' Della replied, 'the pain and emptiness'. The clinician then asked her to think of Della, remembering what she wanted to keep and let go of, and did another set of bilateral stimulation. Della felt more in touch with her love, positive memories, and sense of connection, and less of the pain. Processing continued resulting in more positive memories and emotions arising. Though missing her daughter continued, Della no longer felt 'stuck in tears'.*

What Do You Want to Say to or Do for the Deceased?

Imaginal interactions can be a helpful intervention for grief. Having a conversation, writing a letter and reading it (in imagination) to the deceased, performing a healing ritual, and the like, can be healing. Bilateral stimulation can be helpful to enhance the positive aspects of such imagery. Such interventions are helpful in the context of overall treatment, but given this book is focusing on the standard EMDR protocol, such imaginal interactions are presented as a cognitive interweave to facilitate blocked processing.

When clients are blocked asking them, 'What do you want to say to or do for (name the deceased)?' This can evoke a healing outpouring of sadness, anger, guilt, and even joy (for having known you/loved you). BLS can be added to enhance this interweave.

> *Case Example 15 (What Would You Want to Say or Do in Regard to the Deceased?): James's 28-year-old daughter Jean died of Covid. The death was sudden, with no chance to be physically present when she died. Fourteen months after the death, James requested treatment, feeling sad, guilty, numb, experiencing body aches and having difficulty sleeping. After two sessions of history taking and preparation & stabilization. EMDR therapy started with a memory of his daughter being unconscious in the hospital and realizing 'she is not going to make it'. When processing got stuck, James was asked, 'What would you want to say to Jean?' For the next 25 minutes there was a tearful outpouring of love, anger at her premature death, moments of regret and a tearful apology, and meaningful memories, and regrets of her death. At the end of the session, James reported a significant reduction in body tension. The loss was still terrible, but he felt he could better carry his grief with him.*

> Case Example 16 (What Would You Want to Do for the Deceased?): Carrie's son, Peter, was killed in battle. She sought treatment after a month, with EMDR therapy beginning after three months. The first target being an intrusive image of her son dead on the ground. The image was graphic with a grimace of pain and blood. Reprocessing got stuck. She was asked, 'What would you want to say or do for Peter?' She then imagined herself at his side, holding his hand, saying she loved him and that he was not alone now. Then the image of his face shifted, and he now had a peaceful expression, without blood. Carrie felt more at peace at the end of the session.

New Information and Perspectives

Sometimes clients are perplexed, confused, or even frightened about what they are experiencing, and may need explanations or new information. For example, it is not unusual to have a vivid conversation with the loved one or imagine him/her/they saying something that feels quite real. Some clients question, 'Is this real?'

> Example 17 (New Information): Oliver, during EMDR reprocessing of a memory related to his father's death, experienced his father telling him, it is okay for him to go on. Oliver reported he literally heard his father telling him this, and was frightened. The clinician explained this was a common experience and in our grieving for the deceased loved one, conversations can indeed feel quite real, and are meaningful, and one's inner experience can be honoured. After another set of bilateral stimulation, he said, 'My father is still helping me', and he felt a strong sense of peace.

Evoking the Adaptive Inner Representation: A Cognitive Interweave to Deal with Fear of Losing Connection or When There Is Intense Emotion That Is not Resolving

Processing the 'raw felt emotion' seems to lead to the linking in of a heart felt and meaningful memories. If clients are experiencing emotion and it is not shifting after several sets, one option is to ask clients to think of their loved one. Theoretically, if sufficient emotion has been realized (processed), then adaptive information, usually experienced as positive images and memories, is experienced, which can then be enhanced with bilateral stimulation. Further, if clients are worried about losing their connection, asking clients to think of their loved one can evoke the positive memories/images/emotions, enabling clients to feel the positive connection. Clients can further be asked to recognize these memories/images sensations and know that they will always be with them. One clinician asked the client who was worried about losing connection to the loved one, 'Can this ever go away?' When the client affirmed it felt as they would always be with them, further sets of bls enhanced the positive felt sense of connection. If asking clients elicit continued negative material, then perhaps further sets of bls can facilitate processing, or the other strategies described above can be utilized. Example 5 illustrated this interweave, as does the case example below:

Example 18: (Evoking the Adaptive Inner Representation)

A transcript of the session is presented in the Appendix 2 (Case Example 3).

Fiona's daughter committed suicide. Fiona found her hanging and cut her down, and attempted to resuscitate her until rescue personal arrived. She had several years of treatment in the years following her daughter's death. Fiona sought EMDR treatment, 8 years following her daughter's death because she was still haunted by distressing graphic images. The session was very intense, with the client wondering if the pain will ever go away ('I live with that always, and I get better at living with it; what I don't get about working with grief is: how can that ever be okay, and how could that change.'). After several minutes of continued reprocessing and some acceptance of the circumstances, the therapist thinking she was still stuck in the pain asked her to think of her daughter, resulting in positive memories, thoughts and adaptive information about the situation linked in. Fiona was finally able to gain a sense of love and connection with her daughter, which had been immensely missed and an important therapeutic goal for her.

In summary, if a client is experiencing intense emotion that does not seem to be shifting after several sets or is worried about losing the connection, ask 'When you think of (name the loved one) what comes up/what do you experience?' If the positive images/memories/emotions come up enhance with several sets of BLS. Another option is to ask the client to experience the positive sensations and note that they will always be with the client (or ask 'Can this ever go away?'). If distressing emotions are evoked, continue processing with sets of bls, or use one of the strategies described above for blocked processing.

Getting a SUD
When clients' responses are not changing for two consecutive sets, go back to the memory and ask, 'What do you notice now?' If there is a change (i.e., another channel of association opens up), continue processing. When going back

to target elicits positive or neutral responses for two sets, then get the SUD (i.e., 'When you go back to the memory, how disturbing is it on a 0 to 10 scale, where 0 = calm or neutral and 10 = the worst it can be?') The SUD, as described above, may not get to 0, as seen in Case Example 13. If the SUD is low, clinicians can ask 'Where do you feel it in your body?' And do a set of BLS and evaluate if this is leading to change, such as lowering the SUD or the emergence of new material. Clinicians can ask 'What prevents it from going lower?' which may elicit a blocking belief, or open up another channel of association. Alternatively, ask clients 'What is different from when we started?' This question can elicit the pattern of resolution which can then be enhanced with BLS.

Example 18 (Getting to SUDs = 0): Joseph's son was badly burned in a battle. He was in a field hospital overseas for three days and died. The father felt powerless and guilty that he could not help or do anything about his son's suffering. A Skype conversation where he saw his son was suffering was the initial target with a SUD of 10. With processing, the SUD lowered to a 4, and would not go lower. Joseph was asked, 'What is different from when we started?' He responded, 'I am thinking there was nothing more I could do.' Further sets of BLS resulted in, 'It was beyond my control, all I could was be with him when he died, and I was . . . even over Skype he knew I was there, and he is at peace now.' The SUD for the moment that was targeted went down to 0.

SUD = 0 does not mean absence of emotion or that one feels good about what happened.

When getting a SUD, it can be helpful to say, 'How disturbing is it when 0 = calm, neutral, or absence of disturbance, and 10 = the worst it could be, understanding that 0 is *not the absence* of *emotion* or *mean that you feel good about what happened*; a person can experience sadness, for example, and feel calm, without undue distress thinking of a memory. Also, explain that the *SUD does not have to get to 0* when there is appropriate emotion about a tragic event. Quite often, going back to this beginning moment where processing started yields a low SUD because that moment may be reprocessed and integrated even though other emotional material (i.e., channels of association) may have opened up. That is, the emergence of emotional material can have a 'delinking' effect (see Example 2 in this chapter). Further, focusing on the initial moment the reprocessing started can also be containing, preventing other emotional material from opening up. While some clients may still experience distress while bringing up this original moment, many clients indeed are able to get to '0' for the specific moment being processed.

> *Example 19 (Ecological '0'): Estella's son was killed in a motorcycle accident. Targeting an image resulted in a series of disturbing moments coming up, and she described the hospital scene and events that took placed after the death. When the SUD was taken, the therapist asked her to go back to the moment processing began and how disturbing the moment was on the 0-to-10 scale, explaining, '0 does not mean the absence of emotion or that one feels good about it, just calm or no distress, and 10 means it is the worse it could be, Estella said, 'This will always be a horrible tragedy, but I can think about that sad moment and feel calm. . . . It's a sad '0'.*

ECOLOGICAL REASONS SUD MAY NOT GO TO 0

The SUD may not get to 0 because of ecologically appropriate and adaptive emotions. Examples are, 'I'm calmer but it's still a tragedy.' 'It's very sad.' 'A good person died.' 'An event like this will always be distressing.' 'I miss my wife/husband so much.'

When asking what prevents the SUD from going to 0, it is important to differentiate between clients with a SUD above 0 because it is *ecologically adaptive and appropriate*, and clients whose SUD does not go to 0 because of underlying emotional material or blocking belief (e.g., 'If I go to zero, I will forget about my loved one.'). It is not always easy to distinguish between the two. When asking what prevents the SUD from going lower, and getting a response from clients, add another set of bilateral stimulation ('Go with that') and see if new associations and insights emerge. Many clients say they do not think the SUD will go lower but when another set is added, new associations emerge that with further reprocessing often result in a SUD of 0 for the specific memory targeted. When there are ecological reasons for the SUD not going to 0, further sets of BLS often result in the clients reporting that the emotion or perspective they have feels more congruent and appropriate, which lets the clinician know the SUD is ecologically adaptive.

> *Case Example 20 (Ecologically Adaptive SUD Above 0): Louie was processing a memory of being at his wife's bedside when she died. The SUD went from a SUD of 8 to a 2 and would not go further. When asked what prevents it from going lower Louie reported her suffering is over but it was still an awful moment. With continued processing Louie reported, 'It is still a 2, and this feels right, I still feel the loss and that will never go away, but I can live with this.'*

An incomplete session is still helpful. Integration of a traumatic memory can take many sessions and be emotionally painful, but is still helpful. One client was very happy to end a session with a SUD of 5, as described below.

> *Example 21 (Incomplete but Helpful Session): Casey, a police officer, was in a traffic accident where his partner and best friend was killed, and he received only minor injuries. When reprocessing this memory, the SUD started at a 10 and got down to a 5. It would not go lower because the memory was still distressing. However, Casey reported, 'I am happy, I could not live with a 10, but I can live with a 5.' With more sessions, the memory was fully reprocessed.*

Emergence of Positive Memories

As previously discussed, and illustrated in previous case examples and those in the appendix, EMDR therapy often results in the emergence of positive heartfelt emotions as an adaptive inner representation forms, transforming the relationship to the deceased. It can be helpful to continue to provide sets of BLS as the positive memories are coming up, enhancing the positive meaning and sense of connection. This will be further discussed in Chapter 18. It must be emphasized that is it is not abnormal or pathological, if no memories are coming up, nor is the emergence of positive memories always an indication of positive adaptation. It is possible that mourners can avoid realizing the full impact of the loss and the full implication that the loss is permanent by focusing on positive memories. As stated in Chapter 7, the continuing bond is adaptive only if mourners fully accept the permanence of the loss in all of its implications.

Summary

The desensitization phase is usually the longest phase of processing. Intense emotions can arise and then give way to heartfelt, meaningful memories that form an adaptive inner representation. The transformation of the relationship from loving in presence to loving in absence takes place with a sense of connection. Negative memories that emerge, along with other negative memories involving the deceased, also need to be processed. This chapter covered strategies for dealing with intense emotions and how to navigate through blocked processing. EMDR therapy does not take away appropriate emotion: hence, the SUD may not go to 0 for ecological reasons.

18
Phases 5–8

Installation, Body Scan, Closure, and Re-evaluation

The installation and body scan phases finish the active processing of the memory. The closure phase ensures stability at the end of the session. The re-evaluation phase assesses if treatment effects have been maintained, and, based on clients' responses to treatment, the direction of the session is determined.

Phase 5: Installation

The installation phase builds resilience. In the desensitization phase, adaptive information links into the memory networks holding the maladaptively stored information. Reprocessing continues in the installation phase, with the positive cognition (first checked for appropriateness) linked to the original target, and enhanced by further sets of bilateral stimulation (BLS). This further integrates the memory into the wider memory network and provides a basis for adaptive behavior in the future (enhanced by the installation of the future template). This is successfully accomplished by the following:

- *Link positive cognition (PC))** and Target*—Linking the positive cognition identified in the target assessment phase with the original targeted memory and determining its continued appropriateness (i.e., "Do the words (repeat original PC) still fit or is there another positive statement that fits even better?") Not uncommonly, a new PC arises after the desensitization phase.

Example 1 (Link PC and Target): In the example of Sharon (Presented in Appendix 2), whose son was killed in an automobile accident, the negative cognition (NC) and PC) were, "I can't live with this" and "I can go on and thrive." After finishing the

EMDR Therapy Treatment for Grief and Mourning. Roger M. Solomon, Oxford University Press. © Roger M. Solomon 2024.
DOI: 10.1093/oso/9780198881360.003.0019

> desensitization, Sharon's PC evolved into another PC: "I can learn to live with this and it's
> honoring his life." This new PC was then installed.

- *Validity of Cognition (VoC)*—Using the VoC scale to measure the strength
  of the desired PC (i.e., *"When you think of the memory, how true do the
  words,* (repeat the PC above) *feel to you now on a scale from 1 to 7 where 1
  feels completely false, and 7 feels completely true?"*).
- *PC + Target + BLS*—pairing the chosen PC with the original memory and
  utilizing BLS to enhance and strengthen it (i.e., "Hold the memory and
  those words (repeat PC) together." BLS is applied).
- *Tracking*—After each set, the clinician asks, "What do you notice now."
  BLS continues as long as the material is getting more adaptive, until the
  VoC no longer strengthens. The goal of this phase is a VoC of 7 or whatever is ecologically appropriate.

When VoC < 7

Presence of Residual Tension
If clients respond, "I still feel some tension," to one of the queries above, more
reprocessing is needed. When reprocessing continues, new channels of association may emerge. If nothing emerges, clinicians can explore the tension by
asking "Where do you feel it in your body? What images or thoughts are related to it?," and/or by facilitating a floatback and/or affect scan to uncover the
source of the tension (i.e., blocking belief, unresolved memory) so reprocessing can continue to completion.

Presence of Blocking Belief

If a blocking belief emerges (e.g., "I don't deserve to be a 7."), therapists and
clients can explore this belief to find its origins and associations with the original memory and PC.

> Example 2 (Blocking Belief): Ilina's brother died of a massive heart attack while at a
> family gathering. Family members did CPR, called the ambulance, and did all they could
> think of to do. Her NC was, "I'm inadequate," because of her inability at the time to help
> him, and the PC, "I am okay (I did what I could do)" because of the cognitive knowledge

that his death was beyond her control. There was nothing she could have differently that would have saved him. The subjective units of disturbance (SUD) went down
to an ecologically appropriate 1 during the desensitization phase, but during the installation phase the VoC was stuck at a level 5. When asked what prevented it from
going higher (e.g., "What keeps it a 5?"), she said, "I don't deserve to feel okay when my
brother is dead." The therapist continued doing further sets of BLS, but progress was
still blocked. Then, the clinician facilitated the floatback technique with Illina focused
on the negative belief, "I don't deserve to feel okay, and emotions and sensations." What
emerged was a childhood memory where her brother was punished for hitting her when
she was the one who originally provoked him. After reprocessing this memory, the VoC
of 7 was finally achieved for the original memory. Ilina was able to realize, "It's horrible
he is dead, but I know, and I believe he knew, I was there for him." It should be noted
that reprocessing the memory, and having a VoC of 7 does not take away appropriate
emotion. The death was still horrible to Ilene, but now she could think about her brother
without the guilt.

Presence of Other Negative Memories

Negative memories may surface during the installation phase and need to be
reprocessed.

Example 3 (Other Negative Memories): Giovanni's wife died of heart attack. The memory
of seeing her in the hospital was targeted, with a NC of, "I'm powerless," and a PC of,
"I did all that I could do." The memory processed to a 0, but the VoC would only get to
5. When asked what prevents the VoC from going higher, Giovanni replied that he was
thinking of other memories regarding his wife where, "I could have done better. I did not
do my best." The opening of this memory network, and identification of specific memories provided a helpful direction for further EMDR treatment.

Ecological Appropriateness

A VoC may not get to 7 for ecological reasons because, in the aftermath of a
loss, there may be residual sadness, anger, fear, guilt, or self-doubt, or more
time may be needed to reflect on the loss or to see what happens in the everyday life after the session.

Example 4 (Ecological Appropriateness): Maria's brother committed suicide after suffering from depression for many years. When reprocessing a memory of a conversation where she saw how hopeless he felt, the NC was, "I'm inadequate," with the PC of, "I'm capable." The SUD got to 1 with the realization, "I know I can only do so much and am not responsible for his action, but it is still sad." The VoC would only get to 6, "I know I have limitations, and perhaps there were other avenues that I was not aware of." For Maria, a VoC of 7 would mean she did not have limitations, so the VoC of 6 was ecologically appropriate.

Phase 6: Body Scan

The body scan is the final opportunity for any residual negative elements associated with the targeted disturbing memory to be identified, reprocessed, and transmuted into adaptive learning experiences. Once the SUD = 0 (or ecologically appropriate) and the VoC = 7 (or ecologically appropriate), clients are instructed to pair the original memory with the desired PC and scans for bodily discomfort (e.g., tension, tightness, and unusual sensation). If positive or warm body sensations arise, they too can be enhanced and strengthened by further sets of BLS. It is common that positive memories arise, and these can be enhanced with additional sets of BLS, further strengthening the adaptive inner representation (see the section below, An Additional Step: Enhancement of the Adaptive Inner Representation). If there is some tension, more sets of BLS can be administered until the discomfort dissipates. If administering additional sets of BLS does not alleviate negative body sensations, then explore with clients what is happening. Perhaps there is a blocking belief or a feeder memory (an earlier memory feeding the current discomfort) that needs to be reprocessed. If other memories arise, and there is time in the session, therapists are encouraged to continue with clients' reprocessing. However, if there is little time left in the session, and there are indications that other emotional material may arise, it is advisable for clinicians to close the session with the affect management strategies taught in the Preparation & Stabilization phase.

Example 5 (Body Scan): Giorgio's father died a peaceful death at the hospital. Giorgio was present and it was quite a shock to see his father pass away. It reminded Giorgio of his vulnerability, and how, ultimately, we all die. The NC was, "I am not safe," and the PC

> was, "I am safe today." The memory of his father's passing was desensitized to a SUD of 0 and the PC installed to a VoC of 7. During the body scan, tension was felt. Upon exploring this, Giorgio reported it was fear. An affect scan (letting the feeling take him back to the past) revealed childhood memories of a lack of safety. With little time remaining in the session, the clinician explained that these memories could be explored at the next session. The session was closed with relaxation techniques and a safe place. In further sessions these childhood memories were reprocessed.

Note: SUDs may not get to 0 and VoC may not go to 7 because the sadness and sorrow are ecologically appropriate. These appropriate feelings and sensations that accompany a loss may be felt during the body scan. Alternative directions, that take this into account, are the following: "Taking into account the appropriate emotions and body sensations, when thinking of the memory and the positive words (repeat PC), are there other sensations or tensions that you notice?" This may help clients differentiate the tension from the memory from the ecologically appropriate sensations.

An Additional Step: Enhancement of the Adaptive Inner Representation

One of the results of eye movement desensitization and reprocessing (EMDR) therapy with grief and mourning is that it results in an adaptive inner representation composed of positive, heartfelt memories. After completion of the body scan phase, the adaptive inner representation can be enhanced, further promoting integration, healing, and a sense of connection.

1. *Think of the Deceased, Loved One*: This can be done by asking clients to think of the deceased loved one. If positive images, feelings, or memories arise, do a set of BLS. Like installing the safe/calm place or a resource, sets should be slower and fewer (e.g., 4–8 sets adjusted to clients' responses).
2. *Enhancement*: If the emerging memories/feelings continue to be positive, several more sets of BLS can be administered.

Note: This additional step to enhance the positive adaptive inner representation can also be provided after Phase 6, installation, particularly if positive memories/emotions involving the decease are naturally arising.

Of course, the inner representation may be negative, composed of distressing memories with the loved one. Such memories also need to be reprocessed not only to help clients to deal with the loss, but to enhance overall functioning in life.

Phase 7: Closure

During and after a session (i.e., complete or incomplete), clients may feel like they have run a marathon, and be physically tired and emotionally drained. Integration of negative memories often involves the release of a tremendous amount of tension. This is also true when working with grief-related memories. Francine Shapiro often used the phrase, "The client should be able to leave your office and operate heavy machinery." In other words, clients should leave feeling grounded, safe, and stable. Therefore, it is imperative therapists leave adequate time at the end of the session for grounding, if needed, and debriefing. A safety check also should be completed as to clients' ability to function (e.g., drive a car, go to work) with stabilization and affect management techniques and strategies implemented as needed.

Ending a Complete Session

If the session is complete (i.e., SUD = 0, VoC = 7, and clear body scan, ecologically appropriate), clinicians should have an integrative discussion about the session. For instance, therapists may ask "How was the session for you? What is different now? What have you learned?" Now, that distance from the original memory has been achieved, clinicians can instruct clients to focus on it again (e.g., "Think of your loved one. What comes up?"). Quite often, if there was completed processing, positive memories and feelings regarding the deceased arise (the adaptive inner representation) which can be enhanced with BLS.

Example 6 (Ending a Complete Session): Chiara reprocessed a memory of being with her mother when she died. Her mother had been in pain up until the end of her life. Reprocessing resulted in a SUD of 0, a VoC of 7, and a clear body scan. Chiara was then asked, "What is different for you now when you think of the memory?" She replied, "She is at peace now, and I am glad I could stay with her during her most painful moments. She knew I was there, and when I think of holding her hand when she was in pain, I now remember she would look at me with gratitude in her eyes." Chiara felt good about being present with her mother in her worst moments, and now looking back, these were the moments where she felt the closest. A moment of holding her mother's hand, feeling connected, was enhanced with further sets of BLS.

Ending an Incomplete Session

There are often incomplete sessions (i.e., SUD > 0, VoC < 7, and body scan not clear) even after a 90-minute or 2-hour session. Because of the multilayers of trauma and loss, it is often not possible to clear out all channels of association in a single session. If time is running out, therapists can inform clients it is time to stop or begin to "slow down/come down" from the process. Many clients end a session within the window of tolerance and benefit from an integrative discussion of the session, reflecting on what was learned and what is different now. An integrative discussion of the results of the reprocessing facilitates further consolidation of the memory, grounds clients in the here and now, and helps clients put words to the trauma. Further, positive insights can be enhanced with slower and fewer sets of BLS (e.g., 4–8 passes rather than the usual 20–30 passes, adjusted to client response). To further provide a positive therapeutic frame, therapists may offer helpful observations of what took place during the reprocessing, helping clients reflect on what has shifted and recognizing the courage it took to go through the intense memory.

> *Example 7 (Involving Several Clients): Gina had an incomplete session where discussing what was different led to her stating: "I'm starting to realize there was nothing more I could do." This was enhanced with two brief sets of BLS.*
>
> *George had an incomplete session, when asked "What is different now?," he replied, "I am understanding more about the whole situation." This was enhanced with several sets of brief BLS.*
>
> *Wendy had an incomplete session when reprocessing a distressing memory involving the death of her sister. Positive memories were starting to emerge when it was time to start closing down the session. When asked to give her impressions of the session she replied, "It is nice to have those memories." The therapist asked her if this gave her a sense of positive connection to her sister. She replied yes, and "it makes the heaviness of my grief easier to carry." This was enhanced with several brief sets of BLS.*

For clients who continue to experience and express upset at the end of a session, grounding and stabilization exercises are also in order. Clinicians can then implement stabilization strategies that were learned during the Preparation & Stabilization phase and hopefully know how much time at the end of a session should be allotted for grounding and an integrative discussion of what happened for the particular session. Clinicians can explain, if needed, that intense emotion is "realization" of what happened, and clients were able to recognize and experience "now" something that was too much "then." This is part of the healing process and leads to an increase in strength and capacity. Normalizing and validating the emotions that arise during the session are also an important part of therapy. After grounding and normalizing, having an integrative discussion about what was gained or learned during the session can take place.

Debriefing for All Clients

Educate clients that processing may continue after the session. Steve Silver, an EMDR Institute trainer, used the analogy that reprocessing a memory is like clearing out a beaver dam, and the water now can flow. New memories, insights, dreams, perspectives, and the like may arise in between sessions. There may (or may not) be new memories, dreams, or situations that are disturbing coming up. Particularly, after an emotional session, where obstacles have been reprocessed and the mourning process can flow, other memories, emotions, and dreams related to the deceased are quite common. Many EMDR therapists report that with grief more memories of the loved one come up. It can be helpful to explain that painful emotions and memories are a sign of realization and integration, and part of the mourning process. However, if more memories or feelings are not experienced, that is also normal after an EMDR session. Many clients experience a feeling of peace that comes with the sense of connection to the loved one. Clients can trust that the brain will do what it needs to do, and clients can just notice what is happening. It is helpful to keep a journal or log about what is coming up, and this material can be discussed and worked on the next session. As needed, clients can use grounding and coping strategies.

Phase 8: Re-evaluation

Shapiro stated, "The term *re-evaluation* reflects the need for the precise clinical attention and follow-up that frame any EMDR therapy session targeting disturbing material" (2018, p. 192).

General Functioning

The subsequent session should begin with an evaluation about global functioning as well as specifically about the memory that was previously targeted. In the context of the Dual Process model (discussed in Chapter 7), attention should be paid to both how clients are coping with daily life issues (restoration orientation (RO)) and the emotional aspects of the loss (loss orientation (LO)), and if there is a balanced oscillation between LO and RO. Therapists and clients can review the log or journal clients have created and discuss what has happened since the last session. This includes changes in symptoms, reactions to present triggers, and major concerns that have arisen. It is also important to assess how clients handled the EMDR session. What was it like when they got home? Some clients can be exhausted after a session while others are energized. The few days following a session may be intense with much emotion and more memories emerging concerning the deceased. Other clients may be relaxed, feel a weight off their shoulders, and sleep better. Some clients may need further sessions focusing on affect regulation and stabilization, while others are ready to reprocess other negative memories identified during history taking, or present triggers, or have future templates installed. Perhaps issues arose in between sessions that need addressing. Evaluating what has taken place since the last session, the clients' responses to treatment, and current circumstances determine the direction of the session.

The Target Memory from the Previous Session

If the reprocessing was complete in the previous session, therapists can ask clients to refocus on the negative memory targeted to see if the therapeutic gains have been maintained (e.g., SUD = 0, VoC = 7, and clear body scan, or what is ecologically valid and appropriate). If not, reprocessing of the memory should continue. However, if earlier memories, different aspects of the same memory, or other salient issues have arisen, then attention can be focused on what has been surfacing.

If the session was incomplete, reprocessing should continue by asking clients to focus on the previously targeted memory and identify the worst part (e.g., image/picture), emotion(s), SUD, and the location of body sensation(s). It is not necessary to go over NCs and PCs because the previously established cognitions are assumed to still be in place. Of course, if new NCs and PCs have evolved since the last session (a positive indication of reprocessing), they can be utilized.

If the treatment gains have maintained, ask if there are other associations. Often there are related memories or aspects of the same memory that come up and can be targeted. These new associations are important to reprocess.

Clinicians can "follow the brain" and target the memories or new aspects that have spontaneously arisen.

Example 8: Sherry's adult daughter died of cancer. Sherrie had warm memories of her daughter, but the image of her dying continued to be intrusive. Fourteen months after her daughter's death, Sherry received EMDR treatment and successfully reprocessed the worst moment of her daughter's death, with a of SUD 0, a VoC of 7, and clear body scan, though Sherry still felt appropriate sadness. The next session the SUD was at a 5. Reprocessing of the memory continued. It became apparent that the distress pertained to the feeling of helplessness experienced with seeing her daughter suffer just before she died. Continuing the reprocessing of this memory resulted in an incomplete session, with a SUD of 3. The next session the client reported the SUD connected to this memory was still a 3. Exploring what the "3" was related to, it became apparent that Sherry felt like a failure because she could not ease her pain. Feelings of failure were connected to childhood memories. One such childhood memory (the mother's disapproval with a mediocre grade with a NC of "I am a failure" and a feeling of shame) was identified and fully reprocessed. Returning to the memory of her daughter dying, the SUD = 0, the VoC = 7, and clear body scan. The following session, the client reported that the therapeutic effects had maintained, with the memory of her daughter's death still at a SUD = 0, VoC = 7, and clear body scan. Therapy continued, focusing on past memories, present triggers, and future templates related to the theme of failure.

This example illustrates (a) different aspects of the same memory surfacing after reprocessing the worst memory of the daughter's death, (b) incomplete processing of the memory because it was linked to past memories (related to the theme of "I am a failure"), and (c) how identifying and reprocessing past linked memories resulted in complete processing effects of the initial target memory. Incomplete sessions are quite common and reprocessing the memory can continue for several sessions. Blocked processing can be due to blocking beliefs or earlier memories, which need to be identified and reprocessed, as illustrated in the above example.

Option: Assessing the Inner Representation
As a means of evaluating how clients are dealing with their loss, ask what they experienced when thinking of the deceased. Are there positive, heartfelt emotions and memories? Are there other distressing memories and/or emotions arising, present triggers that continue to evoke distress, and past linking memories underlying the distress? In general, asking mourners to think of

their loved one offers insight regarding progress toward integration of the death, difficulties, or stuck points. Positive memories may indicate progress in adapting to the loss. If negative material is emerging, it perhaps is an indication that clients would benefit from more reprocessing. Clinicians can assess if there are stuck points, as illustrated in the Example 9 of Joe below. However, it must be emphasized that sadness and missing the loved one are normal, and the emergence of positive memories does not take away appropriate emotions (e.g., sadness, sorrow, missing the person).

> *Example 9: Joe was very close to his uncle, even more than his father. Joe received a phone call that his uncle was dying and probably would not make it through the night. As Joe was over 1000 miles away, he was not able to make it to the hospital in time to be with his uncle when he died. Joe felt very guilty about this and sought treatment 1 year after the death. The first memory reprocessed was arriving at the hospital and finding out that his uncle had died. The result of the session was that Joe realized he did the best he could to be at the hospital, and no longer felt guilty. The SUD was 0 and VoC 7 ("I did the best I could."). However, the body scan was not clear because Joe was sad about the death. When asked to think of his uncle, Joe reported just sadness, but no particular thoughts or memories. At the following session, Joe reported he still felt no guilt. When asked to think of his uncle he reported he felt sad and "hollow" inside. Further, after feeling guilty for a year, it was strange not to feel it. Viewing the sadness, hollow feeling, and his discomfort at not experiencing the guilt as an indication that further reprocessing was needed, it was decided to continue to reprocess the same memory. After several minutes of processing, meaningful memories emerged having to do with qualities and values his uncle had taught him. Joe described how these memories filled the hollowness he was feeling, and he felt at peace with his uncle's death.*

This example illustrates how thinking of the deceased loved one can be useful in assessing adaptation to the loss. In the above example, Joe had a successful EMDR session resulting in a shift in the guilt he had experienced since his uncle died. When asked to think of his uncle in the next session, he felt sad and hollow and no meaningful memories emerged. Though sadness, hollowness, and lack of positive memories are not necessarily pathological, after 6 months, it can be a signal that there is still maladaptively stored information. In Joe's case, it seemed to indicate that reprocessing of the target memory was incomplete. With continued reprocessing meaningful memories emerged, filling up Joe's hollow space.

Note: An overall evaluation of client functioning is important in assessing adaptation, and the mourner's response to thinking of the deceased is but one data point. The broader picture that takes into account how the client is coping with life dealing with the challenges caused by the death needs to be evaluated.

Summary

This chapter covered the installation, body scan, closure, and re-evaluation phases.

The installation phase, completing the processing phases, enhances resilience, providing an adaptive perspective on the past memory and paving the way for positive coping in the future. The closure phase is important to ensure clients are stabilized at the end of the session, know that other emotional material may arise in between sessions, and have strategies and support to deal with what arises. The body scan is a final check to evaluate if the memory is fully processed. An extra step was introduced: Enhancement of the adaptive inner representation. Positive memories often arise during reprocessing, forming an adaptive inner representation. The positive memories can be enhanced with BLS after the body scan to enhance the positive transformation of the relationship from loving in presence to loving in absence, providing a positive sense of connection to the loved one which aids adaptation to the loss.

19

Grief and Mourning with Complex Trauma and Trauma-Generated Dissociation of the Personality

Roger Solomon, Onno van der Hart, Kathy Martin

Many of our clients come in with complex trauma and dissociative symptoms. It is important that the reader have appropriate training in dealing with complex trauma and trauma-generated dissociation, and assessment of dissociation, before doing eye movement desensitization and reprocessing (EMDR) therapy. EMDR therapy can be very powerful, and doing memory reprocessing without appropriate assessment and preparation and stabilization can result in over activation of the personality system, and the potential for harm. It is beyond the scope of this chapter to provide the necessary guidelines for treating trauma-generated dissociation and intricacies of utilizing EMDR therapy. But it is hoped that it can provide an introduction to trauma-generated dissociation of the personality and how it can inform EMDR therapy, and that the case examples provide useful illustrations of treatment principles. Useful articles for utilization of EMDR therapy and complex trauma and dissociative symptoms can be found in Knipe (2019); Mosquera (2019); Sandra Paulson, Forgash, and Copely (2008); Steele, Boon, and Van der Hart (2016); Van der Hart et al. (2010, 2013, 2014); and Van der Hart, Nijenhuis, and Steele (2006).

Trauma-Generated Dissociation of the Personality

As human beings we are wired to survive. As the Adaptive Information Processing (AIP) model describes, when an experience is too intense, too much to realize, it becomes stuck in time, maladaptively stored and avoided, enabling the person to focus, to some degree, on everyday living tasks

EMDR Therapy Treatment for Grief and Mourning. Roger M. Solomon, Oxford University Press. © Roger M. Solomon 2024.
DOI: 10.1093/oso/9780198881360.003.0020

important for survival. If the traumatizing events occur with ever-increasing frequency and intensity, and start earlier in life (e.g., childhood abuse and/ or neglect), the memory network of maladaptively stored information gets bigger. Continuing traumatization, especially involving caregivers, where the source of safety is also the source of terror ('fright without solution'), can result in an ever-increasing division of the personality into dissociative parts, with some parts engaging in everyday life survival tasks and other parts holding the traumatic memories which are 'too much' to realize. In short, nature has determined that if something is too much, trauma-generated division of the personality enables the person to focus on daily life and survival.

Bowlby (1973) discussed how a death can be so emotionally overwhelming that grief work is blocked. There is avoidance of the realization that the loved one is dead. The implications (e.g., the loved one is not coming back) can be defensively excluded from experience. With the inability to realize the loss, thoughts and feelings are dissociated, operating, in Bowlby's (1980) term as 'segregated systems'. Bowlby described that individuals may possess multiple self-systems, and the integration of these self-systems into an overall integrative system differs from person to person. Bowlby seems to be describing dissociation. We add that these 'segregated systems' have their own sense of self and first-person perspective. This explains how some mourners oscillate between a state of mind where there is awareness that the loved one is permanently gone and another state of mind where the loved one cannot acknowledge (realize) the reality of the death.

Theory of Structural Dissociation of the Personality (TSDP)

A comprehensive theory of personality and dissociation is provided by Van der Hart, Nijenhuis, and Steele (2006): the TSDP. TSDP describes the personality as intimately related to action systems. Action systems are psychobiological systems (e.g., motivational, behavioural, functional, and emotional operating systems) or adaptations that shape personality (Van der Hart, Nijenhuis, & Steele, 2006), They are referred to as *action systems* because they involve an innate readiness or tendency to act in a goal-directed manner. As Van der Hart, Nijenhuis, and Steele point out, 'They do not rigidly determine actions, but provide a propensity to exhibit a particular pattern of behaviours, thoughts, feelings, sensations, and perceptions ... [They] define to a large degree what we find attractive or aversive, and then generate tendencies to approach or avoid accordingly ... They direct us to learn what is relevant for adaptation … & are modified by learning' (p. 32). Hence action systems involve memory networks.

Action Systems

There are two major categories of action systems. One major action system involves defence and involves a variety of efforts to survive imminent threat. The defence action system is geared towards escaping and avoiding aversive stimuli, and includes subsystems such as fight, flight, freeze, and total submission (Porges, 2001, 2003). The other major category of action systems is focused on daily life functions (Panksepp, 1998). These systems include energy regulation (e.g., eating, sleeping), attachment and care-taking, exploration, social engagement (Porges, 2001), play, and reproduction, and involve approaching attractive stimuli (Lang, 1995).

Trauma can be conceptualized as a 'breaking point', where there is a failure of integration of the experience and the inherent action systems, resulting in a dissociation of the personality (Ross, 1941). TSDP proposes that trauma-related disorders (including complex trauma and dissociative disorders) are characterized by a division of clients' personality into different dissociative subsystems or parts. When an individual is traumatized, a division occurs in their personality, not randomly, but along the metaphorical 'fault line' in the evolutionarily prepared two major psychobiological action systems: daily life and defence. The part(s) of the personality engaged in everyday living actions is/are termed the apparently normal part(s) of the personality (ANPs). The person as ANP is engaged in everyday living, and appears to be 'normal', but there are symptoms (e.g., intrusive symptoms, avoidance, amnesia, and somatic symptoms) so the normalcy is only 'apparent'. The part(s) of the personality engaged in (failed) defence are called emotional parts (EPs). EPs live in *trauma time*, fixated in the sensorimotor and highly charged re-enactments of the trauma experience, from which they cannot escape. This includes action tendencies of defence against perceived or real threat (e.g., fight, flight, freeze, and (total) submission) that was activated during the trauma (Van der Hart et al., 2006, 2010).

Each dissociative part has its own psychobiological foundation (Nijenhuis et al., 2002; Van der Hart et al., 2006) and is characterized by its own first-person perspective and sense of self. That is, these dissociative parts have various degrees of mental autonomy and separateness, having their own point of view, including thoughts, feelings, emotions, perceptions, and behaviours regarding themselves, other people (including the therapist), and events. Dissociative clients tend to alternate between one or more *apparently normal parts of the personality* (ANPs) and one or more *emotional parts of the person-ality* (EPs).

According to TSDP, dissociation of the personality is maintained by a se-ries of (dissociative) phobias as well as a lack of integrative capacity and social support (Van der Hart et al., 2006). The term *phobia* usually describes anxiety disorders, understood as a persistent fear for external elements (e.g., animals, social situations) that the individual tries to avoid. However, Janet (1904) described phobic reactions that are directed towards traumatic memories, but the phobia can go further to include internal experiences such as thoughts, feelings, and fantasies, for example (Van der Hart et al., 2006). Chronically traumatized individuals can be extremely fearful of their internal mental life and the external cues which trigger traumatic experiences (Van der Hart et al., 2006). Indeed, the core phobia maintaining the dissociation of the person-ality is the *phobia of traumatic memories*, the essence of which is an avoidance of full realization of the trauma and its effects on one's life (Janet, 1904; Van der Hart et al., 2006). With chronic traumatization, behavioural and mental avoidance is needed to prevent ANP experiencing unbearable realizations about the self, others, and the world.

Case Example 1 (Phobia of Realization): The mother whose only son had died at age 21 years, 1.5 years ago in a traffic accident, states: 'The idea that he will not be there ever again, I don't let that sink into my mind. Otherwise, one becomes crazy. Otherwise, one would indeed not want to continue living. You don't allow that realization? That is my salvation, I think ... somewhere in me is still a glimmer of hope that he will still be there again.' De Volkskrant Magazine, 24 December 2011.

Trauma-related dissociation of the personality can vary in complexity. *Primary dissociation of the personality* involves one ANP and one EP; and applies to single episode posttraumatic stress disorder (PTSD). *Secondary dissociation* involves one ANP and two or more EPs; and usually applies to Complex PTSD, Borderline Personality Disorder, and Otherwise Specified Dissociative Disorder. *Tertiary dissociation* is characterized by more than one ANP and more than one EP, and applies to Dissociative Identity Disorder (DID). These different degrees of complexity of the dissociation are related to more frequent, severe, and earlier traumatization.

EMDR, the AIP Model, and TSDP: Complementary Approaches

According to AIP, traumatizing events result in memories that are dysfunctionally stored; that is, stored in isolation, unassimilated into the comprehensive memory networks of the individual (Shapiro, 1995, 2001). As Shapiro explains, 'The pathological structure is inherent in the static, insufficiently processed information stored at the time of the disturbing event.... [T]he lack of adequate assimilation means that the client is still reacting emotionally and behaviourally in ways consistent with the earlier disturbing event' (2018, p. 15). The dysfunctionally stored information includes memories 'stuck in time' and contains the maladaptive mental and behavioural actions that were present at the time of the event, including the sensorimotor responses, affective responses (e.g., vehement emotions, in Janet's words, e.g., overwhelming fear, anger, shame, or guilt), cognitions, threat perception, and predictions (i.e., expectancies based on the past danger and threat experienced during the traumatizing event).

Janet (1919/1925) wrote: '[T]he (traumatic) memory was morbific because it was dissociated. It existed in isolation, apart from the totality of the sensations and the ideas which comprised the subject's personality; it developed in isolation, without control and without counterpoise; the morbid symptoms disappeared when the memory again became part of the synthesis that makes up individuality' (p. 674). Janet's 'dissociated' and Shapiro's 'in isolation' refer to the same phenomenon. Though AIP is not an elaborated theory of personality, it points to the importance of learning, and hence, to memory networks, as a prime determinant of personality characteristics and behaviour (Shapiro, 1995, 2001; Solomon & Shapiro, 2008). Thus, dysfunctionally stored memories (especially with chronically traumatized populations) can be conceptualized as dissociated from the remainder of the personality, with their own first-person perspective and sense of self (e.g., Emotional Part(s)), that include the wider system of memory networks of adaptively stored information (e.g., ANPs).

TSDP does not speak in terms of 'stored information' and, instead, states that the mental and behavioural actions involved in traumatic memories belong to some conscious and self-conscious dissociative parts of the personality, each of them having its own first-person perspective and sense of self. In AIP terms, then, EP and ANP have their own memory networks, with EP holding the maladaptively stored ('stuck in time') traumatic memories. Highlighting the fact that a dissociative part has a first-person perspective,

EP can be understood as memory networks 'living in trauma time' with their own sense of self. ANP needs to avoid EPs, which are too much to integrate and, when reactivated, may intrude in the present. EMDR therapists need to understand more Preparation & Stabilization is needed when treating clients, beyond simple trauma, when the dissociation of the personality is more complex, when EP(s) have a high degree of autonomy, and when there are intense phobias between ANP(s) and EP(s).

Phase-Oriented Treatment

Treatment needs to follow a phase-oriented approach (Janet, 1898; Van der Hart & Friedman, 1989, Van er Hart et al., 2006) which includes stabilization, treatment of traumatic memories, and personality reintegration and rehabilitation. These phases of treatment can alternate considerably in the more complex cases. For example, after stabilization, memory work begins, but so much distress may be evoked that going back to stabilization is in order. Similarly, one can do successful memory work, enabling the client to try new behaviours, which in turn brings up other memories that need to be reprocessed, and perhaps the need for further stabilization.

Phase 1 of Phase-Oriented Treatment is symptom reduction, stabilization, skill-building, and treating enough of the dissociation to move into memory work. This equivalent to EMDR Phase 2: Preparation & Stabilization. This involves increasing the client's ability to regulate affect (e.g., utilize adaptive actions instead of being overwhelmed by vehement emotions), enhancing integrative capacity including the ability to have dual awareness (e.g., ability to be present in the here and now while experiencing a traumatic memory), and cope with current symptoms. This phase of treatment also involves working with working with the parts to enhance cooperation and collaboration, with ANP leadership. For example, time orientation of parts (e.g., helping EPs know that what happened in childhood is not happening now), reducing the conflicts among the parts, and developing compassion and understanding among the parts and understanding the survival function of the parts.

Phase 2 is treatment of traumatic memories, which overlaps with EMDR Phases 3–8: assessment, desensitization, installation, body scan, closure, and re-evaluation. Phase 3 of Phase-Oriented Treatment is personality (re)integration and rehabilitation. This overlaps with many aspects of EMDR therapy, including Recourse Development and Installation (Korn & Leeds, 2002), the past-present-future three-pronged protocol which emphasizes the reprocessing of underlying negative memories, present scenarios that elicit symptoms, and enabling adaptive coping to future stressors. Further, personality (re) integration is addressed during Phase 8 of EMDR (the re-evaluation phase) which assesses if treatment effects have been maintained, what has occurred during the week, and what needs to be dealt with now (e.g., more stabilization, dealing with another layer of dissociation, further memory reprocessing, reprocessing of present triggers, providing future template, or teaching of new skills). The therapist needs to understand that in very complex cases, such as DID, Phase-Oriented Treatment can take years.

The goal of therapy is increased adaptation to life's challenges and ever more integration of the personality, which involves synthesis and realization. Synthesis is the sharing of traumatic memories (including information, emotions, and bodily sensations) among parts so that they link their memories from their different perspectives. Realization is the ability to assimilate reality, make sense and meaning of it, and adapt to it. Realization involves two important processes: personification ('It happened to me, and I am aware of how it affected my life, my sense of self, and how I view the world.': personal ownership) and presentification ('I am aware of the present and how my past affects me in the present and in the imagined future. What happened is over, and in the past.').

Disorganized Attachment and Complex Trauma

Brown and Elliot (2016) point out the importance of disorganized attachment in the development of Complex PTSD and dissociative disorders:

> Simple PTSD is associated with single or cumulative specific trauma events, whereas complex trauma is primarily associated with insecure attachment aggravated by abuse or trauma in later childhood or adulthood. There is little support for the view that complex trauma is a function of early trauma per se or a function of multiple-event trauma or cumulative abuse—rather early childhood insecure attachment is a key ingredient in the eventual development of complex trauma, in combination with abuse or trauma later in childhood. (p. 219)

Given the primary role attachment style plays in grief and mourning, mourners with disorganized attachment may be particularly vulnerable to complicated grief. Application of EMDR therapy for reprocessing traumatic memories should be done after sufficient Preparation & Stabilization. Brown and Elliot (2016) point out, 'a consistent focus on trauma processing per se in patients with complex trauma-related disorders runs the risk of aggravating disorganization of mind, which is a feature of insecure attachment ... ' (p. 220). Hence, in treating complex trauma and dissociation, the clinician must help the client raise the integrative capacity of the client to enable dual awareness.

EMDR Therapy and Complex Trauma

The therapist working with complex trauma and trauma-generated dissociation of the personality should have specialized training and be familiar with the treatment literature. It is important the clinician do an assessment of the client for dissociation. The Dissociative Experiences Scale is an often-used screening instrument (Carlson & Putnam, 1993), which, however, includes questions of phenomena not per se being dissociative in nature. The Trauma and Dissociation Symptoms Interview (TADS–I) (Boon, 2023) and SCID-D (Steinberg & Hall, 1997) are more thorough diagnostic instruments.

Phase 1: History and Treatment Planning

Depending on the level of dissociation, history-taking may need to take place slowly. With the more severely affected clients, it may be helpful to begin with stabilization and grounding exercises before taking a detailed history. Treatment planning should take into account that an extended Phase 2 (Preparation & Stabilization) will be needed. The client's response to Phase 2 interventions helps determine the pace and direction of treatment, and when to deal with the death. As described in the integrative model presented in Chapter 10, when there is complex trauma, past memories (unresolved trauma, losses, and negative attachment experiences) underlying current difficulties in adaptation may need to be treated before targeting memories related to the death. Where and when to start memory reprocessing depends on many factors, such as the client's readiness, motivation, capacity, and clinical priorities. Target selection and the treatment plan are continually updated depending on the needs of the client and response to treatment.

Phase 2: Preparation & Stabilization

Readiness for memory processing is determined not so much by time as by meeting criteria to a 'good enough' level (Steele, Boon, & Van der Hart, 2017), such as:

- *Ability to lower arousal/access resources*—the ability to calm and access re-sourceful frames of mind are the first essential skills needed by clients for affect regulation and to start their journey in dealing with their trauma.
- *Stabilize harmful behaviours*—behaviours such as cutting, substance abuse, and other behaviours that are substitute actions (behaviours that are engaged in to avoid experiencing painful emotions and memories).
- *Stabilized social environment*: the client is handling everyday living tasks and is no longer in crisis mode.
- *Compassion of ANP towards parts*—work with the ANP (e.g., the execu-tive functioning self-engaged in daily living) to have compassion towards the EPs.
- *Development of co-consciousness, cooperation, and collaboration among parts of the personality, with ANP providing executive functioning leadership*—Techniques like Fraser's Dissociative Table (Fraser, 1991), where parts can meet in an imaginary conference room or another type of meeting place, can be helpful in getting to know the parts, their func-tions, and facilitate cooperation, collaboration, and ANP leadership within the system.
- *Reduction or elimination of the phobias between/among parts*—Many times these phobias are identifiable by conflicts between parts or groups of parts. For example, a part defending against the attachment cry and feelings of helplessness (which may be experienced as an angry or critical part) blames the part caught in the attachment cry (may be experienced as a 'vulnerable child' part) for being weak or a 'baby'. This keeps the entire person focused on the internal conflict rather than addressing the underlying unprocessed pain of previous attachment wounds. These conflicts, left untreated, will block processing in later phases of EMDR therapy. Understanding that parts, in terms of the AIP model, are memory networks 'living in trauma time' with their own sense of self, doing such work with parts is aligning the different memory networks. Parts that could block processing or get triggered and become overly activated are dealt with before memory repro-cessing, which makes the reprocessing go smoother and helps keep the client within the window of tolerance.
- *Increase the window of tolerance and integrative capacity*—as the ANP is able to develop more self-leadership for stabilization and the ability to stay present with emotion increases, the window of tolerance grows.
- *Dual awareness within the system is necessary before beginning reprocessing*—This is keeping one foot in the past and one foot in the pre-sent. ANP leadership and presence within the system is necessary to help maintain dual awareness.

- *Time orientation of parts (to the extent possible)*—work with parts to know that what happened in childhood is not happening now: the danger of childhood is over.
- *Personification and presentification*—The ability to claim 'the history is my history, and I am part of this one person: is necessary for complete repro-cessing. That is, parts can realize what happened, in the past, to one part happened to all parts. For example, an angry part (e.g., defending against the attachment cry and helplessness) that blames the 'child' part for the abuse may not realize the abuse is in its history as well. Helping parts realize what happened to one part happened to all because there is only one person with one brain, with one personality divided into parts makes memory reprocessing easier, with the client better able to stay within the window of tolerance. Nonpersonified parts can block the reprocessing. Although full personification throughout the entire personality is impos-sible prior to the memory processing phases, sufficient personification and presentification of the memory are necessary to get some reprocess-ing accomplished. Time orientation, (which involves some presentifica-tion), developing compassion among parts, understanding the survival function of each part, eases the conflicts among parts and enables per-sonification ('It happened to all of me.'). As more personification and pre-sentification happens, more reprocessing can be effective.
- *Adaptive information to deal with maladaptive beliefs*—Clients may be-lieve that the abuse or neglect they experienced was their fault, or that they deserved it, or that the world is always dangerous. Clients need to have realistic adaptive information, at least at a cognitive level, to deal with such cognitive distortions.
- *Increased integrative capacity*—ANP and EPs need to be able to stay pre-sent (some degree of presentification) with emotions experienced during reprocessing. The client should be able to talk about the memory (details are not necessary), identify the pathological kernels (worst moments or aspects), and have the integrative capacity to stay within the window of tolerance when confronted with the traumatic memory (e.g., not go into hyperarousal or hypoarousal).

The establishment of a trusting, collaborative, therapeutic relationship is imperative. A disorganized attachment style may involve a dissociative pat-tern of alternation between attachment and defence (rapid switching between parts that are mediated by attachment and defence action systems). Therefore, it is important that the therapeutic relationship provide the safety that child-hood did not. The therapeutic relationship is always the vehicle for change, and is essential for safety and increasing the client's capacity for reprocessing traumatic memories. Thus, it is essential that the therapist can stay present and help the client maintain or regain a sense of safety.

Phases 3–8: Memory Reprocessing

Before doing memory reprocessing, it is important to determine what parts can be present and what parts cannot (or should not) be present and, therefore, should be in their inner safe places. For example, a traumatic memory can be too much for some parts (e.g., an abuse memory can be too much for a 'child' or 'baby' part, but the adult (ANP) and an adolescent part (EP) can and need to be present). Later, the memory, which has lost some of its overwhelming force, can be reprocessed again, with the other parts present. Another clinical choice is to continue to work with the parts that cannot be present until they are able to be participate in the memory reprocessing. Indeed, what happened to one part happened to all—there is one brain, one personality, divided into parts (Martin, 2018). Whether to reprocess the memory with the parts that can be present or wait until further work is done until all relevant parts can be present is a therapeutic choice-point. However, with clients with DID the option of working with parts that can be present, and parts that cannot being in their own safe place, is often imperative.

With parts considered to be memory networks having their own sense of self, and first-person perspective, working with the dissociative system is an integrative process. Promoting co-consciousness, cooperation, and person-ification with ANP leadership can prevent their sudden emergence during memory work which can block processing or be 'too much' for the client. Preparing the personality system (working with parts) makes memory repro-cessing easier, more contained, and helps the client stay within the window of tolerance. In earlier years, as we were taught to do in EMDR therapy basic training, when a client would experience intense emotion, I (RS) would do longer sets and often increase the bilateral stimulation to get the client through the reprocessing. As I began learning how to integrate TSDP into EMDR Therapy, I used Fraser's Dissociative Table Technique to work with parts and orient them to present time. The processing went much smoother as a re-sult. Clients reported that usually they had to prepare themselves for EMDR reprocessing because it would be so intense, but was worth it since they were getting better. After doing the parts work before memory reprocessing, cli-ents reported that reprocessing was much less intense, and they could now approach EMDR sessions without dread. I use the metaphor of reprocessing a memory without Preparation & Stabilization (of parts) for clients suffering from trauma-generated dissociation is similar to a dentist drilling on a tooth without a pain medication.

Case Example 2: (Rose, a Client with Secondary Dissociation): Rose, a 42-year-old woman and mother with one child aged 7 years. Her presenting problem was two miscarriages and the death of her mother within a 10-month period. In her words, she felt 'bereavement overload'. She was depressed. Her functioning at work and home was, at best, adequate. She alternated between numbness and sadness regarding the miscarriages. She was conflicted about mother's death, feeling both sad and angry.

Her history included mother's alcoholism which worsened when Rose was 5 years of age. The family lived in a community where treatment was not available and was perceived as a source of considerable shame upon the family if the family pursued it. By age 10 her mother's alcoholism had progressed to mother being completely non-functional. One day Rose's father took her aside and told her she was now the 'woman of the house'. She was given the tasks of caring for her two younger siblings, cooking, and cleaning. She did what she could but felt inadequate and unable to cope as a child in an adult role. She also tried to look after her mother who continued to drink. This reinforced Rose's sense of 'I can't cope.' Another traumatic memory was at age 15 when she and her boyfriend found mother passed out in an alcoholic stupor. They carried mother to the bedroom. At age 17, Rose left home and moved to a different country. She seldom saw or spoke to her parents again.

Rose had secondary dissociation of the personality: One ANP and a number of EPs. The first 4 months of therapy were devoted to stabilization and getting to know the parts of the personality. Fraser's Dissociative Table Technique found four EPs: (1) EP age 5 years experienced as 'scared and vulnerable', (2) EP age 10 carrying the 'I can't cope' experience, (3) EP experienced as an angry teenager, and (4) dragon who was a protector part functioning to distract from all emotions through substitute actions such as drinking and exercising in excess and numbing.

After learning about the parts and noticing they were stuck in the past, time-orientation interventions were used. For example, 'Does the part experienced as 5 know that childhood is over, and you are an adult woman now?' Helping the ANP understand the survival function of each part during childhood conditions developed ANP compassion for the internal parts. It also helped develop the ANP's ability to stay present with these parts and provide time orientation when necessary. Overall, these first 4 months of treatment developed communication, cooperation, collaboration, and self-compassion within the system with the leadership of the adult executive functioning self (ANP). After 4 months, she met criteria for the memory reprocessing phase of treatment.

The system agreed to begin the reprocessing phase on the memory when father told her she was the 'lady of the house' at age 10. All parts agreed to participate and agreed this memory happened to them. Using the Standard Protocol reprocessing phases of EMDR therapy, the reprocessing went well. Then the 15-year-old's memory of finding mother passed out on the floor was reprocessed. By this time in treatment the parts experienced as children were more connected to the ANP and the rest of the system. They didn't feel so 'alone'.

The treatment moved into addressing mother's death which occurred 10 months prior. An assessment was made of each part's personification and presentification, as well as some presentification, of the mother's death: (1) Does each part know that mother was their mother, and (2) does each part know that mother was dead? All parts agreed that mother was their mother. The part experienced as 10 years old did not know mother was dead. Here is an excerpt of the client's (as ANP) response: 'I don't want her to know because I want to preserve what little childhood attachment that part has. As a child I did not have much of a childhood . . . I did not have much of a mother . . . I don't want the 10-year-old part to lose the only mother she had.' In response, Rose as ANP, reported internally hearing the EP as 10-years-old's attachment cry: 'Mother, don't leave me, don't leave me.' The therapeutic dialogue continued, recognizing and understanding that the loss of the mother was too much to realize for this part. After offering more time orientation to the EP, the therapist then asked Rose to go back to the previously reprocessed memory of her father telling her that she was lady of the house. Rose (as ANP) reported that the 10-year-old EP was not alone, and the parts were having a 'group hug'. This was comforting to Rose. The therapist, recognizing a moment to strengthen this treatment gain, asked Rose to hold the comforting feeling of the 'group hug' with all parts present, along with the 10-year-old EP feeling connected. A short set of eye movements to enhance the good feeling was given. All parts, including the ANP were present for this comfort and knowing. Rose reported that the 10-year-old was okay because 'she has the rest of us . . . she is not alone.' This was enhanced with another short set of eye movements. Then Rose reported that the 10-year-old part knew mother had died. Because this part was connected to all the other parts and felt comforted, the 10-year-old part of self could claim the truth about mother's death. Treatment then successfully worked on mother's death, targeting the moment she received the news of her mother's death.

The next topic was her miscarriages. Because of the work that was accomplished on her mother and the mother's death, including the personification of the parts, the increase of the window of tolerance, the increased communication, cooperation, and collaboration within the system, this work was not as difficult as Rose originally imagined it would be. Rose reported that there was grief and loss, sadness, and anger (over the way the hospital personnel behaved), but it no longer felt as 'too much'. It felt too much *in the beginning of treatment because the miscarriages and death of her mother 'compounded and piled on top of each other. Now the miscarriages don't feel overwhelming, but something that feels more understandable that sometimes happens to people. It's sad, but not destructive like before.'*

Further therapy involved the reprocessing of more childhood memories related to abandonment by the mother, anger at her father for putting too much responsibility on her, and reprocessing of the miscarriages. Therapy concluded 1 year later with her personality integrated, in the sense that unification of parts had taken place.

This case example shows the importance of working with the personality system before memory reprocessing. The 10-year-old part did not know the mother had died, and the ANP (adult Rose) was afraid for this part of her to know because it would be too much for this part. However, this is also a statement that realization of the death is too much for the full person. Blaming the 10-year-old part keeps the personality system distracted from what is still overwhelming for the whole personality system. Given the 10-year-old part is, of course, a part of the whole person, this dynamic illustrates that full realization of the childhood trauma, and the death of the mother was too much to be realized for the full person. To begin with reprocessing the loss of the mother (i.e., starting with getting the news) potentially would have led to too much vehement emotion, beyond Rose's window of tolerance, arising or to blocked processing. This would have been due to either (a) the 10-year-old part not knowing the mother had died, which indicated it was 'too much' for the whole person to realize, or (b) fear on the part of the ANP that the 10-year-old EP knowing the mother had died would cause more emotional damage (e.g., inability to cope with the realization of further abandonment). Reprocessing of earlier memories enabled more realization (i.e., personification and presentification), with the 10-year-old part feeling connected to the other parts (including ANP), now able to 'know' that the mother had died. Reprocessing the death of her mother (starting with getting the news) resulted in Rose achieving a more adult perspective of her loss, able to reflect on the past and be grounded in the present. Rose experienced sadness for her mother's death and that, as an adult, she had not gotten to know her mother more. Further, Rose could experience compassion for her mother's problems. In other words, she experienced increased personification and presentification with regard to her mother's death. Further, there was generalization of treatment results to the grief over the miscarriages. Though still impactful, they no longer felt 'destructive'. Hence, this case example shows how working with the parts prior to memory work went beyond integration of the distressing memory to generalization to other traumatic memories (miscarriages) and, consequently, further integration of the personality.

Case Example 3 (Offered by Kathy Martin—Jill a Client with Secondary Dissociation): Jill is a 38-year-old woman who entered treatment to address her grief over her husband's death 12 years prior. At intake, she presented as if the death had just occurred. She was weepy and felt alone and lost; she reported flashbacks of how she learned about the death; and she said that she never grieved him. She was entering a new relationship with a man and said she needed to do her grieving so she could be emotionally available to him.

Jill's husband died suddenly in a heavy machinery accident. At the time of his death, they had an infant and a 1-year-old child. They had been married 2.5 years. Upon his death, she had to find work to support the family. She believed she had not grieved him because she was too busy as a single working mother over the last 12 years.

Although she was weepy talking about her husband, she had a shut-down quality about her. She met criteria for a clinical depression. She was on an SSRI antidepressant since his death. She reported she felt that she was 'going through the motions' of being a mother and not fully present for her children. She loved her children but reported not enjoying the time she spent with them. She particularly hated when each of them was between the ages of 4 and 10 years.

Jill was an only child to middle-class parents. She reported her history was unremarkable until her parent's separation when she was 4.5 years old. Her father initiated the separation after an affair. There were periods of separation with the father leaving the home and returning, only again to leave because of the marital conflict. The marriage ultimately ended in divorce when she was 10 years old. She never heard from him again. Hence, Jill's difficulties with her children when they were aged between 4 and 10 years was linked to her own trauma between the same ages.

Her mother's response to the marital conflict and break-up was shut down and depression. Once the divorce was final, her mother found work to support her and her daughter. She told her daughter to never talk about her father again and to forget about him because he would never come back. The client complied to minimize conflict with her mother and to maintain that attachment.

In the initial session, the therapist observed there was a childlike quality to her when she was weepy. She also made the statement, 'Daddy will come back for me', in a voice that that had a little-girl quality to it. In the next few sessions, calming skills were introduced and developed, increasing her ability to self-regulate. She also reported enjoying her children more and the depression began to decrease. She reported functioning better at work.

Fraser's Dissociative Table Technique was administered once she met readiness for it, which included having calming skills, self-agency regarding self-regulation, a wider window of tolerance, and an ability to stay more present with her internal experience. She did not meet criteria for a DSM-5 Dissociative Disorder, but, clearly, there was Complex PTSD as evidenced by the childlike weepiness and behaviour. The table technique found an isolated EP experienced as aged 5 years, a young adult part experienced as aged 24 years, and a shut-down part experienced as aged 9 years.

The part that was experienced as 24 years old functioned as a protector to keep the other two parts from intervening into consciousness. The 9-year-old part also served as a protector to 'shut up' the 5-year-old and to block against anger. Jill, as ANP, initially thought she was 'making this stuff up', but she couldn't deny that she always felt like a little child when she dropped into the weepiness. With this insight, she became engaged in the treatment of her dissociative inner world to help resolve the grief.

The 5-year-old part was caught in attachment, crying for her father, and didn't know that her father had left for good. This part also did not know that she was a grown woman. Although she knew her husband, the 5-year-old part couldn't claim she had been married and didn't know the husband had died. The part experienced as 9 years old also could not claim the husband was her husband but knew the husband had died. One of the 9-year-old part's functions was to keep the 5-year-old part from knowing that both father and husband would not come back.

As the treatment of the dissociation of her personality progressed, it became clear that 5-year-old part was caught in attachment cry for father while the 9-year-old and 26-year-old parts were caught in the defence against the attachment cry. The focus on father defended her from realizing the anger, disappointment, and powerlessness she faced as a child and adolescent in response to the family chaos, and the fact that neither parent was able to properly attune to her and help her manage her feelings. She was particularly angry at mother's requirement to never talk about father again.

Jill came to realize what blocked her grief and mourning process for her husband. When her husband died, she was emotionally overwhelmed, and the earlier childhood losses were triggered. As a result, her phobia of realizing her losses became stronger. She could not afford to grieve the husband because it threatened to open up the earlier unhealed losses and pain.

Time orientation of all parts took centre stage. As expected, the 5-year-old EP was the hardest to time orient. The attachment crying for her father carried an idealization defence: he is a good father and he would never leave me. The hope he would come back served to maintain a dissociative cognitive error that she would someday be a 'happy little girl with a normal childhood with two loving parents'. The 5-year-old experienced a lack of personification that it happened to her. This was gradually treated, which allowed the 9-year-old and the 24-year-old parts to also personify the father's abandonment (i.e., realize it happened to them as well). This then allowed personification and some presentation by all parts regarding the husband and his death to gradually occur.

When enough time orientation and personification occurred, Jill was ready for the memory processing phase of treatment. There was cooperation and collaboration among the parts, with ANP (the adult) leadership. The memory chosen to start this phase was the 4-year-old's memory of listening to her parents fight about the affair. Her mother uncontrollably raged at her father, threatening to leave with their daughter and never allow him to see the child again. In this fight, the mother said hurtful things including. 'If you loved your daughter, you wouldn't have done this to her.'

All parts agreed to participate in the memory reprocessing session, with communication going through the adult. Reprocessing of this memory went well, until anger was accessed. The 5-year-old EP defended against the anger by returning to the attachment crying for her father: that is, the 5-year-old part cried for her father to return. When this happened, reprocessing was blocked, and the client shut down, experiencing no emotion. This was the system's way of defending against what was still intolerable. Jill was then given several more sessions focusing on stabilization, which included more sessions of calming and working with parts on time orientation and personification. The part experienced as 5 years old increased her realization that she was part of this grown woman and that the memories and feelings are from the past (increased personification and presentification).

Memory reprocessing then continued with Jill able to stay within her window of tolerance for longer lengths of time before shutting down occurred. When shutting down occurred, the therapist would stop the memory reprocessing and guide the client into calming and more time orientation reminders (presentification), and more work on personification. With continued stabilization sessions in between memory processing sessions, Jill was also able to reprocess the many associations to other traumatic memories such as marital fights, her father leaving, and her mother shutting down.

The anger, powerlessness, disappointment, and annihilation fears gradually lessened. Jill reported enjoying her children more. She understood why when they were aged between 4 and 9 years it was so hard for her as a parent: It had triggered the trauma she experienced around the same age. She grieved her inability to be present during those ages. She also reported being more emotionally available to her new lover.

With the reprocessing of her father's abandonment, her mother's rages and shutting down, and how alone she felt during all those growing up years, Jill felt she had, in her words, 'a new lease on life'. Treatment then moved into the trauma of her husband's accident and death. Because of the earlier work this went easily and quickly. EMDR memory reprocessing sessions were rarely stopped by a part returning to its defensive avoidance. When a defence occurred, it was easy to re-establish access to the adaptive information that the pain was from memory and she was not being abandoned all over again. As expected, working on her husband's death associated into a deeper level of anger and deep disappointment to the earlier parental abandonments. This was also reprocessed successfully (i.e., fully integrated into her life history and personality).

After 1 year and 9 months in treatment, Jill was clear of disturbance from both the family-of-origin abandonments and the death of her husband. She had gone off her SSRI antidepressant about 6 months previously with her doctor's approval and remained stable. She was pleased with the quality of connection she enjoyed with her children. She proudly announced one day that she accepted her lover's proposal for marriage. Treatment successfully terminated after some final clean-up of fears of future abandonment, with the unification/integration of the parts of the personality. Jill left knowing that if she lost her next husband that she would have the skills to handle it and would get through it. She was not scared of her future nor stuck in the past.

Conclusion

The above case examples illustrate the importance of working with the personality system before reprocessing memories. Meeting the criteria (to a 'good enough' level) of co-consciousness, cooperation, and collaboration with ANP leadership is essential before memory reprocessing to avoid overwhelming the client and enable integration, including realization (with its components of personification and presentification), of the loss. Assessing if the different EPs know the deceased has died is an important step in helping the client realize the loss and prepare the client for memory reprocessing. With complex trauma, the loss can certainly trigger past attachment trauma which may have to be dealt with prior to dealing directly with the loss. Consequently, reprocessing past attachment trauma may be helpful before reprocessing the trauma of the loss.

A Final Note on Grief and Mourning in Treatment

All integrative work includes dealing with grief, even when it does not involve the death of a loved one. For every step forward, every accomplishment, there is both joy (Janet's 'act of triumph') and grief—the realization of what was lost (and sometimes will never be regained; Steele et al., 2017). These losses also have to be reprocessed. For example, a woman who was sexually abused as a child utilized a calming technique where she would visualize herself as an octopus because an octopus could escape from tight places. After a particularly integrative session she declared, 'I am not an octopus ... (the abuse) happened to me ... and I lost myself, and I can never get it back' (personification). This realization was a turning point in her therapy, with EMDR therapy focusing on reprocessing her losses such as loss of childhood innocence, sense of safety, and loss of social confidence. Ultimately in building her integrative capacity and internal resources and facing the powerlessness resulting from the abuse, she did get 'herself' back.

Summary

This chapter described how the TSDP can guide EMDR therapy. When a person experiences significant trauma or neglect, especially in early childhood, there can be a division of the personality into dissociative parts, with one or more parts engaging in everyday living (i.e., APNs) and one or more parts engaged and stuck in failed psychological defence (i.e., EPs). Each part has its own sense of self. Therapy needs to follow Phase-Oriented Treatment, consisting of (1) stabilization, (2) memory work, and (3) personality (re)integration and rehabilitation. The eight phases of EMDR therapy can integrate within a Phase-Oriented Treatment approach. Notably, there needs to be an extended Preparation & Stabilization phase of EMDR therapy to treat the dissociation and promote readiness for memory reprocessing.

20
Closing Thoughts

Loss is painful and can impact all facets of life. Eye movement desensitization and reprocessing (EMDR) therapy does not eliminate the pain but rather reprocesses the obstacles that complicate the grief, to facilitate progression through the mourning process, enabling adaptation to the new world without the deceased. Mourners can move from a sense of "I cannot connect" to "I can connect," through the formation of an adaptive inner representation composed of meaningful, heartfelt memories. This book has elaborated how the Adaptive Information Processing model guides clinicians to target past memories underlying present dysfunction, to address present triggers, and to develop an adaptive future template for each trigger. However, in order to have an accurate inner representation, negative memories also have to be dealt with. If mourners' responses to loss are complicated or processing is blocked, then past traumas, losses, memories related to the deceased, and attachment-based memories need to be assessed and dealt with.

Other frameworks can inform EMDR therapy. Attachment Theory helps clinicians understand where to look for developmental memories that underlie stuck points and complicated response to loss. Continuing Bonds theory informs us that the bond with the loved one does not go away, it transforms and continues. The Dual Process model provides an overall view of mourning that guides clinicians toward assessing the balance between Loss Orientation and Restoration Orientation. The "R" processes provide a framework to understand the psychological processes necessary for adaptation to a traumatic loss.

EMDR Therapy Includes Positive Adaptation

EMDR therapy does much more than treat trauma, it focuses on positive adaptation. Consistent with Neimeyer's (2013) model of "meaning reconstruction," EMDR therapy can help mourners integrate traumatic memories, rebuild their assumptive world, and find meaning through the emergence of adaptive perspectives. As painful as a loss is, posttraumatic growth (Tedeschi & Calhoun, 2008) can occur, enabling mourners to attain life-enhancing

EMDR Therapy Treatment for Grief and Mourning. Roger M. Solomon, Oxford University Press. © Roger M. Solomon 2024.
DOI: 10.1093/oso/9780198881360.003.0021

perspectives experienced as positive change. *Posttraumatic growth, a* widely validated concept, is defined as the experience of positive change in one's life beyond the point of mere recovery of previous functioning, which comes as a result of a traumatic experience (Tedeschi & Calhoun, 2008). Tedeschi, Orejuela-Davila, and Lewis (2018) point out, "Bereavement can usher into a person's life new considerations of how to live, as a loss requires changes in perspective, habits, and relationships" (p. 31). Struggles with loss have been present with people through the ages and have created challenges in adaptation. Managing these changes can lead to greater personal development, enhanced resilience, and posttraumatic growth. EMDR therapy, focusing on traumatic memories, present triggers, and implementing adaptive future templates, fosters posttraumatic growth.

EMDR Therapy Is a Paradigm of Resilience

Resilience is the positive capacity people have to cope with stress; it is a dynamic process where people exhibit positive behavioral adaptation when they encounter significant adversity or trauma (Luthar, Cicchetti, & Becker, 2000). As Solomon and Shapiro (2012, pp. 286–287) said:

> In terms of the Adaptive Information Processing model, resilience, coherence and resourcefulness are responses based upon the affects and perspectives that characterize the memories that are stimulated by the current experience. When people are confronted by adversity, adaptive information stored in their memory networks is available for coping with the challenge. A high level of resilience, sense of coherence, and learned resourcefulness results from the person's ability to make full use of functionally stored information and abilities acquired in his or her life.

After a significant loss, life may never go back to the way it was. Therefore, we have to move through and integrate adverse circumstances and create a new normal. "What happens to us becomes part of us. Resilient people do not bounce back from hard experiences; they find healthy ways to integrate them into their lives" (Greitens, 2015, p.23).

As Solomon and Shapiro (2012) state:

> EMDR therapy is designed to identify and process the past memories that underlie difficulties in coping, to address present situations that trigger disturbance, and to enable the development of a positive memory template for future adaptive behavior. The processing of pivotal memories facilitates a rapid learning experience that

transforms the negative perspective and affects into more neutral or even positive ones. These then become the basis of resilience by enhancing one's ability to cope effectively with subsequent related stressors. Processing the dysfunctionally stored memories that underlie current maladaptive behaviors enables a person to bring to bear on future adverse circumstances the full potential of his or her functional capacity and available personal resources. (p. 287).

This book is full of examples of how EMDR therapy brings about post-traumatic growth, finding meaning, and enhancing resilience. It is hoped these examples not only illustrate important teaching points about EMDR therapy but also highlight the strong human spirit that EMDR therapy draws upon to integrate distressing memories and enable the bereaved to move through life challenges in an adaptive way.

Take Care of Yourself

Working with grief and mourning is painful for clinicians. My first time working with a large group of survivors of police officers killed in the line of duty deeply impacted me. The "wall of grief" I encountered in working with this group was immense. Indeed, working with loss triggers one's own vulnerability. How does one cope? Here is what has helped me:

1. *Accept the Pain*—Accept the pain our clients bring. Our clients are people who are experiencing tremendous pain because of what happened to them. Having a boundary between clients and ourselves is very important. We must remember, what happened to our clients did not happen to us. (If it did, then we need to deal with what happened in a constructive way that models what we do for others.) Their pain is normal and appropriate given what has happened, and our role is to be part of their support team and accompany them through the treatment process.
2. *See the Client, Not Just the Pain*—So many people overidentify with what happened to clients, reacting to the circumstance and failing to see the suffering person, making it difficult to be fully present with them. It is important we see the people, beyond the circumstances, who are experiencing the pain, knowing we are part of their healing process.
3. *Deal with Our Own Vulnerabilities*—Dealing with other people's pain can trigger our own vulnerabilities. Indeed, for ourselves and our clients, we have to actively deal with our own fears and personal reactions that get triggered when working with clients.

4. *Create Personal Support*—Have your personal support team, social network, circle of trust, or whatever you call the people you can engage with that give you comfort and safety. Who can you talk to, are there sources of professional consultation for a complicated case, is there a source for personal therapy to deal with whatever is being triggered, and people you can have plain old fashion fun with?

5. *Work with a Team*—Working with a team helps. I have worked with wonderful colleagues as part of a team in providing services to traumatized people. Working with others can provide a buffer to the emotional work of grief and trauma therapy. If you are working alone, have a support network of other people you can check in with regularly.

6. *Have Balance in Your Life*—Engage in your own life-enhancing activities to balance your life. Have fun, do things that engage you in life, engage in meaningful and life satisfying pursuits, both big and small. For me, enjoying a different flavor of gelato goes a long way toward seeing the sweet things in life.

7. *Physical Self-Care*—Take care of yourselves physically. Our job is mentally and emotionally exhausting. Having a regular routine of physical exercise to relieve stress, build stamina, and clear your mind is essential in our profession.

8. *Believe in Humanity*—A belief in human potential, curiosity and an optimistic outlook on life is essential. My friend, Charles Figley, who has done much work on compassion fatigue (1995, 2002), once asked me what has prevented my burnout, and I have reflected much on this question. I sit down with a client, and see the person, not just their pain. I believe a person has an inherent strength, albeit sometimes difficult to find, but it is there. I strive to sense and connect with this humanness, the spark of life strength all of us have, and then join the client to collaboratively go through the healing journey. Though I am guided by other therapeutic frameworks, EMDR therapy is the core of what I do. EMDR therapy is effective, harnessing the healing power within, and I am continually surprised and delighted at how clients find their way out. I playfully think of EMDR therapy as a James Bond movie. As a young child, I would watch a James Bond movie (Sean Connery, of course), and when danger was all around him, I would wonder How is he going to get out of this one? But he always did. There have been many times in an EMDR session when I have wondered How is the client going to get out of this one? But they do. Being part of the client's healing process, watching the resolution and integration progress take place in front of me, and "going

with that," is as engaging for me as it is for my clients, and has taught me more about human nature and the patterns of integration than any book possibly could. I continue to learn from my clients, being curious and always striving to understand not only what the problem is, but what the client's way to integration is. Accompanying clients through their healing process is meaningful and personally enriching and gives me a feeling that I am part of something greater than myself.

Some people, for any of a number of reasons, do not progress in therapy. The impact of physical or organic factors, heredity, and early childhood trauma (including prenatal) can combine to make progress slow. Clients continue to come back for an important reason—for some people all they have to look forward to each week is their session with you. This, in and of itself, is helpful and therapeutic, and I never lose sight of that.

May I ask you, the reader What is your personal outlook on what you do that keeps you going?

A Final Caveat

This book focused on the EMDR Standard Protocol for Treatment of Grief and Mourning. But. there is so much more that can be done to help the bereaved. Other methods include writing letters to the deceased, having meaningful conversations with the deceased, visualizing being at the scene of the death (if one was absent) and offering comfort, healing rituals and memorials, and the like. Bilateral stimulation, utilizing the principles and methodology of Resource Development and Installation (Korn & Leeds, 2002) can enhance the positive aspects of such methods and can help mourners go through the mourning process. Also, clinicians should realize that coping with a loss requires more than reprocessing negative memories. It includes many hurdles such as coping with the loneliness that occurs when one's life partner and main source of support is gone, finding a new way to live when one was quite happy with the life one had, and finding a way to live with pain that will never cease. This requires helping clients do the following: (a) learn new skills, (b) find the motivation and strength to go on, (c) see new directions, and (d) have hope. EMDR clinicians need to provide a wholistic approach, using all the tools and effective methodologies at their disposal, and stand with clients side by side in collaboration to provide a healing presence and support.

Eye Movement Desensitization and Reprocessing (EMDR) Therapy Treatment of Grief and Mourning with Death Caused by Covid-19

The Covid pandemic of the last few years has irreparably impacted the people of our world. Death caused by Covid-19 can compound the trauma of a loss. Mourners have to deal with relevant incidents such as: (1) the loss of a loved one, (2) complications caused by Covid-19 that include risk factors for traumatic bereavement (e.g., sudden and unexpected death), and (c) the disruption to one's personal life caused by Covid-19. Also, the distress of adapting to Covid-19 and grief reactions can be further complicated by prior unresolved losses and trauma, and attachment-related trauma.

The Covid-19 pandemic has resulted in many losses at individual, community, national, and international levels that interact and compound the grief resulting from death of a loved one. These layers of losses can include loss of physical contact with family and friends, loss of employment and financial security, loss of control, loss of personal freedoms, loss of familiar routines and future plans, loss of safety and predictability. There is also the potential for contracting a life-threatening illness. Wang et al. (2020) studied the psychological impact of the Covid-19 outbreak, finding that 53.8% of respondents rated the psychological impact as moderate or severe; 16.5% reported moderate to severe depression symptoms; 28.8% reported moderate to severe anxiety symptoms; and 8.1% reported moderate to severe stress levels.

The loss of a loved one can have a significant impact that can be complicated by the restrictions resulting from Covid-19. Social distancing and quarantine prevent loved ones from being present in person at the bedside of a loved one to provide comfort, express their love, or say what is needed to be said before the death of a loved one. Religious and memorial ceremonies were required to be online, with friends and family offing comfort from a distance. Further, the impact of Covid-19 on one's personal life can be quite distressing, and along with loss, can violate basic assumptions about the world (e.g., safety, a meaningful world where there is control and predictability, and about the self being worthy). Consequently, often, mourners are forced to deal with the trauma of the loss and the trauma of the circumstances that surround it alone. Loss by Covid-19 involves the following risk factors:

1. *Suddenness and Lack of Anticipation*—Contracting Covid-19 and dying as a result can be sudden and unexpected. The hopeful expectation for recovery can make a death more impactful.
2. *Unnaturalness of the Death*—There are many atypical occurrences associated with Covid-19: Visitation for Covid-19 patients is strictly prohibited. Friends and families are unable to be present to hold a loved one's hand and say a last, 'goodbye' at the time of passing. Funerals must be watched from afar or delayed for weeks or months, depriving friends and family of the traditional rituals and moments of togetherness so important and comforting to people during their grieving process.
3. *Physical or Emotional Suffering*—It is distressing to watch loved ones suffer when there is nothing one can do. The sense of helplessness and powerlessness of knowing a loved one

is suffering and realizing there is nothing one can do is magnified because of the inability to provide face-to-face comfort.

4. *Preventable Deaths*—Death that is preventable can be more impactful than those caused by natural disasters (e.g., hurricane, earthquake, and tornado). With Covid-19, some people may view the death as preventable for a variety of reasons: (a) the government's delayed response to the severity of the Covid-19 threat and in providing personal protective equipment to healthcare facilities and workers, (b) nonexistent or insufficient preventive guidelines or protective gear at workplaces, or (c) disregard by the deceased to recommended precautions (i.e., wearing a mask, social distancing). Mourners may struggle with the senselessness of a death and may experience strong feelings of anger (e.g., 'It was preventable and should not have happened.').

5. *Randomness* of an event can be best characterized by 'being in the wrong place at the wrong time'. Covid-19 is invisible and, therefore, uncontrollable. Even with lockdown conditions and restricted movement, one can contract it at the grocery store, gas station, or from a family member. Death can occur as a result of these necessary activities or contacts.

6. *Multiple Deaths* may occur within one household. This can create what is called a 'bereavement overload' (Rando, 1993, 2013) and becomes more difficult to deal with.

7. *Threat to One's Own Life*—The mourner's life may also have been put at risk because of exposure to the loved one who died of Covid-19. Further, if the mourner also had Covid-19 and survived, there can be trauma as a result of having the disease and guilt for surviving when the loved one died.

8. *Untimeliness*—The loved one's dying of a disease can be regarded as premature and untimely when the death occurs at an inappropriate stage of life in the life cycle (e.g., childhood, adolescence, and young adulthood). Intense feelings of anger, injustice, and sadness are often felt because of the loss of a life of unrealized potential.

9. *Social Support* is an extremely important resource when dealing with distressing life experiences. In the days and nights of quarantine and social distancing, lack of direct, face-to-face rituals, such as religious ceremonies, funerals, and visits from family and friends, and lack of social support can compound the trauma and grief of the loss.

Case Conceptualization for Loss in Times of Covid-19

EMDR therapy involves processing the negative memories underlying present difficulties, the present triggers that evoke the distress, and installing a positive future template for each present trigger. The death of a loved one in the times of Covid-19 can create three levels of problems:

1. Loss of a loved one.
2. Traumatic or complicating circumstances attributable to Covid-19 (e.g., risk factors, such as a sudden, unexpected, untimely death involving suffering) and/or previous unresolved losses or traumas, including attachment-based trauma.
3. The impact of Covid-19 on personal functioning.

The loss of a loved one, exacerbated by the risk factors of Covid-19, may interfere with a person's ability to cope with current stressful circumstances, which in turn can interfere with progressing through the mourning process. Consequently, treatment must deal with the loss, the trauma of the loss, and the impact of present stressful circumstances.

This book focuses on the loss of a loved one. However, similar treatment principles apply to treating the distress of Covid-19. Present difficulties in coping with the distress of Covid-19 may be compounded by unresolved losses and past traumas. Adapting to the social isolation conditions can be aggravated by attachment-related memories of abandonment and loneliness. Earlier memories of powerlessness and vulnerability can be triggered by the danger of Covid-19 and interfere with present coping.

The following case example was previously published by Solomon and Hensley (2020).

Case Example: Jerry

'Jerry' is a 46-year-old man whose father died of Covid-19.

Phase 1: History-Taking and Treatment Planning

After Covid-19 restrictions were imposed, Jerry isolated himself at home with his wife and two young adult children. His father contracted Covid-19, was hospitalized 1 week later, and died 1 week after that. As Jerry and his family had not seen the father in over 3 weeks, they felt confident that they were not at risk from the father's illness. The family sought treatment from a family clinician 3 weeks after his father died, and, as a result, Jerry was referred for individual treatment.

Jerry knew that his father could die, but his death was still a shock because of his hope for his father's recovery. It was distressing to be at such a distance. He had to watch his father's rapid decline in health and obvious discomfort on a computer screen, talk to him and say goodbye online, and communicate his emotions and love to his father in a way that felt inadequate. The funeral service was held online with only the family members and the chaplain present to view his father's closed casket. At the graveyard, with no other people in attendance, the family watched the burial service from their car. A virtual memorial service and online chats with friends and family were helpful, even heartwarming, but also troubling to Jerry and his family. Because of the lack of physical proximity, it felt distant and impersonal.

Jerry experienced intrusive negative images of his father in the hospital (e.g., his father's suffering, his father on the respirator). His father's illness also triggered the memory of his grandfather's stroke and eventual death. Jerry had been close to his grandfather, who lived with the family, and died when Jerry was 6 years old.

Jerry described an ambivalent relationship with his father. His father was loving and provided for the needs of the family when Jerry was growing up but also had a quick temper. Several memories of his father yelling at him were surfacing. Jerry reported having a pervasive negative belief of, 'I'm not good enough', which he understood was linked to negative memories involving his father. He and his father had established a good relationship after Jerry got married, especially after his children were born, and he was confused by these intrusive memories, saying, 'I know it's in the past and different from the present, but I just can't sort it out.'

Jerry said he was feeling anxious, having difficulty concentrating on his work with his recurrent belief of 'I am not good enough.' Since his father's death, he felt insecure while working and experienced self-doubt about his capabilities. The computer on which he worked was the same one he used to talk with his father, and it triggered images of his father's suffering. Further, he was isolating more and not engaging in his usual level of conversation and activity with his family.

Jerry's Case Conceptualization

Jerry was experiencing traumatic bereavement with risk factors including: (a) sudden and unexpected death, (b) unnaturalness of the death, (c) father's suffering, (d) randomness, and (e) an untimely death.

Jerry had an anxious attachment to his father. His insecurities and negative self-belief, ('I'm not good enough.') stemmed from childhood and heightened after the death of his father, interfering with work and his emotional availability to his family. Jerry's oscillation between loss orientation (LO) and restoration orientation (RO) was off balance. Jerry was overly focused on LO. His suffering from the loss of his father was complicated by the triggering of previous losses (e.g., grandfather's death and attachment-based memories of father yelling at him). Consequently, his ability to deal with daily living (i.e., RO), such as concentrating on his work and engaging with his family, was diminished.

Jerry's treatment plan was as follows.

1. *Preparation & Stabilization:*
   - Balance the oscillation between LO and RO by helping Jerry with: (a) affect regulation to lower his anxiety, (b) Resource Development & Installation (RDI) to help him function better at working, and (c) a new routine that included regular family time.
2. Target Memories Related to the Immediate Death:
   - The last time he saw his father alive in the hospital on the respirator (i.e., watching from his computer).
   - Images of his father suffering.
   - Unusual circumstances of the funeral, (i.e., virtual visitation and memorial, lack of physical comfort from immediate friends and family members, and watching the burial from his car).
3. Target Memories Stemming from Previous Losses and (Attachment) Trauma:
   - His grandfather's having a stroke.
   - Memories of his father yelling at him and his brother.
4. Target Present Triggers:
   - Being at his computer while working and having images of his father's suffering coming up.
   - Moments where he wanted to be more talkative and involved with his family at home but found it difficult.
   - Reminders of his father, such as seeing his picture of his father.
5. Future Templates:
   - Being able to work on his computer without distraction.
   - Being able to engage comfortably with his family.
   - Being able to think of his father with a sense of peace and love.

Phase 2: Preparation & Stabilization

EMDR therapy was explained during this phase, including the use of bilateral stimulation (BLS). For the virtual sessions, the butterfly hug (i.e., with thumbs locked as Jerry bilaterally tapped on his chest (Jarero & Artigas, 2020)) and knee tapping were introduced as BLS methods. Jerry tapped on his chest during the Safe/Calm Place and resource exercises, and on his knees during reprocessing. This differentiation allowed the butterfly hug to be associated with safety, comfort, and stability. Having been instructed that the clinician would indicate when to start and stop the processing, Jerry was assured that he could stop at any time for any reason.

Jerry had four online Preparation & Stabilization sessions within a 2-week period, involving history-taking and affect management. Safe/Calm Place and breathing exercises assisted in affect management. RDI (Korn & Leeds, 2002) helped Jerry deal with working at his computer. Specifically, a memory where he successfully dealt with a challenging situation at work 2 years prior was utilized to focus on his ability to summon up strength and courage in difficult situations. Another memory of getting an award helped him capture feelings of competence and 'I am good enough.' As the clinician facilitated a future rehearsal, Jerry was able to successfully imagine feeling courage, strength, and competence. Implementation of a more structured daily routine was also beneficial, focusing on his work schedule with breaks, daily exercise through an online programme that he and his wife could do together, and meal and leisure time with the family. This assisted Jerry in maintaining a more balanced oscillation between LO and RO and meet criteria for memory processing.

Along with the usual instructions and education given to clients for EMDR memory processing, with sessions taking place virtually, the importance of collaboration with the therapist was emphasized. He should report if there was any physical or emotional discomfort and let the therapist know what he needed.

Phase 3–8: Target Assessment, Desensitization, Installation, Body Scan, Closure, and Re-evaluation

Originally, the clinician and Jerry had agreed to start work with the memory of seeing his father for the last time on the respirator and not being able to offer comfort. However, as he focused on this memory, the childhood memory of his grandfather having a stroke kept intruding. Therefore, it was decided to first focus on this memory of his grandfather, Jerry described it as:

TARGET: 'My grandfather is lying on his bed, suddenly he got up, made a noise and spit blood, and laid down again.'

IMAGE: the grandfather making a noise and seeing the blood in his mouth.

NEGATIVE COGNITION: Bringing up the memory evoked the experience of being powerless, afraid, and not good enough. After initially thinking about the words, 'I'm not capable', he realized what was most impactful was the terror he felt. Consequently, the negative cognition selected was, 'I'm not safe.'

Note: This interchange highlights the importance of having a clinical dialogue regarding what is the most felt negative cognition. Several negative cognitions came to mind with the 'I'm not safe' being the most felt.

POSITIVE COGNITION: 'I am safe.'

VALIDITY OF COGNITION (VoC): 3/7.

EMOTION: Fear.

SUBJECTIVE UNITS OF DISTURBANCE (SUD): 8/10.

LOCATION OF BODY SENSATION: chest area.

Processing commenced with Jerry focusing on the image, his negative cognition 'I'm not safe', and noticing the sensations in his body. His fear increased after the first set and remained the same for several more sets. With the processing seemingly blocked, the clinician introduced a cognitive interweave, 'As you feel this fear, do you know you are safe today?' Jerry responded, 'Yes.' The clinician then asked, 'Can you bring that awareness to this memory?' When Jerry nodded, 'Yes', the clinician continued processing. Jerry indicated that the fear was subsiding by saying, 'Seems like I'm not so scared ... it's a bit strange, the image of my grandfather on the bed is disappearing gradually ... his death does not terrify me.' With continued processing Jerry reported, 'My grandfather was important in my life. I could laugh with him and cry with him.... I feel gratitude toward him.' When the clinician went back to the target memory and asked Jerry what he noticed, Jerry reported, 'I can see his head. It is bright, and I don't see any blood on his face.' After another set, other memories of his grandfather spontaneously emerged (e.g., grandfather reading him a story, eating an apple with his grandfather). The clinician then went back to target, the initial image had faded, and Jerry reported only feeling gratitude and love for his grandfather. The clinician asked for the SUD, which was 0, and it stayed 0 after another set. Then the positive cognition 'I am safe' was installed with a VoC of 7. The body scan was clear. Jerry was asked to think of his grandfather, and positive memories with associated positive affect arose, which were strengthened with short sets of BLS.

At the end of this session, Jerry was happy but tearful. After a review of affect regulation and coping strategies, and a reminder of his safe place, the session ended.

Next Session (a Week Later)

Jerry reported that he felt calmer during the week and more able to focus on work and was enjoying more interaction with his family. The memory of his grandfather no longer bothered him. Further, he felt more comfortable thinking about his father.

The target for this session was the memory of seeing his father for the last time on the respirator. Jerry was on the computer at the time and was not able to be present to offer comfort.

IMAGE: The father on the respirator looking weak and haggard.
NEGATIVE COGNITION: Jerry had feelings of powerlessness for not being able to do more and resonated with 'I am powerless.'
POSITIVE COGNITION: Jerry initially had difficulty coming up with a positive cognition. After going over what he was in control of and what was beyond his control, he offered, 'I did the best I could.'
VoC: 3/7.
EMOTIONS: sadness and a feeling of resignation.
SUD: 7/10.
LOCATION OF BODY SENSATION: chest area.

After the first set of bilateral stimulation (BLS), Jerry started to cry. With continuing sets, his tears abated. He remembered his final conversation with his father before he went on the respirator. The discomfort had changed, and Jerry reported that he felt at a deep level his father knew he was not alone, and that Jerry loved him. Upon going back to target, he reported his father was no longer suffering. With continued processing, positive and heartfelt memories of his father alive emerged (e.g., family picnics, his father playing with the grandchildren). The SUD went to 2 and did not decrease with further sets. A discussion with Jerry revealed it was a 2 because this was a tragic and sad event, so was ecologically appropriate (*Note*: it was checked using BLS before designated ecologically appropriate.) The positive cognition changed to 'I was there in the best way I could be', and installed until a VoC = 7. The body scan was clear. When asked to think of his father, positive memories came up and were enhanced with brief sets of bilateral stimulation. He could now think of his father with a sense of peace and connection. Further, he reported that the memories of his father's suffering, though sad, no longer bothered him. He could imagine his father being at peace. This illustrates that treatment effects generalized to other negative memories of his father.

At the next session, Jerry reported that he felt a greater sense of peace and connection with his father, though memories of his yelling were still on his mind. He was engaging more with his family and reported working more efficiently, but still felt sad about his father. The funeral, which had disturbed him before because the family was alone, no longer bothered him. It now felt like a quiet and peaceful time for Jerry and his family to remember his father.

In this session, a childhood memory of his father yelling at him was targeted.

IMAGE: The father's angry and loud voice.
NEGATIVE COGNITION: 'I am not good enough.'
POSITIVE COGNITION: 'I am good enough.'
VoC: 4/7.
EMOTION: sadness and anger.
SUD: 5/10.
LOCATION OF BODY SENSATION: Chest area.

With reprocessing, other memories (e.g., childhood memories of his father yelling at his brother and himself) surfaced. Jerry was emotional and reported, 'I did not deserve to be treated that way.' With continued processing, an adult perspective emerged, 'We had our diffi-cult moments, and I know he felt bad about it as well.' With continued processing, he acknowl-edged his father's efforts to make their relationship better and that he was a good grandfather. When going back to target, the memory felt over and in the past, with a SUD of 0. The positive cognition of 'I am good enough' was installed with a VoC of 7, and he had a clear body scan.

The next session Jerry reported feeling good and engaged with his family. His work was going much better, and, although still sad, he could continue to think of his father with a sense of peace. He was no longer negatively triggered by reminders of his father. For example, he could look at pictures of his father and feel warmth and recall positive memories.

The focus of the next session revolved around moments when he felt a surge of incompe-tence. A recent memory (i.e., present trigger) when he was working at his computer and dealing with a difficult situation was targeted.

IMAGE: Looking at his computer screen with an email detailing the work situation.
NEGATIVE COGNITION: 'I am incompetent.'
POSITIVE COGNITION: 'I am competent.'
VoC: 5/7.
EMOTION: anxiety.
SUD: 4/10.
LOCATION OF BODY SENSATION: chest area.

During the processing, Jerry realized that the work problem was one of the most challenging issues in his job. It was a difficult assignment, but he had completed it and said, 'I am up to the challenge.' At the end of processing, the SUD was 0, and a new positive cognition emerged, 'I am up to the challenge', and was installed with a VoC of 7. The body scan was clear.

A future template was then installed. Jerry thought of dealing with a similar situation at work, with the positive cognition, 'I'm up to the challenge', and a feeling of confidence. Using BLS, the positive feeling enhanced. The positive cognition was installed with a 7. Thinking of his positive cognition, a movie with his dealing with the situation was installed. Another chal-lenging situation also was identified (i.e., his initial attempts failing), and a future template of adaptive handling of the situation (i.e., calling some colleagues for consultation) was installed.

Termination
After completing the processing of memories related to his grandfather's death, his father's death, past childhood memories, processing present triggers, and installing future templates, Jerry had a balanced oscillation between LO and RO. Though he was sad and missed his fa-ther, he could think of his father with a sense of peace and could reflect on meaningful, positive memories of him. Jerry was more engaged with his family, adapted to the new schedule, and was able to be focused while working. Treatment terminated with an agreement to check back if he felt he was getting out of balance.

Discussion

EMDR therapy was utilized to treat the three layers of Jerry's loss, consisting of the loss of his father, the compounding factors caused by Covid-19, and the distress emanating from life changes caused by Covid-19. The Preparation & Stabilization phase, focusing on enhancing RO, involved helping Jerry cope with life changes resulting from Covid-19 by learning affect regu-lation strategies and implementing a more structured daily routine. The loss, and its traumatic impact, was dealt with in five steps, by processing (1) unresolved childhood losses, (2) memo-ries related to attachment trauma, (3) the most painful memory (or memories) regarding the loved one's death, (4) and present triggers, and (5) installing future templates for each trigger to further enable adaptation to the loss and present circumstances. Positive, heartfelt memories emerged as a result of processing distressing memories, illustrating the formation of an adaptive inner representation. This gave Jerry a positive sense of connection with his father, aiding in the transformation of the relationship from loving in presence to loving in absence.

Conclusion

The loss of a loved one is painful, and it can be complicated by the distressing circumstances of Covid-19. Therefore, treatment needs to help clients deal both with the loss (which is distressing by itself) and the present distressing circumstances which complicate the trauma of the loss. Further, previous losses and past disturbing memories can exacerbate the current distress and need to be treated.

Transcripts of Sessions

The following are partial transcripts of eye movement desensitization and reprocessing (EMDR) therapy sessions with mothers whose children were killed. Each of these sessions was very emotional. The printed words, of course, cannot really illustrate the emotionality of the client or clinician involvement. Being present with clients with facial expression, body language, supportive 'nurturing through' by helping clients gain distance by saying, 'just notice it', to gain distance or joining through saying things like 'I know it hurts' and 'I am with you' to join with clients. Occasionally, cognitive interweaves are used to help clients through the process. Notes in the transcripts illustrate the clinician's thinking and highlight the important teaching points. In these three cases, the therapists elicit the inner representation (see Chapter 18 on Phases 5–8) at the end of the reprocessing session by asking the client to think of their loved one, and enhancing the positive memories and feelings that arise with further bilateral stimulation (BLS).

In the transcripts, **. will signify a set of eye movements (with the clinician saying 'Go with that') and asking 'What do you notice?'

Case 1: Death of an Infant

Anabia's infant son died when he was 3 months old. She sought EMDR consultation 6 years after the infant's death.

Anabia, aged 28 years, grew up in a family that was very religious, and religion was an important part of her adult life. For Anabia, being a mother was an important life goal. She married at age 20 and had a son at age 21, who died when 3 months old. Though she since had two more children, she still suffered from the death of her firstborn. Anabia had previously engaged in grief therapy (individual and group) from several sources, but still her grief seemed neverending. She was advised to 'find the meaning', but never could. Anabia felt guilty. Either God was good, and she did something wrong and was being punished, or God was not good. She felt angry at God. She understood cognitively, as told to her numerous times by religious leaders that she could not have done anything so bad that God would punish her in this way, and that we may not know the reasons for what happens. However, she still blamed herself: 'God does not give so much pain to somebody who doesn't deserve it.' After three sessions of history-taking, and Preparation & Stabilization, Anabia and the therapist decided to initially focus EMDR therapy on the trauma of her son dying.

Phase 2: Preparation & Stabilization

The Safe/Calm Place exercise and several resource installation exercises were provided during the first three sessions, along with history-taking.

Phase 3: Target Assessment

IMAGE: Holding her baby who is not breathing.
NEGATIVE COGNITION: I am helpless.
POSITIVE COGNITION: I did the best I could.
VALIDITY OF COGNITION (VoC): 1/7.
EMOTION: sadness and guilt.
SUBJECTIVE UNITS OF DISTURBANCE (SUD): 10/10.

Phase 4: Desensitization

Therapist: Bring up the image and the words, 'I am helpless', notice the sensations in your body, and follow my fingers. (Eye movement starts.)
Note: Anabia was very emotional during the reprocessing. After 38 minutes, positive memories started to come up. She remembered the day she became a mother.
Anabia: It was, you know, the happiest I could ever remember. It was such a beautiful day I felt so much gratitude, so much love, so much warmth.... and then, it just turned upside down in literally a second.
Therapist: **.

With continued processing of the suddenness of the loss, more positive feelings arose.

Anabia: I feel just that love, that peace, that calm in me ... I feel warm, that nurturing feeling ... I feel that connection, I feel the connection to him.
Therapist: **.
Note: Then, Anabia became stuck, feeling an intense 'crushing' pain. The therapist explored the crush, by asking 'What is good about the crush?' Anabia had the insight that the pain keeps the memory alive.
Anabia: But I feel stuck, I can't move on, and I don't know why. I feel as intense pain like crushing, like you know, it crushes you every day.
Therapist: What is good about the crush ... what does it do?
Anabia: I guess it keeps the memory alive.
Therapist: So if you let go of the 'crush?'
Anabia: I may forget ... Even though he's such a part of me ... I have so few memories of him, he was only 3 months old.
Note: At this point the therapist provided a cognitive interweave, and explained EMDR would not take away what was needed, including the cognition. Further, the therapist continued with another cognitive interweave, asking her to recognize both the pain and the sense of connection at the same time. The purpose of this interweave was to foster co-consciousness and integration of both important aspects of her experience.
Therapist: EMDR will not take away anything that you need.... Think of the connection you feel now, you will not lose this.... Let's recognize, on one hand there is a 'crush' and you fear 'if I lose this crush, I lose this positive feeling.' But can you recognize that you're feeling some positive, warm feelings when you think of your son?
Anabia: Yeah.
Therapist: Can you feel both the pain, and the sense of connection you have?
Anabia: Yes, and I can feel the warmth.
Therapist: **.
Anabia: The pain subsides. It's a much better feeling.

Therapist: **.

Anabia: I felt ... I was ... holding my son, just feeling that bond, feeling that warmth and that love, and not even focusing on the pain.

Therapist: **.

Anabia: I'm still focused on that positive feeling of holding my son.

Therapist: **.

Anabia: I can feel that strength. The strength of our hearts bonding together.... This is wonderful, I haven't felt like that in a long time, just enjoy that feeling of holding him again. I have not felt this in a long time, it was just the crushing pain.

Note: With more sets of BLS, more positive memories arose.

Anabia: This is amazing ... I am remembering the birth, remembering the positive, remembering the good and happy moments with him which I never remembered. Which I had forgot about.

I remember when he was born, first holding him, the joy that I felt when I first held him. You know, even though for a short time, 3 months, but it's just ... the feedings, the nighttime feedings, just being there, wrapping him up, holding him, just looking at him....

Note: This next part of the session showed the transformation of the relationship with Anabia who was now feeling a connection to her son. It is surprising and confusing to her how she could feel she could still be his mother and love him, even though he was not physically present.

Therapist: **.

Anabia: I feel very grateful, that even though he would be just, you know, living 3 months, I had that time with him, and I made the most that I can with him, and I will always be his mother.

Therapist: **.

Anabia: I can't physically do anything for him anymore, I can't fulfil any physical needs, but I can still be his mother.

Therapist: **.

Anabia: I don't know why the relationship has to be this way, that I am a mother to a child who is not here, but I'm going to do whatever I can, and I can still be his mother.

Therapist: **.

Anabia: It's a hard concept, to love a child that's not here, not physically here, but it's still ... the relationship does exist.

Note: In these last two sets, the transformation of the relationship from loving in presence to loving in absence took place. Her feeling the connection to her son who is no longer living arose naturally, despite being confused about how this can be. Given she had no previous conception of how such a sense of connection could be felt, and it seemed to arise organically, it is hypothesized that the development of an internal representation through positive, meaningful memories with associated feelings is nature's inherent way of integrating a loss. There is not only the experiencing of heartfelt memories, but an enhancement of her identity as a mother. In the next interchange, Anabia described how the sudden, unexpected trauma of her son's death interfered with adaptation.

Anabia: It's a hard concept to understand. I guess when it happens so quickly it was just, you know, that I had to go literally go from one second to the next, from taking care of a child physically to all of a sudden to loving him, you know, just as a spirit, and I didn't know how to do it. It is like, I don't have any training for this ... I don't know how or what to do. How can you love a child who is not here?

Note: The therapist did a cognitive interweave to help her get in touch with her felt sense of connection. Processing the trauma of her son's death enabled a sense of connection, as illustrated in the dialogue below.

Therapist: Um hmm, and what's different now for you, what do you experience when you think of your son?

Anabia: That I understand that you can love a child even though they are not here. I don't feel that shock anymore, that crazy feeling of helpless, I think it's okay, I'm going to be okay. I can do this ... I feel like it's going to be hard, and there will be times where I'll be confused, as how to have this relationship, but I can do it, I can do it. I can love a child who's just not here and realizing that attending to his physical needs is not my only way of connecting with him.

Note: After another set where she again reiterated, she felt a positive sense of connection, the therapist returned to target and asked for a SUD.

Therapist: When you return to the original memory, how disturbing is it, 0 to 10? Zero is not the absence of emotion, or that you feel good about it. ... zero means calm or no distress, and 10 is the worst it can be.

Anabia: It is about a 1; my body is calm, but it will always be something awful. But I feel a sense of peace; he is still my son, and I am still his mother.

Note: The therapist does one more set, and the SUD remains at 1, which is deemed to be ecologically adaptive, and then the positive cognition is installed.

Phase 5: Installation

Therapist: Do the words 'I did the best I could' fit or are there other words that may be more suitable?

Anabia: Those words fit, but I like the words, '*I am still his mother.*'

Note: The words *I am still his mother* were installed as the positive cognition. Though this was not a traditional positive cognition about the self, it was adaptive and positive because it was very meaningful to Anabia, describing a felt connection to her son, an important goal of EMDR therapy with loss.

Phase 6: Installation:

The memory and the positive cognition 'I am still his mother' were held together, with Anabia scanning for tension. The result was a warm feeling, which was enhanced with another set of BLS.

Next, the therapist elicited the inner representation.

Therapist: When you think of your son, what comes up?

Anabia: I feel the love, the connection.

Therapist: **.

Note: At this point, the therapist asked Anabia about God.

Therapist: I would like to ask you, now, about God. What happens now when you think of God, now that you feel the connection and knowing you can love your son without the pain?

Anabia: Yeah, the anger is not there.

Therapist: Can you tell me more?

Anabia: I'm still confused, and I want God to help me through it, to just give me guidance.

Therapist: Okay, is that different from before?

Anabia: Absolutely, before I was angry and I felt like I was at fault, and I felt like I deserved that punishment, because I could not make sense out of it, and now it is more like I understand these things can happen, for whatever reason that I don't understand and I'm okay with that, my child was supposed to die at 3 months old. But I still have a relationship with him. I am still trying to understand this relationship, but I'm hoping that God will be able to show me, that God will be able to help me through it.
Therapist: **.
Anabia: I can pray for God to help me.

Phase 7: Closure

Anabia felt grounded at the end of the session, and described she felt connected to her son. She now experienced a sense of meaning that came from realizing that she is still a mother to her son, even if he is dead.

Phase 8: Re-evaluation

The next session, Anabia reported she still felt she was the mother to her son, and had a sense of connection. She also felt sadness at his loss. She also now understood how the trauma of the death kept her stuck in powerlessness, and unable to fully realize the loss. EMDR reprocessing continued with the next target being a ceremony at his gravesite following the death. She was no longer angry at God and was able to ask God for guidance.

Discussion

This case illustrates three important points that interfered with integration of the loss:

1. The trauma of the loss resulted in feelings of powerlessness.
2. Anabia feared that losing her pain would result in loss of any connection she had with her son.
3. Her religious belief was that she was being punished by God.

EMDR therapy first dealt with the trauma of her son dying. It was an emotional session. After 32 minutes of emotional reprocessing, positive memories were experienced. However, the reprocessing stalled because of her blocking belief that if she lost her pain, she would lose her connection. It is not uncommon that the connection to the lost loved one is through pain. The cognitive interweave that she would not lose anything she needed, and recognizing that she had both the positive feelings and the pain, resulted in positive, heartfelt memories of her son coming up. Then, a wonderful moment happened as Anabia felt a sense of connection to her son, and realized that she could still have a relationship to her son. She was amazed that she could still be his mother: 'I can love a child that's just not here, and realizing that attending to his physical needs is not my only way of connecting with him.' This was confusing to Anabia who before could not conceive of this idea. This points to the inherent and natural pattern of healing from loss, and the potential in all of us to move from, 'I cannot connect' to 'I can connect', through heart felt memories. Lastly, Anabia's faith in God was restored. With the processing of the trauma, and the feeling of connection, her anger at God dissipated. Her felt connection to a person no longer living was new and confusing. But now she felt she could ask God for help.

Case 2: Sharon, Teenage Son Killed in a Car Crash

Phase 1: History-Taking

Sharon was described in Chapter 13 History-Taking and Treatment Planning. Her teenage son, Joe, was killed in an auto accident. Sharon and her husband were receiving grief counselling. Sharon was referred for EMDR treatment 22 months following the death to deal with the trauma of Joe's death. Sharon had a stable family situation, and was utilizing her support system of friends, was participating in grief counselling with her husband, and had hobbies she enjoyed prior to the death of her son. Therefore, Sharon had minimal stabilization needs and appeared ready for EMDR therapy targeting the trauma of her loss. The two sessions focused on history-taking and teaching the Calm/Safe Place. The third session targeted the getting the news of Joe's death, when the police knocked on the door to deliver the death notification. This moment was successfully reprocessed. After this session, however, it was difficult for her to think of her son. She would experience deep pain when realizing he was dead, and this was too much for her.

This session described below, 2 months later, took place on the second anniversary of Joe's death. Sharon focused on her difficulty in thinking of Joe.

Phase 2: Preparation & Stabilization

With Sharon currently in ongoing counselling, she met criteria for EMDR therapy. After two sessions of history-taking and teaching a safe place exercise, EMDR therapy began with targeting, 'the knock on the door', and receiving the news of Joe's death. The session described below focused on her difficulty in thinking of Joe. Below is a partial transcript of the second EMDR session.

Phase 3: Target Assessment

In most instances, when thinking of Joe, she would realize he was dead, and become devastated. A recent example (present trigger) of driving while trying to think of Joe was targeted.

IMAGE: Driving while thinking of Joe's 'beautiful smiling face'.
NEGATIVE COGNITION: I can't go on living.
POSITIVE COGNITION: I can go on and thrive.
VoC: 2/7.
EMOTION: sadness.
SUD: ?/10.
LOCATION: Heaviness in her chest

Phase 4: Desensitization

Sharon was crying as she described the heaviness in her chest, so BLS was begun, with the therapist saying, 'Just following my fingers.'

Therapist: provides a set of BLS, and asks, 'What do you notice?'
Sharon: (crying) I think the one thing that comes up is just this major resistance.
Therapist: **.

Note: Sharon continued to cry for the next minute, as BLS continued, and the therapist gently talked to her to nurture her through the difficult moments.

Therapist: Just notice ... I know it hurts, ... I'm with you as we process this ....

Sharon: It's just hopeless.

Therapist: **.

Note: Sharon continued to cry, and found it difficult to follow the eye movement. The therapist, with permission, started to tap her hands, and continued by saying, 'I know it hurts ... just notice ....'

After a 90 second set, the therapist continued.

Therapist: Lets pause, take a breath, and what do you notice?

Sharon: I just feel better right now.

Therapist: **.

Note: Sharon continued to cry, and the therapist continued to nurture her through, 'I know it hurts ... just notice.'

After about 1 minute of BLS, with Sharon crying:

Sharon: What comes up is I can see Joe's smiling face, with his curls.

Therapist: **.

Note: Sharon began to cry again, and the eye movement continued for about another 40 seconds. It is common in EMDR sessions involving loss that waves come up and are reprocessed, followed by another wave of emotional pain. This ebb and flow of emotional pain is quite usual and comes with the unfolding levels of the realization of the loss. In the next sets of BLS, Sharon reported she felt better, but then another wave of pain was experienced.

Sharon: Better.

Therapist: **.

Sharon: It's not so deep and hopeless.

Therapist: **.

Note: Sharon continued to cry, with the therapist nurturing through ('I know it hurts, we will get through this ... '

Sharon: I just had a realization ... that it's like a kind of, being robbed the second time. Because, when I looked at his face, think about his beautiful smiling face ... instead of being able to experience that love and that person that is Joe.... It's just horrible (Sharon cries). The universe is not even allowing me to enjoy that.

Therapist: **.

Sharon: I feel like I could have more of a sense of believing I will be able to heal. It is worth making the effort, although I'm still feeling sad (crying continues).

Therapist: (Continuing eye movement and nurturing through) I know ... Just notice....

Sharon: I was just thinking maybe I will be able to miss him without being devastated, and then the next wave hit.

Note: Sharon's above statement illustrated how horrible the loss had been for her. Progress was noted as she wondered if she could miss him without the devastation, and then the next wave of pain/realization hit.

Therapist: **.

Sharon: I feel sad, but I feel a lot more peace than I had before, I don't know if it will be true 10 minutes from now, but I feel much more peace about the fact that if I continue to heal it does not mean I am going to lose him again.

Note: Sharon felt that if she healed, she would lose him again, and now was realizing that if she healed, she would be able to connect with him more.

Therapist: **.

Sharon: I feel that if I heal, I will be able to connect with him more.

Therapist: **.

Sharon: It just came to me that I don't have to expend so much energy fighting the fact that Joe is dead. I guess maybe I could possibly come back to trusting the universe a little.

Therapist: **.

Sharon: It doesn't feel so emotionally charged.

Therapist: **.

Sharon: This is the first time I can think about Joe's image and smiling face without hurting so bad.

Several sets later:

Sharon: I feel more relaxed, as if a burden was lifted.

Therapist: **.

Sharon: I feel more at peace. I know I can continue to heal.

Therapist: **.

Sharon: I can't say that I've totally accepted his death, but I'm feeling more willing to move through the process because I want to honour him.

Note: She now realized moving through the process was a way to honour—to connect with— Joe, as was seen after the next set.

Therapist: **.

Sharon: I can learn to live with this and honour his life.

Therapist: **.

Sharon: Yes, I can think of Joe, and healing is a way to honour him.

At this point, Sharon was brought back to target and the therapist asked for the SUDs.

Therapist: How distressing is the memory of driving, on a scale of 0 to 10 where 0 is not the absence of emotion or that you feel good about it, but 0 means calm in your body, or no distress, and 10 = the most distressing?

Sharon: It's a 1 or 2.

Therapist: Go with that.

Sharon: I can think of Joe, his love, and I can feel happy, but I also feel sad, its bitter-sweet.

Therapist: **.

Sharon: I just feel pretty good and peaceful at this moment in time.

Therapist: **.

Sharon: I feel better.

The therapist took Sharon back to target, including thinking of Joe.

Sharon: I get a feeling of warmth and love and sadness mixed together.

Therapist: **.

The therapist took Sharon back to target, and when Sharon responded that she felt more at peace, the therapist took the SUDs, which continued to be a 1. The SUDs of 1 was thought to be appropriate, so the Installation Phase was initiated.

Phase 5: Installation

Therapist: Do the words: *I can go on and thrive* still fit, or are there other words that may be more appropriate?'

Sharon: I can learn to live with this and it's honouring his life.

Therapist: When you think of the memory and the words *I can learn to live with this and it's honouring his life?*, on a 1 to 7 scale, with 1 being totally false and 7 being totally true, how true is it?

Sharon: It feels pretty true. Like, a 5 or a 6 or 7, somewhere in there.

Therapist: Go with that ... Now how true are the words *I can learn to live with this and its honouring his life*, on a 1 to 7 scale, with 1 being totally false and 7 being totally true?

Sharon: They feel pretty true. I know that Joe would want that, and I would be honouring his life.

Therapist: **.

Therapist: How true are the words again?

Sharon: It's a 6; it feels pretty true.

Note: The VoC remained at a 6 because, to Sharon, it was still a tragedy, and there were other painful memories that still haunted her.

Phase 6: Body Scan

The body scan was skipped because it was thought that other painful memories may surface, and it was time to end the session.

The therapist elicits the inner representation.

Therapist: When you think of Joe, what do you notice?

Sharon I can see his beautiful smiling face, and feel love.

Therapist: **.

Phase 7: Closure

The therapist and Sharon discussed the session.

Therapist: What was this like for you?

Sharon: Well, overall, it's difficult to go there but I do all the time anyway. But what was good was being able to move through it ... I feel some sort of, resolution, you know. Some small bit of, I don't know, like, some sense of accomplishment.

Note: This last statement showed that reprocessing a trauma increased her sense of resilience, a sense of accomplishment, that can strengthen her for dealing with future challenges.

Sharon: I have read that a lot of people do not want to let go of their grieving because of the fear that fear that you'll lose that little remnant of connection. And I think, there is definitely a certain amount of truth in that for me. I was able to realize that internally during the session ... But now I know that it's not true. In fact, it's just the opposite, you know. Hanging on is what was preventing me from connecting.

Phase 8: Re-evaluation

This session was lifechanging for Sharon. She could now think of Joe's 'smiling face' with love, and her adaptive belief, that healing was a way to honour Joe maintained over time.

Discussion

The sudden, unexpected death of Joe was traumatic for Sharon, and she could not fully realize her loss. Trying to think of her son led to her, 'being robbed a second time', and she would feel devastated. Interestingly, she commented during the session how much emotional energy it took to avoid the realization of Joe's death. Avoiding the realization of loss can be exhausting. With reprocessing of the trauma, she was able to picture her son, and realize that going through the mourning process was a way to honour him. As with other examples in this book, Sharon came to understand during the reprocessing that she wanted to hold onto the pain out of fear she would 'lose that little remnant of connection'. With reprocessing her trauma, she came to know she could connect with Joe, and honour him, by moving through the mourning process. In doing so, she felt a sense of accomplishment, illustrating posttraumatic growth.

Case 3: Daughter Committed Suicide

Phase 1: History-Taking

Fiona's daughter, Jean, was 14 years of age when she committed suicide by hanging. She had a psychotic disorder that was due to a medication side effect. The side effects of the medication were not understood until after she died. Fiona sought EMDR treatment 8 years after her daughter's death. She had previously had therapy to deal with her grief. However, she still had not dealt with the worst moment, discovering her daughter hanging, cutting her down, and attempting mouth to mouth resuscitation.

Fiona knew her daughter was suicidal and for 12 days, she stayed with her daughter all the time, even sleeping on a mattress in her room. When Fiona left the room for 10 minutes to check on her other children, Jean hanged herself.

Phase 2: Preparation & Stabilization

Fiona's previous therapy had provided sufficient stabilization so that she met criteria for EMDR therapy. After four sessions of history-taking, and teaching the Safe/Calm Place, Fiona felt ready to process her worst memory of finding her daughter.

Phase 3: Target Assessment

> IMAGE: My daughter on the ground and I'm beside her, getting ready to work on her.
> NEGATIVE COGNITION: This is too big, too much. How could this have happened? (And after further discussion) I'm powerless.
> POSITIVE COGNITION: I can manage.
> VoC: 3/7.
> EMOTION: 'It's almost too big to have a name. . . . Overwhelmed.'
> SUD: 10/10.
> LOCATION: very deep in the stomach.

Phase 4: Desensitization

> Therapist: Bring up the image, the words *I am powerless*, notice the sensations in your body, and follow my fingers. (Eye movement starts.)
> *Note:* During the BLS the client was crying and verbalizing what she was thinking. The client was not talking to the therapist, but like many clients, was reprocessing as she was talking.

The therapist continued BLS as she was talking. Fiona reported, 'I left her', meaning that she had continually stayed with her daughter for 12 days, knowing she was suicidal, and left for 10 minutes to check on her other children.

Fiona: (Crying). This is awful … Horriblest thing is that it's Jean, it's my girl, it's Jean, that's so bad. It's dreadful. I've been living with this. And I couldn't, couldn't save her; I tried everything I could do. I didn't know enough. I didn't know enough to save her. Sorry. Just didn't know enough to save her; I did what I could, did everything I could do. I didn't know enough; and I left her, I left her, I left her, I left her. Ten minutes, and that's all it took. I was tired of watching her; I'd been watching her for 12 days. I was sleeping on the mattress in her room with a T-shirt rolled up behind my back, so I wouldn't go to sleep.

The psychiatrist was telling me I had to stop watching her. I said, 'You don't understand.'

Note: The therapist did not understand what the client meant, and thinking it was an important point, asks for further details.

Therapist: Who said that?

Fiona: The psychiatrist said that I had to stop watching her, I said, 'You don't understand.' Jean told my son, a couple of days before she died, that me watching her was driving her crazy but she was really glad I was doing it. She knew I loved her … I didn't think I could go with all of this. I don't know if it's ever going to get totally better.

Therapist: I can appreciate that; let's just acknowledge that. **.

Fiona: I am going to live the rest of my life without her, and I live with my kids who lost her. It's tough. There is a part of me that chimes in, and I don't know what part it is, but it says: 'Why don't you give up the struggle, why don't you give up living with it'; 'Why don't you give in to the pain … it's just too hard.'

Therapist: **.

Fiona: This is so hard.

Note: With her saying it was 'so hard' twice, she was brought back to target, which also offered structure and containment (see Chapter 17 on desensitization).

Therapist: So, let's go back to the memory; what do you notice?

Fiona: Her, on the ground; check plaids, jumper, socks, hair … the face has changed. Yeah … but it is her; that's what comes back. I stayed with her; I stayed with her; until the paramedics came, I stayed with her. And that's pretty good, pretty big; and I can stay with her now.

Therapist: **.

Fiona: (Crying). I had to work on her, and I didn't know if she was still alive or dead, I didn't know.

Part of me wanted to run away, part of me wanted to hold her, and I had to do what I knew, to try to save her.

Therapist: **.

Fiona: I made the right choice. I did what I had to do. Another strange thing of me being with her is that she's dead, and she's also there. And she knows what I'm doing and she's like, approving … approving. It's pretty silly, but that's the sense I had.

Note: The client was feeling a sense of presence as she was providing resuscitation, which was experienced as positive ('she's like, approving …'). The therapist offered a supportive response before continuing BLS.

Therapist: I understand that. **.

Note: With this next set, the client described in more detail what was happening. It is quite typical when reprocessing a traumatic incident that the client starts to get in touch and describe the details of what happened.

Fiona: I kind of see, I did the right thing, but while I was doing that, my three other kids are in three other places in the house. My daughter is in her bed, hearing what is happening.

My youngest son, number three in the family, is downstairs, knowing something really bad has happened but not knowing who it is. My oldest boy, who has just helped me get her down, is calling the ambulance and dealing with them, and calling my husband to tell him what's happened, and he's telling him, 'Come home now.' So, they are all doing something ... and I'm not helping them, I've abandoned them; I can't be in four places, I know I didn't even remember my youngest daughter, until much later; that feels bad; understandable, but bad. It was too much, but I did my best, but it really weighs on me because I couldn't save her (meaning Jean), I couldn't save her.

Therapist: **.

Fiona: (Crying) I didn't save her and she's dead; took me a long time to realize that. I just ... I wish she wasn't; I wish she wasn't; I wish she wasn't; I would give anything. But she is. I wish she wasn't.

Therapist: I know you do ... **.

Fiona: (Crying) I miss her so much ... Can I ask you, I ... I live with that always, and I get better at living with it; what I don't get about working with grief is: how can that ever be okay, and how could that change?

Note: The client asked the therapist a question, how can the loss ever be okay? The therapist, rather than give her an explanation that could interrupt the flow of processing, was thinking that with continued reprocessing of the 'raw felt emotion', he would be able to go back to target and elicit positive, meaningful memories that represented the formation of an adaptive inner representation (see Chapter 14 on the desensitization phase). He asked her to continue the processing for a few more minutes.

Therapist: I know how hard it is, but let's continue to process some more first ... let's acknowledge just how awful this is.

Fiona: (Crying) And it's the rest of my life's forever and it's my kids' forever, too; and it's my ex-husband's forever.

Therapist: **. (When beginning eye movement, the therapist made supportive statements: 'Yes, you can really feel that pain, be present with that.').

Client: And I'm tired of it, I'm really tired of it.

Therapist: **.

Note: After 3 minutes of continued emotional reprocessing, the client said:

Fiona: It's just what it is; it's just what it is.

Note: The above response seemed to convey both acceptance and resignation, but also looping (being 'stuck') in distress. Hypothesizing that now, with more realization of the traumatic circumstance, thinking of her daughter would bring up positive memories, and facilitate adaptive information linking in, breaking the 'loop'.

Therapist: Think of your daughter ... what comes up?

Fiona: (Laughing) She's great; she was so great, I loved her, she was amazing. Jean. I used to talk about the joy and pain question with raising kids, and my sons were hard work, you know; but Jean was mostly joy, and I can honestly say that she was so much joy.

Therapist: **.

Fiona: At a soccer game people asked me 'Which one is your daughter?' I'd say to them, 'The one with the great big smile.' And she was, she was the one with the great big smile on her.

Note: Sets of BLS continue with Jean describing happy memories with Jean). Then the therapist takes Fiona back to target.

Therapist: So, let's go back to the memory we started with, what comes up?

Fiona: I can still see her, it's not as distressing; not as distressing. I kind of feel bad saying that, but it's not as distressing, I feel I can be there; that's my daughter, she died.

In the next set, another wave of distress arose, which is quite common in doing grief work, as we saw with Sharon in the previous example, and was reprocessed.

Therapist: **.
Fiona: And I wasn't there.
Note: Fiona meant she was not there when her daughter suicided. It still hurts. It's just that's real, that's what happened; and ... It's there forever. It's horrible.
Therapist: **.
Fiona: I tried so hard. At the coroner's inquest, the coroner looked me in the eye and said: 'You could not have done anymore, you have done over and above, you could not have done anymore.'

Reprocessing continued, with Fiona later describing what she found in her daughter's diary.

Fiona: In the end, she was in a very bad way. I read her journal in February, and she died in May. It was dreadful what she went through. She was really psychotic, and she was really in a bad way, and she thought she had an evil spirit in her that was making her hurt people. My understanding of the journals, it is crazy, but I think she thought she might kill her little sister, and I think that's possibly what she could have done. She adored her little sister when she was herself. And what she went through was dreadful ... she left a note, and she must have written it before I left, and then taped it to the window. And she said she did it so that she wouldn't hurt anyone else.
Note: Adaptive information and understanding is linking in with Fiona's understanding why her daughter suicided. Adaptive information continues to link in is seen in the next sets of BLS.
Therapist: **.
Fiona: She was wrong; it wasn't an evil thing in her, it was that poison you know, the medication that changed her. It was what the coroner called a 'different adverse reaction'. It's a drug called xxxx (drug purposely not named), and you cannot get it anymore.

Therapist brings the client back to target.

Fiona: I know I did my best. There are some things you can't prevent. There are things you can't know, and there are things you can't prevent.
Note: In the next few minutes, Fiona described how she came to understand the side effects of the medication Jean was taking. Then, the therapist took her back to target.
Therapist: Well now, when you go back to where we started, what do you notice?
Note: Fiona has a deeper level of realization of the death.
Fiona: I'm seeing less of the image actually. I'm seeing the bit of her that wasn't affected by what happened to her. So, just sort of the body and the legs, and ... it's true, she is dead, it took me a long time to work that out. It's awful, it's horrible, it's true, and now I just do my best to live with it.
Therapist: **.
Fiona: Okay, this is a bit of a new thought, and not a very nice one. There were times after she died where I could have taken the opportunity to hold her. One was when I had to formally identify her in the hospital, and the other was with my then husband to look at her in the coffin; I couldn't, because I was horrified of her body, and I hate that I didn't. I wish I could have gotten over the horror, so that I could have. My dad was with me when I identified her, and he went over, and he kissed her on her forehead. I'm glad he did; but I wish I could have....
Therapist: **.
Fiona: You know you have to give clothes, and she had a coat on, one that she really liked, you know. They buttoned it up and I knew that was so uncool. And I said, 'No, they've buttoned it up, they shouldn't have', and my husband unbuttoned it for her .... I couldn't.
Therapist: Yes; I can understand that. **.

Fiona: This is hard, but I think maybe for the first time I am actually admitting that was her in the coffin.

Note: Next Fiona experienced more realization, and the ability to be present with the awful memory of her daughter in the coffin.

Therapist: **.

Fiona: It's a hard thing to see this again; I wish I had stayed. I can stay now.

Therapist: **.

Fiona: I can't remember her face very much in that memory, but I can just see the rest of her.

Note: After a few minutes, the therapist takes Fiona back to target.

Fiona: And I lost her. But she was already gone. She'd already gone by then. I feel like I worked on some of this before, but I guess it's just deeper, going deeper.

Therapist: **.

Fiona: Yeah, and I guess I got a glimpse of, you know, the broader perspective, And that's probably good, that's probably okay.

Therapist: **.

Fiona: It's okay, it is okay now.

Go back to target.

Therapist: So now, when you go back to the memory, what do you experience?

Fiona: I see Jean as she was before she died, I see her room, the curtains I made her. The bedspread that we bought together. The room. So, the memory is bigger, it isn't just her, it's gotten a bit bigger.

Therapist: **.

Fiona: It is better now.

Therapist: So, I'm going to ask you, on the 0 to 10 scale; where 0 is not the absence of emotion and doesn't mean you feel good about it; but 0 is being able to think about it without distress, and calm, not that it has to be a 0, and 10 = the most disturbance.

Fiona: I know what you're saying, yeah. I don't know what to say; there's certainly a calmness. I've gotten to this place where I've been able to stay in her room and have it grow, and feel that calmness and kind of be there as long as I needed to; and I feel like I'm doing that again, and it does feel, you know, okay. But then, I know that although I've done it before I still got that massive distress, so I don't know if it's 0 or not. Does that make sense? I don't know when you get there, I don't know. So, I don't know how to rate it; I don't know how to rate it.

Therapist: How about for only right now, just in terms of level of distress.

Fiona: I'm okay, I'm okay.

Therapist: That's why I'm very careful to say 0 is not the absence of emotion; it just means you can be calm at this moment.

Therapist: **.

Fiona: I can be calm at this moment, and access that memory, and it's not hitting at me again. I'm okay, I'm calm when accessing that memory.

Therapist: **.

Fiona: Yeah, I can be quite calm and stay connected to the memory.

Note: The therapist understood Fiona's calmness as 0, or close to 0, and did not want to insist on having a number. Next, is the Installation Phase.

Phase 5: Installation

Therapist: So, we talked about the words *I can manage.*

Fiona: Yes, they're the right words.

Therapist: So when you bring up the memory and the words *I can manage*, how true do they feel now: 1 = totally false and 7 = totally true?

Fiona: It's a 6; I got just a little bit of a surge of emotion, so probably 6.

Therapist: Okay, bring up the memory, and 'I can manage' together, and follow my fingers.

Fiona: Surging doesn't mean I can't manage. I've been managing it for a long time. I sat in here and I managed.

Therapist: **.

Fiona: I manage, I manage, don't know how, but I do. . . . It is a 7.

Therapist: **.

Fiona: I guess it's more about who she was. She wasn't who she was at the end.

I was just remembering the psychiatrist who helped me through a lot of this,

saying to me—and she wasn't a 100% right—that I lost her long before I lost her. And that's sad.

Note: The therapist, wanting to check for an adaptive inner representation, asked Fiona to think of her daughter.

Therapist: And now, think of her again; what comes up?

Fiona: She was so much more than what happened to her at the end. Yeah, and that's the Jean I want to keep.

Phase 6: Body Scan

Therapist: So, there is probably more; let's get to the body scan.

Body Scan is completed with Fiona feeling calm.

Fiona: I can think of Jean and know it wasn't my fault.

Note: This next interchange illustrated a beautiful, heartwarming integration where the transformation from pain to love was experienced.

Fiona: You know, in lots of ways I just don't want to go there again. It's always just been so hard for me to connect to her. I get little flashes of her here and there, you know. And that's something I really want to do, is to connect to her more. And I think that it is possible, and this is probably helping with that.

Therapist: Connect with her?

Fiona: Yes ... You know, you grow this child inside you and they stay inside you, they're just not there anymore. But they're still inside you.

The therapist enhanced the inner representation, the felt connection to Jean who was still 'inside', through simply asking her to focus on her experience.

Therapist: Can you feel that?

Fiona: Yes.

R: **.

Fiona: (Very enthusiastic). My love for her does not have the person out there to land on, but I guess it can land on what's still there inside me. And that's good, but sad. But it's okay, I can love ... it's okay, I can do that, can't I? I can do that.

Therapist: Yes.

Fiona: That's okay, I can still love her. That's big. It's really big; it's really big. And maybe it doesn't make sense, I can still love her.

Therapist: It totally makes sense. **.

Fiona: But it makes sense that it feels good.

Therapist: That's right, you can still love her. Go with that again. **.

Phase 7: Closure

Fiona discusses the session.

> Fiona: The realization that I could still love my daughter, that I can still have a connection with her. I struggled to find a connection with her, I've envied people that felt they had a connection with— the person they've lost. I have been searching around and found nothing to land on ... Now, I can land on her; that's what has changed, and that's okay, and I just think that's going to get better.
> Therapist: Right, the sense of connection with the love.
> Fiona: Yes, and with her, through the love.

Phase 8: Re-evaluation

The trauma remained reprocessed, and the internal feeling of love and connection remained with Fiona over time.

Discussion

This was a very emotional session with a courageous client facing an awful moment she had been avoiding for years. During a very tearful moment, the client asked if the grief and loss could ever change. Continued processing led to a sense of acceptance and resignation ('It's just what it is'), but the client appeared someone stuck in the distress. The client was asked to think of her daughter, and positive memories and thoughts came to mind. This illustrated that a strategy of having the client think of their loved one, after sufficient distressing emotion had been experienced, helped Fiona out of a loop of negative affect and elicited positive, meaningful memories. If negative material emerged, reprocessing could continue, at the pace appropriate for the client. The end of the session was perhaps the most meaningful moment of the session. When Fiona talked about carrying her child inside of her before she was born, she got in touch with her love for her daughter. She then could, finally, feel a loving connection to her daughter that she had sought since her death. For these clients, BLS was utilized to enhance their felt sense of love and connection, the adaptive inner representation.

Note: Realistically, these were exceptional sessions with exceptional clients. Of course, not all sessions are so transformative. Quite commonly, shifts are subtle; progress much slower than illustrated in the cases above; processing often gets blocked; and there are many incomplete sessions. However, these cases illustrate informative teaching points about the EMDR therapy process with grief and mourning.

Psychological First Aid

The eight phases of eye movement desensitization and reprocessing (EMDR) therapy are always provided within the context of support and caring, with a collaborative relationship that empowers the client. Death of a loved one can be a traumatic event, leaving a person experiencing shock, disorientation, disbelief, and numbness. In the immediacy of a traumatic event, these mourners do not need 'therapy' or 'fingers in their face', they need Psychological First Aid (PFA) (Watson & Brymer, 2012). PFA is an attitude of attending, supporting, comforting, normalizing, being available as needed (and not intruding), and certainly not doing deep psychological probing—which can really be an intrusion when someone is in shock. I think of it as 'chicken soup', which is comforting. What do you do when someone is very upset and emotional? The best answer I have comes from an army chaplain who provided support to the family of a veteran who committed suicide shortly after returning home from war. The family was very upset, and they directed their anger at him. I asked the chaplain what can you do in such a situation? He said, 'All you can do is love them.' To me this means being present, with respect and acceptance of the survivors and what they are experiencing. Much is said with a caring presence, without words. A caring presence is needed as one provides EMDR therapy in all of its phases.

Below is a brief description of the principles of PFA.

1. *Contact and Engagement*: Be available to mourners in a nonintrusive, compassionate, and helpful manner, accepting their response. If someone wants to talk, let them. If not, let them be.
2. *Safety and Comfort*: In the wake of a trauma, survivors may be frightened, confused, and disoriented. As possible and appropriate, provide physical as well as emotional comfort. A safe environment, food, concrete comforts (e.g., shower, clothing, or a teddy bear for a child [of any age] to hug) and other things that would provide an atmosphere of security and comfort to enable someone to de-escalate and calm down.
3. *Stabilization (as Needed)*: Many people will be coping adaptively (even if upset) and not need intervention. People who are emotionally overwhelmed or disoriented may need grounding and strategies for calming. For example, for people who are:
   - Disoriented
   - Confused
   - Frantic or agitated
   - Panicky
   - Extremely withdrawn, apathetic, or 'shut down'
   - Extremely irritable or angry
   - Exceedingly worried—
     - Offer stress reduction exercises, be available to talk (or not talk), meeting physical needs, help with immediate planning, and providing a calm atmosphere for de-escalation and calming go a long way towards stabilization. Other strategies are discussed below and in Chapter 14 on EMDR Phase 2 (Preparation & Stabilization).
     - Talk to another person for support (friends, family, your physician, and clergy).
     - Get adequate rest.
     - Maintain proper nutrition.

- Participate in exercise (at a comfortable level) to help relieve stress.
- Engage in positive activities (e.g., sports, hobbies, and reading) that provide a balance to distress of present circumstances.
- Try to maintain a normal schedule to the extent possible—our daily routines provide a sense of control, rhythm, and structure.
- Use coping methods that have been successful in the past.
- Contact community support agencies—talking to other people who have experienced a similar tragedy can be helpful, can let you know what to expect, and can let you know you are not alone or unique.

4. *Information Gathering About Current Needs and Concerns*: What are the mourner's immediate needs and concerns? Gather information about the mourners and their situation. Tailor support and intervention to meet these needs.

5. *Practical Assistance*: Offer practical help to address immediate needs and concern. What are the immediate needs and how specifically can these needs be met? People who are disoriented and in shock may need help in problem-solving and in getting what they need (e.g., funeral arrangements, contacting family and friends, dealing with everyday day demands and basic care needs, and specific plans for coping and dealing with the next few days (and weeks)).

6. *Connection with Social Supports:* Social support is important in coping. Provide assistance, as needed, to establish brief or ongoing contacts with primary support persons including family members, friends, medical aid, clergy, and community resources.

7. *Providing Information*: In the wake of a traumatic loss, people benefit from information. Mourners need two kinds of information: facts about what happened and information to help mourners understand their reactions and the reactions of others (Dyregrov & Kristensen, 2020). Regarding facts about what happened, mourners usually want to know what happened and how it happened, and not having this information can be very distressing and preoccupying. Mourners may need assistance in getting this information from law enforcement or hospital sources. A support person can be present when the family gets this information, which can be very upsetting.

8. *Getting Information*: Getting information on trauma, grief, and coping is very important. As one father described after the immediate loss of his 13-year-old son, 'I felt overwhelmed, I did not understand my reactions, and on hindsight I would have benefitted from information on reactions and coping.' See the information in the next section on coping with stress and trauma.

9. *Linkage with Collaborative Services*: link mourners with available community resources and services as needed at the time or in the future.

10. *Empower Clients*: It is important to have a helping relationship that encourages competence, self-efficacy, and autonomy. Rather than foster dependency, it is important to have a collaborative relationship where therapists can offer guidance, support, and respect that clients are experts on their lives. Mobilize their strengths and encourage them to use their resources, with clients knowing that you are available to accompany them through the grief and mourning process.

11. *Hope*: After a tragic incident, people may view life as having stopped with no way for things to ever get better. When I hear this, I say I really understand how life can seem this way now, and I have heard this from many people in similar circumstances. However, if I may plant the seed, that it does get better. It may not seem this way now, but the future holds promise.

Information on Coping with Tragedy

These are the important kinds of information to tell those who are coping with tragedy:

1. You have experienced a tragedy. Life has changed, and it can be difficult to both cope with the loss of a loved one and adapt to new circumstances. I am here to accompany you, and provide support and assistance as wanted.
2. All reactions and feelings are normal. Strong feelings of shock, sadness, anger, guilt, despair, and relief (in certain circumstances) are normal. Some people feel numb, with the death not seeming real, even though you know it happened. Other people are highly upset and experience deep sadness, fear and anxiety, anger, and deep pain. Emotions can alternate between waves of pain and numbness.
3. Everyone is different, and it is important to respect how others are reacting, as well as how you are reacting.
4. It is normal to think about your loved one, yearn for them, think of them, and miss them deeply. This is how we start to come to grips with what happened, understand, and adapt to the loss.
5. Physical reactions such as muscle tension, crying, changes in eating or sleeping patterns, feeling tired, or having difficulty concentrating are quite common.
6. Grief reactions can indeed be intense, but usually get better with time and positive, constructive coping. Grief is not something we resolve; it is something we adapt to. It takes time for the reality of the death to sink in, mourn our loss, and learn to live without our loved one present.
7. People tend to oscillate between feeling the pain of the loss and putting the distress aside to focus on everyday living tasks and adaptation. This oscillation is normal.
8. We don't lose our attachment to a loved one, the attachment and connection continue through love that is experienced through heartfelt memories. If memories are negative and complicated, they can be dealt with through therapy, particularly with EMDR therapy to reprocess the negative memories and build resilience.

Information on Coping with Stress

In general, the following strategies can be helpful:

1. *Identify Your Needs and Fulfil Them*—Get the rest you need, recognize your limits, and separate things that must be done from those that can wait. If you need to reschedule commitments or adjust your work schedule, most people will understand.
2. *Reach Out to Others*—Being with other people with whom one is comfortable helps one cope with tragedy. Initially, a mourner may want to isolate and withdrawal. But soon the client may be ready to check in friends, visit with old friends, and re-engage in the social world.
3. *Talk to Others*—talking to people you are comfortable with, to clergy, your physician, a therapist, can facilitate healing.
4. *Express Yourself*—for example, write a letter to your loved one, keep a journal, or paint a picture to express what is in your heart.
5. *Avoid Making Major Decisions*—During times of crisis and emotional distress, it may be difficult to see beyond one's pain. Impulsive decisions, made during moments of distress, are not necessarily the best decisions. If an important decision needs to be made immediately, talk it over with a trusted person(s).

6. *Honour Your Loved One's Memory*—Remember your loved one in comforting, meaningful ways. Make a collage of pictures or create a scrapbook of letters and mementos, plan a memorial activity, plant a tree or flower in their name, visit places where there are pleasant memories, remember the loved one with a prayer or a toast at holidays or special occasions, and/or contribute money to a cause or charity in the name of your loved one.

7. *Use Self-Care*—The stress of grief can impact one physically as well as emotionally. Get proper rest, including times when you can just relax. Eat well with regular nutritious meals and snacks. Exercise, even with a brisk walk, can lift spirits. It may be helpful for the client to check in with their physicians just to let them know about the loss in case medical intervention may be needed now or in the future.

8. *Avoid Numbing Feelings with Chemicals*—it is one thing to have a glass of wine or a beer, but overdoing brings on a host of other problems and only prolongs the pain.

9. *Engage in Recreational/Leisure Activities*—Healthy grief involves a balance between recognizing and expressing grief reactions and putting the grief aside to focus on everyday living tasks. Part of everyday living is leisure. As possible, indulge in leisurely activities that were enjoyed before the loss. Reading a book, playing cards with friends, going to a movie, watching a favourite television show are ways of taking a break from focusing on grief that can help get through the painful mourning process.

10. *Plan Ahead for Special Days*—Birthdays, anniversaries, holidays, and other special days can be very stressful after the loss of a loved one, especially during the first year. Talking to family members and friends about any concerns and thinking about what would be meaningful (e.g., a new tradition or ritual) can greatly assist coping with special days.

11. *Maintain Routines*—Keep up your old routine when possible and plan and engage in new routines necessitated by the change in circumstances. After a traumatic event, people may be sad and low in energy and may want to withdraw from usual activities. However, our daily rituals provide a sense of control and predictability. Engaging in usual activities and routines, with appropriate modifications (e.g., working less hours or postponing stressful activities until capacity is approaching normalcy) can help one adapt to the loss.

12. *Pace Change*—The loss of a loved one may require a more drastic change than described with Joe. For example, moving to a new neighbourhood or having to cut back on expenses can disrupt one's major life routines. Though clients may have little control on what has to change, there is often some control over the timing of the change. Taking the time to plan and pace change, rather than react impulsively, can mitigate the stress of change.

Eye Movement Desensitization and Reprocessing (EMDR) Protocol for Recent Critical Incidents and Ongoing Traumatic Stress (EMDR-PRECI) and EMDR Recent Event Protocol (R-TEP)

In Chapter 15, the Recent Event Protocol, eye movement desensitization (EMD), and focused reprocessing are discussed. Two other EMDR methodologies for dealing with recent events are the EMDR Protocol for Recent Critical Incidents and Ongoing Traumatic Stress (EMDR-PRECI) (Jarero, Artigas, & Luber, 2011) and the EMDR Recent Event Protocol (R-TEP) (Shapiro & Laub, 2008).

The EMDR-PRECI is an eight-phase, three-pronged protocol especially designed to treat recent, present, or past prolonged adverse experiences where related stressful events continue for an extended time and there is no posttrauma safety period for traumatic memory consolidation (e.g., sexual and/or physical violence, interpersonal violence, pandemic casualties, and ongoing or prolonged traumatic stress). EMDR-PRECI conceptualizes the continuum of prolonged adverse experiences as an extended event that does not give the distressing or pathogenic memories sufficient time to consolidate into an integrated whole. This creates a cumulative, trauma-exposure memory network of linked pathogenic memories with similar emotional, somatic, sensorial, and cognitive information that extends into the present moment and often produces maladaptive or catastrophic concerns about the future (Jarero & Artigas, 2020). The example below illustrates treatment of the trauma and grief of a frontline worker's experience dealing with Covid-19.

EMDR Protocol for Recent Critical Incidents and Ongoing Traumatic Stress (EMDR-PRECI)

Case Example 1 (EMDR-PRECI, Submitted by Ignacio Jarero): María is a 38-year-old nurse who has been working in a hospital with Covid-19 patients for the last 8 months. She experienced significant posttraumatic stress disorder (PTSD), depression, and anxiety symptoms. Targets for reprocessing included imagining her children getting Covid-19, the expression of terror of patients when they were notified that they needed to be intubated, and the never-ending sounds of the ventilator machines.

Seven days later, Maria attended her second session. She reported a significant decrease in PTSD, anxiety, and depression symptoms and a present trigger, the piles of cadavers in the hospital waiting for days to be recovered by their relatives. After reprocessing this pathogenic memory, she did not find another disturbing memory and the clinician proceeded to the Future Template Prong. Fifteen days after finishing treatment, Maria reported subclinical scores in her PTSD, anxiety, and depression symptoms.

EMDR Recent Traumatic Episode Protocol

The EMDR Recent Traumatic Episode Protocol (RTEP) of Shapiro and Laub (2013) provides an eight-phase, three-pronged approach which includes EMD and focused processing that the authors term EMDR. Utilizing the eight phases of EMDR therapy, a history phase, and Preparation & Stabilization phase, readiness for reprocessing can be assessed, and the protocol and be used to teach the client emotional regulation skills. After going over the trauma episode (period from the onset event up to the present including thoughts about the future), moments of disturbance (called Points of Disturbance) are identified, and targeted individually. Hence, the cumulative and ongoing effects of a traumatic event are taken into account. During the desensitization phase, associations are followed as long as these associations relate to the current episode. Associations that open up earlier issues are acknowledged but are not followed at this time (though can be later), with the client being guided back to the target. This has been termed EMDR. EMD, going back to the target after each set or very frequently can be utilized, especially for intense moments and to minimize the opening up of other material.

Case 2 (EMD & EMDR strategies of the EMDR R-TEP Protocol, Submitted by Elan Shapiro): A 35-year-old woman was seen 10 days after finding her partner hanged in their bedroom. She presented with a full range of significant acute stress symptoms. After being assessed, the client met the guidelines for reprocessing trauma, and she gave a detailed narrative of the episode. The first target selected was the intrusive image of her partner hanging in their bedroom, which was constantly retraumatizing her. A narrow-focused EMD strategy was provided. Within twelve sets of bilateral stimulation (BLS), she moved from the shock and dissociation, where she was stuck, to sadness, and had a subjective units of disturbance (SUD) of 2. The intrusive image was now distant, and the client could begin normal grieving. At the second session, 6 days later, the target selected for reprocessing was a scene from the night before the suicide, which in her mind had become part of the traumatic event. The client experienced significant guilt. This target was reprocessed using EMDR, a focused strategy to limit associations to only the current episode. The guilt rapidly gave way to a rational forgiveness of herself and acceptance that even if she was tired and had gone to sleep early that night, she was not responsible for his decision to commit suicide. This 90-minute session ended with an ecologically low SUD and installation of positive cognition recognizing her lack of guilt. In all, she was seen three more times during the 40 days following the suicide, to follow-up and check for sticking points so that the normal grieving could proceed. At a follow-up a year later, she was in a new relationship and had retrained to a healing profession.

Additional Resources

This book cannot cover all the helpful literature, methods, guides, and therapeutic strategies relevant to grief and mourning. Eye movement desensitization and reprocessing therapy, a therapeutic approach in and of itself, can be integrated within wider therapeutic frameworks that include the resources and coping strategies available online.

There are many wonderful resources and books for grief and mourning. The website https://griefcounselor.org/resources/helpful-websites/ lists many of these websites. The website https://nymag.com/strategist/article/best-books-grief.html lists wonderful books on grief and mourning that will benefit both client and therapist alike. Memorials, grief rituals, and coping methods are an important part of healing grief and going through the mourning process, and are described in many of these books and resources available online, but are beyond the scope of this book. Online memorials are important are helpful for mourners, and are described at https://www.everplans.com/articles/the-top-10-online-memorial-websites.

An example of another intervention is guided imagery and imagined conversations. Many imagery and mediation resources can be found on youtube.com. Some examples are the following:

- Imagining a conversation with a deceased loved one, and then changing perspectives and imagining the loved one answering back. Bilateral stimulation can be helpful to enhance mediation resources can be found on youtube.com.
- Write a letter to the deceased and this can be read in session, with the clinician providing bilateral stimulation as the client is reading (Helene Delucci, personal communication, 5 April 2021).

I would like to end this appendix with an imagery exercise described by Francine Shapiro in some of her trainings:

'Imagine your loved one in heaven, with a light connecting your heart to your loved one's … feel it in your body.' If it is positive, bilateral stimulation can be applied to enhance it.

'Go with that.'

And thank you, Francine.

References

Ainsworth, M. D. (1969). Object relations, dependency, and attachment: A theoretical review of the infant-mother relationship. *Child Development, 40*(4), 969–1025.

Ainsworth, M. D. S., Blehar, M. C., Waters, E., & Wall, S. (1978). *Patterns of attachment: A psychological study of the strange situation.* Lawrence Erlbaum.

Attig, T. (2000). Anticipatory mourning and the transition to loving in absence. In T. A. Rando (Ed.), *Clinical dimensions of anticipatory mourning.* Research Press.

Bartholomew, K., & Horowitz, L. M. (1991). Attachment styles among young adults: A test of a four-category model. *Journal of Personality and Social Psychology, 61*(2), 226–244.

Becker, C. B., Darius, E., & Schaumberg, K. (2007). An analog study of patient preferences for exposure versus alternative treatments for posttraumatic stress disorder. *Behaviour Research and Therapy, 45*(12), 2861–2873.

Boelen, P. A., & Prigerson, H. G. (2013). Prolonged grief disorder as a new diagnostic category in DSM-5. *Complicated Grief: Scientific Foundations for Health Care Professionals,* 85–98.

Boelen, P. A., Van Den Hout, M. A., & Van Den Bout, J. (2006). A cognitive-behavioral conceptualization of complicated grief. *Clinical Psychology: Science and Practice, 13*(2), 109–128.

Bonanno, G. A., Wortman, C. B., Lehman, D. R., Tweed, R. G., Haring, M., Sonnega, J., . . . Nesse, R. M. (2002). Resilience to loss and chronic grief: A prospective study from preloss to 18-months postloss. *Journal of Personality and Social Psychology, 83*(5), 1150.

Bonanno, G. A., Wortman, C. B., & Nesse, R. M. (2004). Prospective patterns of resilience and maladjustment during widowhood. *Psychology and Aging, 19*(2), 260.

Boon, S. (2023). *Assessing trauma-related dissociation with the trauma and dissociation symptoms interview.* Norton.

Bowlby, J. (1960). Separation anxiety. *The International Journal of Psychoanalysis, 41,* 89–113.

Bowlby, J. (1969). *Attachment and loss: Vol. I.* Basic Books.

Bowlby, J. (1973). *Attachment and loss: Vol. II. Separation, anxiety and anger.* Basic Books.

Bowlby, J. (1980). *Attachment and loss: Vol. III. Loss,* sadness and depression. Basic Books.

Bowlby, J. (1982). Attachment and loss: Retrospect and prospect. *American Journal of Orthopsychiatry, 52*(4), 664–678.

Bowlby, J. (2005). *A secure base.* Routledge.

Bowlby, J. (2008). *A secure base: Parent-child attachment and healthy human development.* Basic Books.

Brennan, K. A., Clark, C. L., & Shaver, P. R. (1998). Self-report measurement of adult attachment: An integrative overview. In J. A. Simpson & W. S. Rholes (Eds.), *Attachment theory and close relationships* (pp. 46–76). The Guilford Press.

Brico, E. (2018). Mental fog, stress, and posttraumatic stress disorder (PTSD). *HealthyPlace.* https://www.healthyplace.com/blogs/traumaptsdblog/2018/02/mental-fog.

Brown, D. P., & Elliott, D. S. (2016). *Attachment disturbances in adults: Treatment for comprehensive repair.* WW Norton.

Brymer, M., Taylor, M., Escudero, P., Jacobs, A., Kronenberg, M., Macy, R., . . . Vogel, J. (2012). *Psychological First Aid for schools (PFA-S): Field operations guide.* National Child Traumatic Stress Network. http://www.nctsn.org/content/psychological-first-aid-schoolspfa.

Carlson, E. B., & Putnam, F. W. (1993). An update on the dissociative experiences scale. *Dissociation: Progress in the Dissociative Disorders.*

Carr, D. (2008). Factors that influence late-life bereavement: Considering data from the changing lives of older couples study.

Carr, D., House, J. S., Kessler, R. C., Nesse, R. M., Sonnega, J., & Wortman, C. (2000). Marital quality and psychological adjustment to widowhood among older adults: A longitudinal analysis. *Journals of Gerontology Series B: Psychological Sciences and Social Sciences, 55*(4), S197–S207.

Cleiren, M. P. (1991). *Adaption after bereavement: A comparative study of the aftermath of death from suicide, traffic accident and illness for next of kin.* DSWO Press.

Cleiren, M. P. (1992). *Bereavement and adaptation: A comparative study of the aftermath of death.* Hemisphere.

Cleiren, M., Diekstra, R. F., Kerkhof, A. J., & Van Der Wal, J. (1994). Mode of death and kinship in bereavement: Focusing on 'who' rather than 'how'. *Crisis: The Journal of Crisis Intervention and Suicide Prevention, 15*(1), 22–36.

Djelantik, A. M. J., Smid, G. E., Mroz, A., Kleber, R. J., & Boelen, P. A. (2020). The prevalence of prolonged grief disorder in bereaved individuals following unnatural losses: Systematic review and meta regression analysis. *Journal of Affective Disorders, 265*, 146–156.

Dyregrov, A. (2008). *Grief in children: A handbook for adults second edition.* Jessica Kingsley Publishers.

Dyregrov, A., Gjestad, R., & Dyregrov, K. (2020). Parental relationships following the loss of a child. *Journal of Loss and Trauma, 25*(3), 224–244.

Dyregrov, A., & Kristensen, P. (2020). Information to bereaved families following catastrophic losses. Why is it important? *Journal of Loss and Trauma, 25*(5), 472–487.

Dyregrov, K. (2003). *The loss of a child by suicide, SIDS, and accidents: Consequences, needs and provisions of help.* Research Centre for Health Promotion, Faculty of Psychology, Center for Crisis Psychology, University of Bergen.

Dyregrov, K. (2004). Bereaved parents' experience of research participation. *Social Science & Medicine, 58*(2), 391–400.

Dyregrov, K., Nordanger, D., & Dyregrov, A. (2003). Predictors of psychosocial distress after suicide, SIDS and accidents. *Death Studies, 27*(2), 143–165.

EMDR Institute Inc. Copyright © 1990–2021, by the EMDR Institute & Francine Shapiro, PhD.

Fairbairn, W. D. (1952). *An object-relations theory of the personality.* New York, NY: Basic Books.

Fields, N.P., Gao, P., & Paderna, L. (2005). Continuing bonds in bereavement: An attachment theory based perspective. *Death Studies, 29*(4), 277–299.

Figley, C. R. (1995). *Compassion fatigue: Coping with secondary traumatic stress disorder in those who treat the traumatized.* Brunner/Mazel.

Figley, C. R. (Ed.). (2002). *Treating compassion fatigue.* Brunner-Rutledge.

Forgash, C. E., & Copeley, M. E. (2008). *Healing the heart of trauma and dissociation with EMDR and ego state therapy.* Springer.

Fraley, R. C., & Bonanno, G. A. (2004). Attachment and loss: A test of three competing models on the association between attachment-related avoidance and adaptation to bereavement. *Personality and Social Psychology Bulletin, 30*(7), 878–890.

Fraser, B. J. (1991). Two decades of classroom environment research. In B. J. Fraser & H. J. Walberg (Eds.), *Educational environments: Evaluation, antecedents and consequences* (pp. 3–27). Pergamon Press.

Freud, S. (1917). *Mourning and melancholia.* Hogarth.

Gallagher-Thompson, D., Futterman, A., Farberow, N., Thompson, L. W., & Peterson, J. (1993). The impact of spousal bereavement on older widows and widowers. In W. S. M. S. Stroebe & R. O. Hansson (Eds.), *Handbook of bereavement: Theory, research and intervention* (pp. 227–239). Cambridge Press.

Germain, A., Caroff, K., Buysse, D. J., & Shear, M. K. (2005). Sleep quality in complicated grief. *Journal of Traumatic Stress, 18*(4), 343–346.

Greitens, E. (2015). *Resilience: Hard-won wisdom for living a better life.* Houghton Mifflin Harcourt.

Grimby, A. (1993). Bereavement among elderly people: Grief reactions, post-bereavement hallucinations and quality of life. *Acta Psychiatrica Scandinavica, 87*(1), 72–80.

Holland, J. M., & Neimeyer, R. A. (2011). Separation and traumatic distress in prolonged grief: The role of cause of death and relationship to the deceased. *Journal of Psychopathology and Behavioral Assessment, 33*(2), 254–263.

Holmes, J., & Slade, A. (2018). *Attachment in therapeutic practice.* Sage Publications, Inc.

Hornsveld, H. K., Landwehr, F., Stein, W., Stomp, M., Smeets, M., & Van den Hout, M. (2010). Emotionality of loss-related memories is reduced after recall plus eye movements but not after recall plus music or recall only. *Journal of EMDR Practice and Research, 4,* 107–112.

Janet, P. (1898). *Le traitement psychologique de l'hystérie. Dans: A. Robin, Traité de thérapeutique appliquée.* Rueff.

Janet, P. (1904). L'amnésie et la dissociation des souvenirs par l'émotion. *Journal de Psychologie, 1,* 417–453.

Janet, P. (1919). Les médications psychologiques (3 Vols). *International Journal of Psycho-Analysis, 2,* 123–141.

Janet, P. (1925). *Psychological healing: A historical and clinical study.* Macmillan,

Janoff-Bulman, R. (1989). Assumptive worlds and the stress of traumatic events: Applications of the schema construct. *Social Cognition, 7*(2), 113–136.

Janoff-Bulman, R. (1992). *Shattered assumptions: Towards a new psychology of trauma.* The Free Press.

Jarero, I., & Artigas, L. (2020). The EMDR therapy butterfly hug method for self-administer bilateral stimulation. *Beschikbaar.* op: www.researchgate.net/publication/340280320.

Jarero, I., Artigas, L., & Luber, M. (2011). The EMDR protocol for recent critical incidents: Application in a disaster mental health continuum of care context. *Journal of EMDR Practice and Research, 5*(3), 82–94.

Jordan, A. H., & Litz, B. T. (2014). Prolonged grief disorder: Diagnostic, assessment, and treatment considerations. *Professional Psychology: Research and Practice, 45*(3), 180.

Kamp, K. S., O'Connor, M., Spindler, H., & Moskowitz, A. (2018). Bereavement hallucinations after the loss of a spouse: Associations with psychopathological measures, personality and coping style. *Death Studies, 43*(4), 260–269.

Kimiko S (2010). The effect of PTSD treatments after stillbirth: Eye movement desensitization and reprocessing (EMDR) combined with hypnotherapy. *Journal of Psychosomatic, Obstetrics and Gynecology, 31*(98), 0167-482X.

Klass, S., Silverman, P. R., & Nickman, S. (Eds.). (1996). *Continuing bonds: New understandings of grief.* Routledge.

Knipe, J. (2018). *EMDR toolbox: Theory and treatment of complex PTSD and dissociation.* Springer.

Korn, D. L., & Leeds, A. M. (2002). Preliminary evidence of efficacy for EMDR resource development and installation in the stabilization phase of treatment of complex posttraumatic stress disorder. *Journal of Clinical Psychology, 58*(12), 1465–1487.

Kosminsky, P. S., & Jordan, J. R. (2016). *Attachment-informed grief therapy: The clinician's guide to foundations and applications.* Routledge.

Kübler-Ross, E., & Kessler, D. (2014). *On grief and grieving: Finding the meaning of grief through the five stages of loss.* Simon and Schuster.

Laliotis, D. (2020). Letting steam out of the pressure cooker: The EMDR Life Stress protocol. *Journal of EMDR Practice and Research, 13*(4), 150–162.

Lang, P. J. (1995). The emotion probe: Studies of motivation and attention. *American Psychologist, 50*(5), 372.

Lanius, R. A., Williamson, P. C., Densmore, M., Boksman, K., Neufeld, R. W., Gati, J. S., Menon, R. S. (2004). The nature of traumatic memories: A 4-T FMRI functional connectivity analysis. *The American Journal of Psychiatry, 161,* 36–44.

Lazarus, R. S., & Folkman, S. (1984). *Stress, appraisal, and coping.* Springer.

Lee, S. A. (2015). The persistent complex bereavement inventory: A measure based on the DSM-5. *Death Studies, 39*(7), 399–410.

Liotti, G. (1992). Disorganized/disoriented attachment in the etiology of the dissociative disorders. *Dissociation, 5*(4), 196–204.

Luthar, S. S., Cicchetti, D., & Becker, B. (2000). The construct of resilience: A critical evaluation and guidelines for future work. *Child Development, 71,* 543–562.

Mary, M. (1990). Cross-cultural studies of attachment organization: Recent studies, changing methodologies, and the concept of conditional strategies. *Human Development, 33*(1), 48–61.

Main, M. (1995). Recent studies in attachment: Overview, with selected implications for clinical work. In S. Goldberg, R. Muir, & J. Kerr (Eds.), *Attachment theory: Social, developmental, and clinical perspectives* (pp. 407–474). Analytic Press, Inc.

Main, M., & Solomon, J. (1990). Procedures for identifying infants as disorganized/disoriented during the Ainsworth Strange Situation. In M. T. Greenberg, D. Cicchetti, & E. M. Cummings (Eds.), *Attachment in the preschool years: Theory, research, and intervention* (pp. 121–160). The University of Chicago Press.

Marwit, S. J., & Klass, D. (1996). Grief and the role of the inner representation of the deceased. In D. Klass, P. R. Silverman, & S. L. Nickman (Eds.), *Continuing bonds: New understandings of grief* (pp. 297–309). Taylor & Francis. (Reprinted in modified form from "Omega—Journal of Death and Dying," 30(4), 1994/1995, pp. 283–298)

Martin, K. M. (2018). Structural dissociation in the treatment of trauma and eating disorders. In A. Seibert & P. Virdi (Eds.), *Trauma-informed approaches to eating disorders* (pp 221–233). Springer.

Mikulincer, M., & Shaver, P. R. (2008). An attachment perspective on bereavement. In J. Cassidy & P. R. Shaver (Eds.), *Handbook of bereavement research and practice: Advances in theory and intervention* (pp. 87–112). American Psychological Association.

Mikulincer, M., & Shaver, P. R. (2014). An attachment perspective on loneliness. In (Eds.), The handbook of solitude: Psychological perspectives on social isolation, social withdrawal, and being alone (pp. 34–50).

Mikulincer, M., & Shaver, P. R. (2011). An attachment perspective on interpersonal and intergroup conflict. In J. P. Forgas, A. W. Kruglanski, & K. D. Williams (Eds.), *The psychology of social conflict and aggression* (pp. 19–35). Psychology Press.

Mikulincer, M., & Shaver, P. R. (2016). *Attachment in Adulthood, Second Edition: Structure, dynamics and change.* Guilford Publications.

Mosquera, D. (2019). Working with Voices and Dissociative Parts: A trauma-informed approach. Instituto Intra-Tp, S.L.

Mosquera, D., & Knipe, J. (2018). EMDR therapy and physical violence injury: 'Best moments' protocol. In M. Luber (Ed.), *Eye movement desensitization and reprocessing (EMDR) therapy scripted protocols and summary sheets: Treating eating disorders, chronic pain and maladaptive self-care behaviors* (p. 251). Springer.

Murphy, S. A., Chung, I. J., & Johnson, L. C. (2002). Patterns of mental distress following the violent death of a child and predictors of change over time. *Research in Nursing & Health, 25*(6), 425–437.

Murphy, S. A., Clark Johnson, L., Wu, L., Fan, J. J., & Lohan, J. (2003). Bereaved parents' outcomes 4 to 60 months after their children's deaths by accident, suicide, or homicide: A comparative study demonstrating differences. *Death Studies*, 27(1), 39–61.

Murphy, S. A., Johnson, C., & Lohan, J. (2003). The effectiveness of coping resources and strategies used by bereaved parents 1 and 5 years after the violent deaths of their children. *Omega-Journal of Death and Dying*, 47(1), 25–44.

Murray, K. (2012). EMDR with grief: Reflections on Ginny Sprang's 2001 study. *Journal of EMDR Practice and Research*, 6(4), 187–191. doi:10.1891/1933-3196.6.4.187

Neimeyer, R. A. (2006). Complicated grief and the reconstruction of meaning: Conceptual and empirical contributions to a cognitive-constructivist model. *Clinical Psychology: Science and Practice*, 13(2), 141–145.

Neimeyer, R. A. (2013). The staging of grief: Toward an active model of mourning. In S. Kreitler & H. Shanun-Klein (Eds.), *Studies of grief and bereavement* (pp. 1–17). Nova Science Publishers.

Neimeyer, R. A. (2015). Treating complicated bereavement: The development of grief therapy. In J. M. Stillion & T. Attig (Eds.), *Death dying, and bereavement: Contemporary perspectives, institutions and practices* (pp. 307–320). New York, NY: Springer Publishing.

Neimeyer, R. A., & Sands, D. C. (2015). Containing the story of violent death. In R. A. Neimeyer (Ed.), *Techniques of grief therapy: Assessment and intervention* (pp. 306–311). Routledge.

Nijenhuis, E. R., Van der Hart, O., & Kruger, K. (2002). The psychometric characteristics of the Traumatic Experiences Checklist (TEC): First findings among psychiatric outpatients. *Clinical Psychology & Psychotherapy*, 9(3), 200–210.

Nolen-Hoeksema, S. (2001). Gender differences in depression. *Current Directions in Psychological Science*, 10(5), 173–176.

Nolen-Hoeksema, S., & Larson, J. (1999). *LEA series in personality and Clinical Psychology: Coping with loss*. Lawrence Erlbaum Associates Publishers.

O'Connor, M., Lasgaard, M., Shevlin, M., & Guldin, M. B. (2010). A confirmatory factor analysis of combined models of the Harvard Trauma Questionnaire and the Inventory of Complicated Grief-Revised: Are we measuring complicated grief or posttraumatic stress? *Journal of Anxiety Disorders*, 24(7), 672–679.

O'Connor, M. F., & Sussman, T. J. (2014). Developing the yearning in situations of loss scale: Convergent and discriminant validity for bereavement, romantic breakup, and homesickness. *Death Studies*, 38(7), 450–458.

Osterweis, M., Solomon, F., & Green, M. (1984). *Bereavement: Reactions, consequences, and care*. National Academy Press.

Panksepp, J. (1998). The periconscious substrates of consciousness: Affective states and the evolutionary origins of the self. *Journal of Consciousness Studies*, 5(5–6), 566–582.

Park, C. L., & Halifax, R. J. (2011). *Religion and spirituality in adjusting to bereavement: Grief as burden, grief as gift*. Routledge.

Parkes, C. M. (1972). *Bereavement: Studies of grief in adult life London*. Tavistock.

Parkes, C. M. (1988). Bereavement as a psychosocial transition: Processes of adaptation to change. *Journal of Social Issues*, 44(3), 53–65.

Parkes, C. M. (2006). *Attachment, bonding, and psychiatric problems after bereavement in adult life*. Routledge.

Parkes, C. M. (2011). Introduction. The historical landscape of loss: Development of bereavement studies. In R. A. Neimeyer, D. L. Harris, H. R. Winokuer, & G. F. Thorton (Eds.), *Grief and bereavement in contemporary society: Bridging research and practice* (pp. 1–6).

Parkes, C. M. (2015). *Death and bereavement across cultures*. Routledge.

Parkes, C. M., & Prigerson, H. G. (2010). *Bereavement: Studies of grief in adult life* (4th ed.). Routledge/Taylor & Francis Group.

Pearlman, L. A., Wortman, C. B., Feuer, C. A., Farber, C. H., & Rando, T. A. (2014). *Treating traumatic bereavement: A practitioner's guide*. Guilford.

Porges, S. W. (2001). The polyvagal theory: Phylogenetic substrates of a social nervous system. *International Journal of Psychophysiology, 42*(2), 123–146.

Porges, S. W. (2003). The polyvagal theory: Phylogenetic contributions to social behavior. *Physiology & Behavior, 79*(3), 503–513.

Porges, S. W. (2014). *Polyvagal theory: Neurophysiological foundations of emotion, attachment, communication, and self-regulation*. Norton.

Prigerson, H. G., Boelen, P. A., Xu, J., Smith, K. V., & Maciejewski, P. K. (2021). Validation of the new DSM-5-TR criteria for prolonged grief disorder and the PG-13-Revised (PG-13-R) scale. *World Psychiatry, 20*(1), 96–106.

Prigerson, H. G., Frank, E., Kasl, S. V., Reynolds, C. F., Anderson, B., Zubenko, G. S., … Kupfer, D. J. (1995). Complicated grief and bereavement-related depression as distinct disorders: Preliminary empirical validation in elderly bereaved spouses. *American Journal of Psychiatry, 152*(1), 22–30.

Prigerson, H. G., Horowitz, M. J., Jacobs, S. C., Parkes, C. M., Aslan, M., Goodkin, K., … Maciejewski, P. K. (2009). Prolonged grief disorder: Psychometric validation of criteria proposed for DSM-V and ICD-11. *PLoS Med, 6*(8), e1000121.

Prigerson, H. G., & Jacobs, S. C. (2001). Traumatic grief as a distinct disorder: A rationale, consensus criteria, and a preliminary empirical test. In M. S. Stroebe, R. O. Hansson, W. Stroebe, & H. A. W. Schut (Eds.), *Handbook of bereavement research: Consequences, coping, and care* (pp. 613–647). American Psychological Association.

Prigerson, H. G., Maciejewski, P. K., Reynolds III, C. F., Bierhals, A. J., Newsom, J. T., Fasiczka, A., … Miller, M. (1995). Inventory of Complicated Grief: A scale to measure maladaptive symptoms of loss. *Psychiatry Research, 59*(1–2), 65–79.

Rando, T. A. (1993). *Treatment of complicated mourning*. Research Press.

Rando, T. A. (1995). Anticipatory grief and the child mourner. In T. Rando (Ed.), *Beyond the innocence of childhood: Vol.3. Helping children and adolescents cope with death and bereavement* (pp.). Baywood Publishing Company.

Rando, T. A. (2000). *On the experience of traumatic stress in anticipatory and postdeath mourning. Clinical dimensions of anticipatory mourning*. Research Press.

Rando, T. A. (2013). On achieving clarity regarding complicated grief. In (Eds.), Complicated grief: Scientific foundations for healthcare professionals (pp. 40–54).

Rando, T. A., Wass, H., & Neimayer, R. A. (1995). *Grief and mourning: Accommodability to loss. Dying, Facing the Facts*. Taylor and Francis.

Ross, J. M. (1941). Haemorrhage into the lungs in cases of death due to trauma. *British Medical Journal, 1*(4176), 79.

Rynearson, E. K., & Salloum, A. (2011). Restorative retelling: Revisiting the narrative of violent death. In (Eds.), Grief and bereavement in contemporary society: Bridging research and practice (pp. 177–188).

Schut, H. A., Stroebe, M. S., van den Bout, J., & De Keijser, J. (1997). Intervention for the bereaved: Gender differences in the efficacy of two counselling programmes. *British Journal of Clinical Psychology, 36*(1), 63–72.

Shapiro, E., & Laub, B. (2008). Early EMDR intervention (EEI): A summary, a theoretical model, and the recent traumatic episode protocol (R-TEP). *Journal of EMDR Practice and Research, 2*(2), 79–96.

Shapiro, E., & Laub, B. (2013). The Recent Traumatic Episode Protocol (R-TEP): An integrative protocol for early EMDR intervention (EEI). In M. Luber (Ed.), *Implementing EMDR early mental health interventions for man-made and natural disasters: Models, scripted protocols, and summary sheets* (pp. 193–207). Springer.

Shapiro, F. (1989). Eye movement desensitization: A new treatment for post-traumatic stress disorder. *Journal of Behavior Therapy and Experimental Psychiatry, 20*(3), 211–217.

Shapiro, F. (1995). *Eye movement desensitization and reprocessing: Basic principles, protocols and procedures.* Guilford Press.

Shapiro, F. (1999). Eye movement desensitization and reprocessing (EMDR) and the anxiety disorders: Clinical and research implications of an integrated psychotherapy treatment. *Journal of Anxiety Disorders, 13*(1–2), 35–67.

Shapiro, F. (2001). *Eye movement desensitization and reprocessing: Basic principles, protocols and procedures, 2nd ed.* Guilford Press.

Shapiro, F. (2018). *Eye movement desensitization and reprocessing (EMDR) Therapy: Basic principles, protocols and procedures, 3rd ed.* Guilford Press.

Shapiro, F., & Forrest, M. (1997). *EMDR: The breakthrough therapy of overcoming anxiety, stress, and trauma.* Basic Books.

Shear, K. T., Houck, P., Melhem, N., Frank, E., Reynolds, C., & Sillowash, R. (2007). *An attachment based model of complicated grief including the role of avoidance.* Eur Arch Psychiatry Clinical Neuroscience.

Shear, K., & Shair, H. (2005). Attachment, loss, and complicated grief. *Developmental Psychobiology, 47*(3), 253–267.

Shear, M. K., Boelen, P. A., & Neimeyer, R. A. (2011). *Treating complicated grief converging approaches.* In R. A. Neimeyer, D. L. Harris, H. R. Winokuer, & G. F. Thornton (Eds.), *Grief and bereavement in contemporary society: Bridging research and practice* (pp. 139–162). Routledge/Taylor & Francis Group.

Shear, M. K., Simon, N., Wall, M., Zisook, S., Neimeyer, R., Duan, N., ... Keshaviah, A. (2011). Complicated grief and related bereavement issues for DSM-5. *Depression and Anxiety, 28*(2), 103–117.

Smith, A. J., Abeyta, A. A., Huges, H., & Jones, R. T. (2014). Persistent grief in the aftermath of mass violence: The predictive roles of posttraumatic stress symptoms, self-efficacy, and disrupted worldview. *Psychological Trauma: Theory, Research, Practice, and Policy.* Advance online publication. http://dx.doj.org/10.1037/tra0000002.

Solomon, R. M. (2008). Critical incident interventions. *Journal of EMDR Practice and Research, 2,* 160–165.

Solomon, R. M. (2018). EMDR Treatment of grief and mourning. *Clinical Neuropsychiatry, 15*(3), 173–186.

Solomon, R. M., & Hensley, B. J. (2020). EMDR Therapy Treatment of Grief and Mourning in Times of COVID-19 (Coronavirus). *Journal of EMDR Practice and Research, 14*(3), 1–13.

Solomon, R. M., & Rando, T. A. (2007). Utilization of EMDR in the treatment of grief and mourning. *Journal of EMDR Practice and Research, 1*(2), 109–117.

Solomon, R. M., & Rando, T. A. (2012). Treatment of grief and mourning through EMDR: Conceptual considerations and clinical guidelines. *European Review of Applied Psychology, 62*(4), 231–239.

Solomon, R. M, & Rando, T. A. (2015). EMDR therapy and grief and mourning. In M. Luber (Ed.), *Eye movement desensitization and reprocessing (EMDR) therapy scripted protocols and summary sheets: Treating trauma and stressor related conditions* (pp. 230–252). Springer.

Solomon, R., & Shapiro, F. (2012). EMDR and adaptive information processing: The development of resilience and coherence. In K. Gow & M. Celinski (Eds.), *Trauma: Recovering from Deep Wounds and Exploring the Potential for Renewal.* New York: Nova Science Publishers.

Solomon, R. M., & Shapiro, F. (1997). Eye movement desensitization and reprocessing: An effective therapeutic tool for trauma and grief. In C. Figley, B. Bride, & M. Nicholas (Eds.), *Death and trauma: The traumatology of grieving* (pp. 231–247). Taylor and Francis.

Solomon, R. M., & Shapiro, F. (2017). *APA handbook of Trauma Psychology: Vol. 2. trauma practice*. American Psychological Association.

Solomon, R., & Shapiro, F. (2008). EMDR and the adaptive information processing model: Potential mechanisms of change. *Journal of EMDR Practice and Research, 4*, 315–325.

Sprang, G. (2001). The use of eye movement desensitization and reprocessing (EMDR) in the treatment of traumatic stress and complicated mourning: Psychological and behavioral outcomes. *Research on Social Work Practice, 11*(3), 300–320.

Steele, K., Boon, S., & van der Hart, O. (2017). *Treating trauma-related dissociation: A practical, integrative approach (Norton Series on Interpersonal Neurobiology)*. WW Norton.

Steinberg, M., & Hall, P. (1997). The SCID-D diagnostic interview and treatment planning in dissociative disorders. *Bulletin of the Menninger Clinic, 61*(1), 108.

Stroebe, M. S., & Schut, H. (1999). The dual process model of coping with bereavement: Rationale and description. *Death Studies, 23*(3), 197–224.

Stroebe, M. S., & Schut, H. (2010). The dual process model of coping with bereavement: A decade on. *Omega: Journal of Death and Dying, 61*(4), 273–289.

Stroebe, W., Schut, H., & Stroebe, M. S. (2005). Grief work, disclosure and counseling: Do they help the bereaved? *Clinical Psychology Review, 25*(4), 395–414.

Stroebe, W., Stroebe, M. S., & Abakoumkin, G. (1999). Does differential social support cause sex differences in bereavement outcome? *Journal of Community & Applied Social Psychology, 9*(1), 1–12.

Stroebe, W., Stroebe, M., Abakoumkin, G., & Schut, H. (1996). The role of loneliness and social support in adjustment to loss: a test of attachment versus stress theory. *Journal of Personality and Social Psychology, 70*(6), 1241.

Sveen, C. A., & Walby, F. A. (2008). Suicide survivors' mental health and grief reactions: A systematic review of controlled studies. In (Eds.), Suicide and Life-Threatening Behavior (pp.). Guilford Press.

Tedeschi, R. G., & Calhoun, L. G. (2004). *Posttraumatic growth: Conceptual foundation and empirical evidence*. Lawrence Erlbaum Associates.

Tedeschi, R. G., & Calhoun, L. G. (2006). Time of change? The spiritual challenges of bereavement and loss. *Omega-Journal of Death and Dying, 53*(1), 105–116.

Tedeschi, R. G., & Calhoun, L. G. (2008). Beyond the concept of recovery: Growth and the experience of loss. *Death Studies, 32*(1), 27–39.

Tedeschi, R., Orejuela-Dávila, A. I., & Lewis, P. (2018). Posttraumatic growth and continuing bonds. In D. Klass & E. M. Steffen (Eds.), *Continuing bonds in bereavement: New directions for research and practice* (pp. 31–42). Routledge/Taylor & Francis Group.

Van der Hart, O., & Friedman, B. (1989). A reader's guide to Pierre Janet on dissociation: A neglected intellectual heritage. *Dissociation: Progress in the Dissociative Disorders, 2*(1), 3–16.

Van der Hart, O., Groenendijk, M., Gonzalez, A., Mosquera, D., & Solomon, R. (2013). Dissociation of the personality and EMDR therapy in complex trauma-related disorders: Applications in the stabilization phase. *Journal of EMDR Practice and Research, 7*(2), 81–94.

Van der Hart, O., Groenendijk, M., Gonzalez, A., Mosquera, D., & Solomon, R. (2014). Dissociation of the personality and EMDR therapy in complex trauma-related disorders: Applications in Phases 2 and 3 treatment. *Journal of EMDR Practice and Research, 8*(1), 33.

Van der Hart, O., Nijenhuis, E. R., & Solomon, R. (2010). Dissociation of the personality in complex trauma-related disorders and EMDR: Theoretical considerations. *Journal of EMDR Practice and Research, 4*(2), 76–92.

Van der Hart, O., Nijenhuis, E. R., & Steele, K. (2006). *The haunted self: Structural dissociation and the treatment of chronic traumatization*. WW Norton.

Van der Hart, O., Van der Kolk, B. A., & Boon, S. (1998). Treatment of dissociative disorders. *Volkskrant Magazine*, 24 December 2011.

Wallin, D. J. (2007). *Attachment in Psychotherapy.* Guilford Press.

Wang, C., Pan, R., Wan, X., Tan, Y., Xu, L., Ho, C. S., & Ho, R. C. (2020). Immediate psychological responses and associated factors during the initial stage of the 2019 coronavirus disease (COVID-19) epidemic among the general population in China. *International Journal Environmental Research Public Health, 17*(5).

Watson, P. J., & Brymer, M. J. (2012). Promoting resilience through early intervention. In R. A. McMackin, E. Newman, J. M. Fogler, & T. M. Keane (Eds.), *Trauma therapy in context: The science and craft of evidence-based practice* (pp. 141–163). American Psychological Association.

Winnicott, D. W. (1965). *The maturational processes and the facilitating environment: Studies in the theory of emotional development.* International Universities Press.

Worden, J. W. (2018). *Grief counseling and grief therapy: A handbook for the mental health practitioner.* Springer.

Wortman, C. B. (2016). Coping with death and dying. In J. C. Norcross, G. R. VandenBos, D. K. Freedheim, & N. Pole (Eds.), *APA handbook of clinical psychology: Psychopathology and health* (pp. 567–581). American Psychological Association. https://doi.org/10.1037/14862-027

Wortman, C. B., & Pearlman, L. (2016). Traumatic bereavement. In R. A. Neimeyer (Ed.), *Techniques of grief therapy: Assessment and intervention* (pp. 25–29). Routledge/Taylor & Francis.

Wortman, C. B., & Silver, R. C. (1989). The myths of coping with loss. *Journal of Consulting and Clinical Psychology, 57*, 349–357.

Wortmann, J. H., & Park, C. L. (2008). Religion and spirituality in adjustment following bereavement: An integrative review. *Death Studies, 32*(8), 703–736.

Young, B. H. (2006). The immediate response to disaster: Guidelines for adult psychological first aid. In E. C. Ritchie, P. J. Watson, & M. J. Friedman (Eds.), *Interventions following mass violence and disasters: Strategies for mental health practice* (pp. 134–154). Guilford Press.

Young, I. T., Iglewicz, A., Glorioso, D., Lanouette, N., Seay, K., Ilapakurti, M., & Zisook, S. (2012). Suicide bereavement and complicated grief. *Dialogues in Clinical Neuroscience, 14*(2), 177.

Zech, E. (2016). The dual process model in grief therapy. In R. A. Neimeyer (Ed.), *Techniques of grief therapy: Assessment and intervention* (pp. 19–24). Routledge/Taylor & Francis Group.

Zhang, B., El-Jawahri, A., & Prigerson, H. G. (2006). Update on bereavement research: Evidence-based guidelines for the diagnosis and treatment of complicated bereavement. *Journal of Palliative Medicine, 9*(5), 1188–1203.

Zisook, S., & Shuchter, S. R. (1993). Uncomplicated bereavement. *Journal of Clinical Psychiatry, 54*(10), 365–372.

Index

For the benefit of digital users, indexed terms that span two pages (e.g., 52–53) may, on occasion, appear on only one of those pages.

Tables and boxes are indicated by *t* and *b* following the page number

absentmindedness 27
accidental death 40–41
accommodation phase 22, 90, 97–103
action systems 227–29
acute symptoms 158, 162, 165
adaptation 17–18, 132–33, 245–46
adaptive information processing (AIP)
    model 7, 78, 91, 230
adaptive inner representation 15–17, 209–13,
    218–19
adaptive memory networks 159–60, 163, 166
affect regulation 155–56, 169
affect scan 198
Ainsworth, M. 66
ambiguous death 51
ambivalent attachment 67–68
ambivalent relationships 39
anger 23–24
anxiety 24
anxious attachment 68, 74, 77, 85, 171,
    173t, 201
appetite 27
assumptive world 31–34, 100, 136–45
attachment 65–78
    adaptive information processing 78
    ambivalent/resistant 67–68
    anxious/preoccupied 68, 74, 77, 85, 171,
        173t, 201
    avoidant 67, 74–75, 77–78, 87, 170–71,
        173t, 201
    blocked processing 123–27
    caregiving and 72–73
    case examples 76–78
    classification 66–69
    communication 69–70
    complicated grief 57, 73–74
    deactivating strategies 71

development of attachment style 70–71
    dismissing 67
    dismissive-avoidant 67
    disorganized 68–69, 171, 232–33
    fearful-avoidant 67, 69, 75
    feeder memories 198
    grief response 74–75
    history of relationship with attachment
        figures 156
    hyperactivating strategies 70–71
    implications for EMDR therapy 75–78,
        111–12
    loss in adulthood 72
    loss in childhood 71–72
    mediator of mourning 39, 44
    mirroring 70
    preparation and stabilization phase 170–71
    relevance to EMDR therapy 70
    "R" processes model 91
    secure 66–67, 74, 76–77
    therapeutic alliance 170–71
avoidance phase 21–22, 28, 48, 90, 92–93
avoidant attachment 67, 74–75, 77–78, 87,
    170–71, 173t, 201

balanced life 248
basic assumptions 48
behaviors 27–28
belonging 129–30, 159, 190–94, 206–7
bereavement
    definitions 20–21
    overload 50–51
bilateral stimulation (BLS) 7, 9, 10–11,
    16–17, 196
blame 33, 50
blocked processing 110–11, 122–30, 145–47,
    198–210, 200b–1

blocking belief 199–201, 215–17
body of deceased
    failure to find 52
    viewing 52
body scan phase 11, 177, 217–19
body sensations 10, 193–94
Boelen 13–14
Bowlby, J. 21, 55, 71–72, 227
Brown, D. P. 232

calm/safe place exercise 9, 172
carrying objects 28
case conceptualization 108–10, 157–58,
    160–62, 163–64, 166–67
case examples
    adapting to new life 139b, 140b–41
    adaptive inner representations 16b, 17b,
        18b, 210–13, 224b
    affect regulation difficulties 124b
    assumptive world 136b
    attachment-related issues 123b–24, 145b–46
    attachment styles 76b, 77b–78
    be cautious 179b–80
    blocked processing 200b–1
    blocking belief 200b, 215b–16
    body scan 217b–18
    case conceptualization and treatment
        planning 161b, 164b
    client readiness 181b
    comprehensive treatment for going
        forward 144b
    connection 129b, 137b–38, 206b
    connection through pain 202b
    continuing bonds 81b–82
    control 129b, 205b–6
    delinking 199b
    distressing memories 116b–17
    dual process model 86b, 87b–88
    ecological appropriateness 217b
    emergence of meaningful memories 16b
    ending sessions 219b, 220b
    eye movement desensitization 178b
    feeder memories 198b
    intrusive images 117b
    linking positive cognition and
        target 214b–15
    moment of shock 115b, 116b
    mortality 128b
    negative memories 125b–26, 216b
new identity 142b
new information 209b
new relationships 143b, 144b
nightmares 117b
painful memories 120b–22
phobia of realization 229b
positive memories 126b
previous loss 122b–23
recent event protocol 177b
responsibility 127b, 188b–89, 203b,
    204b
"R" processes model 93b, 95b, 96b, 99b,
    102b, 103b, 135b
safety 128b, 205b
secondary dissociation 237b, 240b
secondary loss 119b
subjective units of disturbance
    (SUDs) 211b, 212b, 213b
target memory 223b
vicarious negative images 118b
what do you want to keep? 208b
what do you want to say to or do for the
    deceased? 208b, 209b
causality 33
child, death of 35, 39, 43, 51
choices 159, 190, 205–6
chronic grief reaction 58
circumstances of death 40–42, 152–53
Cleiren, M. P. 39
closure phase 12, 219–21
cognition
    negative cognition 10, 185, 186–87, 188t,
        190t, 191t, 192t, 192
    positive cognition 10, 177, 186–87, 188t,
        190t, 191t, 192t, 214
    validity of cognition 10, 11, 186–87, 193, 215
cognitive behavioral therapy (CBT) 12–14
cognitive interweave 202–7, 209–10
communication, attachment style 69–70
complex trauma 232–43
complicated grief and mourning 54–62
    assessment instruments 61
    attachment 57, 73–74
    chronic/prolonged grief reactions 58
    clues to 60–61
    defining terms 54–55
    delayed grief reactions 58–59
    depression and 56–57
    exaggerated grief reactions 59

future template 145–47
high-risk factors 153
implication for EMDR 61–62
integrative treatment model 110–11
loss as trauma 55
masked grief reactions 59–60
past memories 122–30
PTSD and 57
separation distress 56
symptoms 57–60
confirmation of death 52
conflicted relationships 39–40
conflictual memories 119–22
confrontation phase 22, 90, 93–99
confrontation with death 51
confusion 26
connection 129–30, 159, 190–94, 201–10
continuing bonds model 15–16, 79–82, 111
control 128–29, 159, 190, 205–6
coping 44, 154, 169, 173t
Cotter 12–13
Covid-19 pandemic 42
criminal justice system 37
crying 27
cultural issues 152

daily life 36
deactivating strategies 71
death notification 52
debriefing 221
delayed grief reactions 58–59
delinking 199
Denderen 13–14
dependent relationships 40
depersonalization 25
depression 29–30, 56–57
derealization 25
desensitization phase 10–11, 195–213
destabilization 47
detachment 71–72
disasters 41
disbelief 26
dismissing attachment 67
dismissive-avoidant attachment 67
disorganized attachment 68–69, 171, 232–33
dispositional optimism 44
dissociative disorder 180
Dissociative Experiences Scale 233
dreams 27

dual awareness 155–56
dual process model 83–89, 111
Dyregrov, A. 38, 39

ecological appropriateness 216–17
Elliot, D. S. 232
emotion
    emotional impact phase 22
    emotional loneliness 24
    intense emotions 195–97
    overwhelming emotional impact 201
    target assessment 10, 193
exaggerated grief reactions 59
extended family 36
eye movement desensitization (EMD) 178–
        79, 197
eye movement desensitization and
        reprocessing (EMDR) therapy
    approach 3–4, 7–8
    attachment theory 70, 75–78, 111–12
    beginning 114
    client readiness 170t, 180–81
    complex trauma 233–43
    complicated grief and mourning 61–62
    continuing bonds model 82, 111
    dual process model 85–88, 111
    EMDR Protocol for Recent Critical
        Incidents and Ongoing Traumatic Stress
        (EMDR-PRECI) 179
    EMDR Recent Traumatic Episode Protocol
        (R-TEP0) 179
    ending sessions 219–21
    goal 15
    initial targets 115–22
    integrative treatment model 107–12
    length of sessions 181–82
    natural therapy 14
    paradigm of resilience 246–47
    phase-oriented treatment 171, 231–32
    phases 8–12
    positive adaptation 245–46
    preparing for 172–74
    progressive nature 14–15
    research on use in grief and
        mourning 12–14
    "R" processes model 92–93, 94–95, 96–97,
        99, 102–3, 111
    studies validating use in trauma 8
    traumatic bereavement 52–53

Fairbairn 16
faith 34, 37, 45
family functioning and relationships 35, 36
fatigue 25
fearful-avoidant attachment 67, 69, 75
feeder memories 198–99
feelings 23–25
Figley, C. 248–49
finality 33
flashbacks 117–18
floatback 198
focused processing 197
Fraser's Dissociative Table 234
Freud, S. 21, 79
future templates 8, 110–12, 133–47, 157, 177

gender differences 43
general (global) functioning 221–22
grief and mourning
    attachment style 74–75
    behaviors 27–28
    complicated, *see* complicated grief and
        mourning
    continuing bonds model 15–16, 79–82,
        111
    definitions 20–21
    depression and 29–30
    dual process model 83–89, 111
    feelings 23–25
    manifestation and impact on daily life 154
    mediators of mourning 38–45
    physical sensations 25
    reactions 22–28, 29*t*
    "R" processes model 14, 90–103, 111
    stages 21–28
    thought patterns 26–27
guilt 24, 33–34, 203–4

hallucinations 26
helplessness 25, 26–27
historical antecedents 43
history-taking and treatment planning
        phase 9, 151–68, 233
homicide 42
Hornsveld 13
humanity 248–49
hyperactivating strategies 70–71
hyperactivity 27
hyperarousal 195–96
hypoarousal 195–96

identity 100–1, 141–43
illusions 26
image 10, 184
imaginal interactions 208
information for clients 171–72
information processing 7; *see also* adaptive
        information processing (AIP) model
inhibited grief reactions 58–59
inner representation 15–17, 197, 223–25
installation phase 11, 214–17
integrative capacity 235
intentional death 50
internal working models 80–82
interpersonal relationships 35–36
Inventory of Complicated Grief
        (ICG/ICG-R) 61

Janet, P. 230
Janoff-Bulman, R. 31
Jordan, A. H. 56–57
Jordan, J. R. 73–74
justice 37

keepsakes 28
Keijser 13–14
kinship 38–39
Kosminsky, P. S. 73–74
Kubler-Ross, E. 21

Lee 12–13
legal system 37
length of sessions 181–82
Liotti, G. 2
Litz, B. T. 56–57
loneliness 24
looping 202–3
loss orientation 83–87, 155–56, 172

masked grief reactions 59–60
meaning of loss 32
Meaning Reconstruction model 17
memories
    adaptive memory networks 159–60, 163,
        166
    attachment-related 198
    emergence of positive memories 2, 27,
        213
    feeder memories 198–99
    information processing 7
    meaningful memories 15–17

negative memories 216
painful memories 119–22
starting with a specific memory 181
target memory 176, 222–25
see also past memories
Meysner 12–13
Mikulincer, M. 73
mirroring 70
mode of death 40–42, 152–53
mortality 128, 189
mourning
definition 20–21
mediators of 38–45
see also grief and mourning
multiple deaths 50–51
murder 42
Murphy, S.A. 39

NASH categories 40
natural death 40
nature of loss 153
negative beliefs 26–27
negative cognition 10, 185, 186–87, 188*t*,
190*t*, 191*t*, 192*t*, 192
negative memories 216
negative self-appraisals 26–27
Neimeyer, R. A. 1–2, 17
new identity 100–1, 141–43
new information 209
nightmares 117–18
Nijenhuis, E. R. 227–28
notification of death 52
numbness 23
nurturing 196

obstacles 133, 143–45
optimism 44

pain 2–3, 94
accepting client's pain 247
connection through 201–10
painful memories 119–22
parental grief 35–36
Parkes, C.M. 1, 32
past experiences 122–23, 156–57, 198
past memories 8, 108–10, 113–30
blocked processing 122–30
complicated grief 122–30
conflictual or painful memories 119–22
flashbacks 117–18

initial targets 115–22
moment of shock/realization 115–16
nightmares 117–18
painful memories 119–22
secondary losses 118–19
target selection 113–14
vicarious negative images 117–18
past trauma and/or loss 122–23,
156–57, 198
Persistent Complex Bereavement
Inventory 61
personality
apparently normal parts (ANPs) 228–29
emotional parts (EPs) 228–29
mediator of mourning 44
theory of the structural dissociation of the
personality 227–31
trauma-generated dissociation 226–32
personification 235
PG-13 61
phase-oriented treatment 171, 231–32
phobias 229, 234
physical self-care 248
physical sensations 25
pining 24–25
positive adaptation 245–46
positive cognition 10, 177, 186–87, 188*t*,
190*t*, 191*t*, 192*t*, 214
positive memories 2, 27, 213
postponed grief reactions 58–59
posttraumatic growth 17, 45, 133, 245–46
posttraumatic stress disorder (PTSD) 47–48,
51, 57
powerlessness 26–27
preoccupation 26
preoccupied (anxious) attachment 68, 74,
77, 85, 171, 173*t*, 201
preparation and stabilization phase 9, 169–
75, 233–36
presence, sense of 26
presentification 235
presenting problem 157, 161, 165
present triggers 8, 110, 131–33, 157, 177
preventable death 49–50
primary loss 1
prolonged grief disorder (PGD) 22–23,
54–55, 56–57; *see also* complicated grief
and mourning
prolonged grief reaction 58
proximity 42–43

psychoeducation 171–72
Psychological First Aid 180

ramifications of death 48
random death 50
Rando's "R" processes 14, 90–103, 111
react to separation 93–95
readiness criteria 170*t*, 180–81
readjust 100–2
recent event protocol 176–79
recognize the loss 92
recollection 95–97
re-enactment 49
re-evaluation 12, 221–25
re-experience 95–97
reinvest 102–3
relationships
    impact of loss 35–36
    mediators of mourning 38–40
    new relationship with deceased 137–38
relaxation 196
relief 25
religious beliefs 34, 37, 45
relinquish 97–99
reminders 28
reminiscing 27
reorganization 72
reprocessing 7, 176–83, 236–43
resilience 246–47
resistant attachment 67–68
resource development and installation 9, 172
responsibility 33, 127, 158, 187–89, 203–4
restlessness 27
restoration orientation 83–85, 87–88,
    155–56, 172
"R" processes model 14, 90–103, 111
run a movie 177

sadness 23
safe/calm place exercise 9, 172
safety 128, 158–59, 189, 204–5
Schut, H. 83
searching 28
secondary gain 45
secondary loss 1, 94, 118–19
secure attachment 66–67, 74, 76–77
segregated systems 55, 227
self-blaming 26–27
self-care 247–49
self-defectiveness 203–4
self-esteem 44

self-reproach 24
sense of presence 26
separation distress 56, 71–72, 108, 131–32
Shapiro, F. 11, 12–13, 14, 107, 196, 219, 221,
    230, 246–47
Shaver, P. R. 73
shock phase 21–22, 23
sighing 27
Silver, S. 221
sleep disturbances 27
social ineptitude 38
social loneliness 24
social support 37–38, 44–45, 156
social withdrawal 28
Solomon, R. M. 11, 12–13, 246–47
soothing imagery 196
Space Shuttle Columbia 34
spiritual beliefs 34, 37, 45
Sprang, G. 13
stabilization, *see* preparation and
    stabilization phase
Steele, K. 227–28
Stewer 13–14
stigmatized death 51
"strange situation" 66
Strauss, P. 192
stress 45
Stroebe, M. S. 83
stuck points 133, 143–45, 198–210
subjective units of disturbance (SUDs) 10–11,
    193–94, 210–13
suffering 34, 49
suicide 41–42
support
    for clients 37–38, 44–45, 156
    for therapist 248
suppressed grief reactions 58–59
symptoms
    acute symptoms 158, 162, 165
    complicated grief symptoms 57–60

talking between sets 196–97
target assessment phase 9–10, 184–94
target memory 176, 222–25
team working 248
"tender loving care" 180
tension 215
theory of the structural dissociation of the
    personality 227–31
therapeutic relationship 169–71
thought patterns 26–27

tracking 215
Trauma and Dissociation Symptoms
    Interview (TADS–I) 233
trauma-generated dissociation of
    personality 226–32
traumatic bereavement 47–53
traumatic death
    impact 47–48
    risk factors 48–52
traumatic distress 108
treatment goals 158, 162, 165
treatment planning phase 108–10; *see also*
    history-taking and treatment planning
    phase

underlying issues 158, 162, 165
unfinished business 119–22
unnaturalness of death 49
untimely death 51

validity of cognition 10, 11, 186–87, 193,
    215
Van der Hart, O. 227–28
vicarious negative images 117–18
viewing the body 52
violent death 49
VoC scale 11
vulnerability 26–27

what do you want to keep/let go
    of? 207–8
what do you want to say to or do for the
    deceased? 208–9
widows/widowers 43
window of tolerance 195–97, 234
Wind River (movie) 2
Worden, J. W 22–23, 24–25, 26, 57, 60

yearning 24–25